REINALDO ARENAS

REINALDO ARENAS

The Pentagonía

Francisco Soto

University Press of Florida
Gainesville / Tallahassee / Tampa / Boca Raton
Pensacola / Orlando / Miami / Jacksonville

Library of Congress Cataloging-in-Publication Data

Soto, Francisco, 1956–

Reinaldo Arenas: The pentagonía / Francisco Soto.

p. cm.

Includes bibliographical references and index.

ISBN 0-8130-1315-1 (alk. paper)

I. Arenas, Reinaldo, 1943– Pentagonía. I. Title.

PQ7390.A72P437 1994

863—dc20   94-26066

Cover illustration: Reinaldo Arenas, by David Levine. Reprinted with permission from *The New York Review of Books*. Copyright 1991 by Nyrev, Inc.

The University Press of Florida is the scholarly publishing agency for the State University System of Florida, comprised of Florida A & M University, Florida Atlantic University, Florida International University, Florida State University, University of Central Florida, University of Florida, University of North Florida, University of South Florida, and University of West Florida.

University Press of Florida

15 Northwest 15th Street

Gainesville, FL 32611

a la memoria de mi padre, el Dr. Fernando F. Soto (1926–1993)

CONTENTS

ACKNOWLEDGMENTS

This book could not have been written without the help and support of a number of individuals. First, I would like to express my most sincere appreciation to Reinaldo Arenas for having inspired me through his writing. For his Cuban hospitality and genuine affection during our interview in 1987, his supportive letters, and his thoughtfulness in sending me the final manuscripts of *El color del verano* and *El asalto* long before they appeared in print, I will be forever indebted.

I would like to thank John Alexander Coleman and Roberto Echavarren for their intellectual stimulus during my years at New York University. At the University of Michigan–Dearborn, I am particularly grateful to Emily Spinelli, Claude Summers, Ted-Larry Pebworth, Neil Flax, and Sheryl Pearson, who all, in their own ways, supported this project. I also gratefully acknowledge the financial assistance that came from the University of Michigan–Dearborn Campus Grants and Diversity Steering Committees, which allowed me to complete portions of the manuscript.

I would especially like to thank Andrew Hurley and Viking Press for providing me with the manuscript of the English edition of *El asalto*. In addition, I would like to give special thanks to Saúl Rosales, Jr., and Elena M. Martínez, two dear Cuban friends whose encouragement, advice, and emotional support got me through this project.

Finally, I thank Mark Albano for his friendship, companionship, and love. And to the memory of my father, Dr. Fernando F. Soto, who taught me to be proud of my Cuban heritage, I dedicate this book.

The publishers of the following copyrighted works by Reinaldo Arenas have generously given permission to use extended quotations:

Cantando en el pozo. Copyright 1982 by Reinaldo Arenas. Reprinted by permission of the author's literary estate.

A NOTE ON TRANSLATIONS

I have used both the original Spanish texts and the published English translations of the works of Reinaldo Arenas throughout this book. In the case of *El asalto,* I have quoted from Andrew Hurley's unpublished translation. For *El color del verano,* not yet translated, and in certain cases where my analysis required a more literal reading, I have done the translation myself. Unless otherwise noted, all other translations are mine. All titles are given in their original language in the text; English versions appear in the bibliography at the end of the book.

INTRODUCTION

Escribir esta pentagonía, que aún no sé si terminaré, me ha
tomado realmente muchos años, pero también le ha dado un
sentido fundamental a mi vida que ya termina. (Writing this
pentalogy, which I still don't know if I'll complete, has in
fact taken me many years, but it has also given a fundamental
meaning to my life, which now ends.)

Reinaldo Arenas, *El color del verano*

Immediately after the publication of his second novel, *El
mundo alucinante* (1969), Reinaldo Arenas (1943–1990) began to receive
critical attention as one of Latin America's most innovative and promising
literary voices. The success of this novel, hailed by Latin American as well
as European critics for its intelligence and wit, catapulted this young
Cuban writer to international status. Long available in Europe in translation (French, German, Portuguese, and Italian), over the past several
years Arenas's work has also become available in English, making him
accessible to an even larger reading audience.[1] Yet despite the overall
agreement by Latin American scholars of the importance of Arenas's work
within contemporary Latin American letters, surprisingly only five book-
length studies in Spanish have been written concerning his work.[2] Apart
from some book reviews, short articles, and notes, few attempts have been
made in English to study Arenas's texts. My study contributes to fulfilling
the need for more serious textual evaluations and analyses of Arenas's
work, especially in light of his recent death. Because of this book's acces-
sibility to the non-Spanish speaker, it also encourages the study of Arenas's
work by a wider range of scholars, thus giving this gifted writer deserved
recognition in international letters as a noteworthy creator of contemporary literature.

Born on July 16, 1943, in the rural poverty of the Cuban countryside, Arenas experienced a childhood that can only be described as wretched. In his autobiography, *Antes que anochezca,* he recounts an early memory of eating dirt because food was scarce. As an idealistic teenager he joined the revolutionary rebel forces of Fidel Castro and fought against the dictatorial government of Fulgencio Batista. Two years after the triumph of the Revolution he moved to Havana, where his literary career officially began. In 1967, at the age of twenty-two, he published his first novel, *Celestino antes del alba,* the story of a child, persecuted by his family as well as by the impoverished conditions of his rural existence, who must rely on his imagination to survive. Shortly after its publication, the novel, a free-flowing narrative that undermines the realistic mode of writing, fell out of favor with the revolutionary cultural policy makers who demanded a literature that clearly contributed to a revolutionary consciousness.

In the mid-1960s, when the Castro regime began to openly persecute homosexuals, Arenas turned away from the Revolution. His dissatisfaction with the government deepened when his writings—transgressive, unconventional, and supportive of the individual's right to self-expression—were declared "antirevolutionary" and censored. Soon afterward, Arenas was no longer permitted to publish on the island. Defiant, he secretly sent his manuscripts abroad where they were immediately published, an act that infuriated the regime, which on various occasions confiscated and destroyed his work and ultimately branded him a nonperson in Cuba. While his novels were being read and praised in Europe and Latin America, Arenas was reduced to living a somewhat picaresque life in Havana, moving constantly and working at odd jobs simply to survive. Finally, in 1980, as a result of a bureaucratic blunder, he managed to escape from the island through the Mariel exodus.

After his arrival in the United States, Arenas settled in New York City. Having been censored in Cuba for so long, the author, as if intoxicated with his newly found freedom, began to write prodigiously: novels, short stories, poetry, dramatic pieces, essays, newspaper articles. For him, writing was both a liberating act of self-expression and an act of fury in which he challenged, undermined, and subverted all types of ideological dogmatism, all forms of absolute "truths."

On December 7, 1990, suffering from AIDS and too sick to continue writing, Arenas committed suicide. In a moving farewell letter sent to the Miami Spanish newspaper *Diario las Américas,* the writer made it quite clear that his decision to take his life should not be interpreted or construed as defeat. "My message is not a message of failure," he declared, "but rather one of struggle and hope. Cuba will be free, I already am."

Arenas's oeuvre is quite extensive. Throughout his life the Cuban writer explored all the major literary genres: novel, short story, poetry, theater, and essay. Moreover, he was an insightful critic, illuminating the works of such important Spanish American writers as José Martí, José Lezama Lima, Juan Rulfo, Gabriel García Márquez, and others. Still, it is the novel that Arenas most consistently cultivated and that was responsible for his critical success and recognition. Arenas took advantage of the novel's open-endedness, its inexhaustible ability to accommodate and incorporate different discourses, its world of play and hypotheses, its metaphysical questioning, to give free rein to his imagination and existential inquiries. The fact that Arenas consistently went back to writing novels after exploring other literary forms indicates his predilection for this broadly encompassing, highly flexible, and ever changing genre. Unlike, for instance, Edgar Allan Poe or Jorge Luis Borges, both advocates of the laconic precision of the short tale, Arenas exploited the novel's potential for growth and change.[3]

At the time of his death, Arenas had written eleven novels, nine that had been published and two that had not.[4] Within this prolific novelistic production, *Celestino antes del alba* (retitled *Cantando en el pozo* in 1982), *El palacio de las blanquísimas mofetas, Otra vez el mar, El color del verano,* and *El asalto* form a five-book sequence—described by Arenas as both a writer's autobiography and a metaphor of Cuban history—that constitutes a unique intradependent unit.[5] Although the interrelated narratives of this pentalogy or quintet provide for the reader a significant insight into the literary concerns and creative processes of the writer—more so perhaps than any single text in Arenas's entire literary production—these texts have not received significant critical attention.[6]

Arenas once stated that he began to write at an early age out of necessity: "Cuando tenía unos diez años ya escribía . . . y ahora me doy cuenta, yo tenía necesidad de escribir, porque si no, no hubiese perdido mi tiempo."[7] (When I was ten years old I was already writing . . . and now I realize I needed to write; otherwise I wouldn't have wasted my time). This exigency to write is evident in *Celestino antes del alba* (1967), Arenas's first novel. This first work, awarded an honorable mention in the *Concurso Nacional de Novela Cirilo Villaverde* (Cirilo Villaverde National Novel Competition) in 1965, heralded the arrival of this innovative and unconventional young writer. However, because only a limited number of copies

(2,000) were issued, Arenas's literary reputation was restricted to a small number of Cubans on the island.

In 1968 Arenas secretly sent the manuscript of his second novel abroad, and the French editorial house Editions du Seuil published it as *Le monde hallucinant*. One year later the novel appeared in Spanish as *El mundo alucinante*. There is no question that his literary reputation has been based on the success of this novel. Among his texts, *El mundo alucinante* has received the most critical acclaim both in Latin America and abroad. Yet, without dismissing the importance of this novel within Spanish American letters, it is essential to consider other, equally provocative and singular works in Arenas's oeuvre.

In 1975 the publication of *Le palais des très blanches moufettes* marked the second time that one of Arenas's novels appeared first in French. In this novel—later to be published in Spanish as *El palacio de las blanquísimas mofetas* (1980)—the writer continues the family saga that he began in *Celestino antes del alba* and, in addition, conceives of these two works as part of a *pentagonía* (pentagony), a neologism for the Spanish *pentalogía* (pentalogy), a word that underscores the *agonía* suffered by the characters in this quintet, who find themselves pressured and persecuted by abusive authoritarian systems and discourses of power. While *Celestino antes del alba* focuses on the experiences of an unidentified child-narrator persecuted by his family as well as by the impoverished conditions of the prerevolutionary Cuban countryside, *El palacio de las blanquísimas mofetas* explores the world of the adolescent Fortunato, a chaotic world of torment and spiritual hardship played out against a backdrop of revolutionary upheaval.

Otra vez el mar, rewritten three times over a period of sixteen years, was finally published in 1982 by the publisher Argos Vergara in Barcelona.[8] While he was alive, Arenas considered this third and central novel of the five-book sequence to be his most important work. In 1983 Severo Sarduy wrote, "*Otra vez el mar* es, con *Paradiso*, una de las mejores novelas que nuestro país ha producido, también una de las más críticas y más cubanas" (*Otra vez el mar* is, with *Paradiso*, one of the best novels that our country has produced, as well as one of the most critical and most Cuban).[9] With an entire history behind him (childhood and adolescence), the adult Héctor of *Otra vez el mar*, now living under an institutionalized revolution, continues questioning his alienation and tortured existence.

Arenas completed *El color del verano* and *El asalto* shortly before his death in December 1990. The novels appeared one year later, published by

Ediciones Universal, Miami. Héctor is reborn in *El color del verano* as Gabriel, who is also identified in the text as Reinaldo and the Tétrica Mofeta (the Gloomy Skunk). With their extravagance and festive laughter the trinity Gabriel/Reinaldo/the Tétrica Mofeta move within a homosexual subculture that challenges the bureaucracy, hostility, and persecution of the dictator Fifo's tyrannical society. In *El asalto,* Gabriel/Reinaldo/ the Tétrica Mofeta are metamorphosed into the nameless narrator, who lives in an abominable future society where individual rights are sacrificed for the good of the state. Ironically, however, this final novel of the pentalogy leaves the reader with a glimmer of hope. The decrepit tyrant El Reprimerísimo Reprimero (the Represident) is destroyed, and the protagonist, who has suffered countless persecutions throughout the five-book cycle, can finally stretch out on the beach and rest.[10]

In his autobiography, *Antes que anochezca,* Arenas recounts his determination, despite his hospitalization from AIDS-related complications, to complete the last two novels of the pentalogy:

> En el hospital comencé a escribir la novela *El color del verano.* Tenía en las manos distintas agujas con sueros, por lo que me era un poco difícil escribir, pero me prometí llegar donde pudiera. . . . Cuando salí del hospital . . . continué trabajando en *El color del verano.* También trabajaba conjuntamente con Roberto Valero y María Badías en la revisión de la quinta novela de la pentagonía, *El asalto.* En realidad se trataba de un manuscrito escrito en Cuba atropelladamente para poderlo sacar del país. Lo que Roberto y María hicieron fue una labor de traducción de un idioma casi ininteligible al español.[11]

> I started to write the novel *El color del verano* in the hospital. Although it was very difficult to write because of the various intravenous needles I had in my hand, I promised myself to go as far as I could. . . . When I left the hospital . . . I continued writing *El color del verano.* Concurrently, I was also working with Roberto Valero and María Badías on the revision of the fifth novel of the pentagony, *El asalto.* In reality, *El asalto* was a manuscript that I wrote helter-skelter in Cuba in order to be able to get it out of the country. What Roberto and María did was a labor of translation from an almost unintelligible language into Spanish.

The inclusion of *El color del verano* and *El asalto* in this book allows for the first time a complete reading and analysis of Arenas's *pentagonía,* a project that he had worked on intermittently since he was eighteen years old and that he labored furiously to complete once he sensed his death was imminent.[12]

While it has been generally observed that Arenas's texts deviate from the normative cultural ideology established in Cuba after 1959, no one has studied precisely how they differ. *Reinaldo Arenas: The Pentagonía* studies Arenas's five-book sequence through the general framework of the Cuban documentary novel tradition, a specific vein within the state-sanctioned literature of the Revolution that provides a meaningful context in which to place these texts that originated in Cuba. This analytical framework allows me to illustrate the differences between the writer's particular view of literature (fiction) and that of the Revolution's official cultural policy makers. Moreover, placing the novels of the pentalogy within this literary tradition better reveals the narrative strategies and the distinct structural and rhetorical techniques present in Arenas's novels, thus allowing for a more comprehensive and critical reading of each text.

The study is divided into two parts. In part 1, chapter 1, I present an overview of the cultural policies instituted in Cuba after 1959 to illustrate how the Revolution actively supported the publication of documentary texts—so much so that a new narrative form, *la novela-testimonio* or documentary novel, was created and legitimated. The Cuban documentary novel is a genre that, when it first appeared, was immediately sanctioned and promoted by the cultural policy makers of the Revolution, who defined the function of literature as a political task of immediate practical utility. Roberto González Echevarría attests in his essay "*Biografía de un cimarrón* and the Novel of the Cuban Revolution" that the Cuban documentary novel is "one of the most popular forms of narrative to emerge in Cuba since the triumph of the Revolution" (p. 110).

Chapter 2 demonstrates how the novels of the *pentagonía* can be read within the general principles of the documentary novel outlined by Miguel Barnet, the genre's most recognized proponent in Cuba. According to Barnet, the documentary novel gives voice to *la gente sin historia* (the people without a history), who would lack a voice within society if not for documentary narratives. This avowed principle has not applied, however, to all marginal members of Cuban society. The characters of the pentalogy—dissidents, "extravagants," dreamers, freethinkers, homosexuals—indeed represent marginal perspectives that should have a voice in documentary novels but have not had one. Therefore, by giving voice to those members of Cuban revolutionary society who have been forgotten, silenced, and overlooked by the government, Arenas reveals the revolutionary system's societal double standard while remaining faithful to the genre's fundamental outlining principle.

In part 2, chapters 3 through 8 illustrate how *Celestino antes del alba, El palacio de las blanquísimas mofetas, Otra vez el mar, El color del verano,* and *El asalto*—although positioned within the general outlining principle of the documentary novel—simultaneously expand, undermine, subvert, transgress, and build off the genre's particular characteristics and features. In these chapters I study, in order, the documentary novel's use of the first-person narrative voice to establish authenticity and verisimilitude, the use of so-called real witnesses, the chronological presentation of events, the use of documentation to authenticate the testimony given, mistrust of literary forms, and the reinterpretation and rewriting of recorded history from the perspective of an official revolutionary historiography. By transgressively undermining these specific characteristics and features that place more value on the documentary nature of the text over its aesthetics (fiction), Arenas illustrates how fiction, free of propagandistic constraints, can indeed express much more than overt and unmistakable political messages. Unlike recorded documents, fiction has the particular gift of being able to portray life in its full immediacy and brilliance; it is not merely a recording of life, but a vivid form of life itself.

In his study *Tradition,* Edward Shils defines literary tradition as a normative transmission of literary forms and styles from past to present. Arenas, inimical to the imposition of rules, conventions, and canons both in life and in art, distrusted what we might call tradition's propensity for establishing models, norms, "classics." (The concept that certain texts achieve the distinction of becoming classics within a literary tradition was a notion that Arenas challenged, for example, when he wrote *La Loma del Angel,* a parodic recreation and dethroning of the famous Cuban novel *Cecilia Valdés.*) While it is true that "the traditions of literary works are less sacrosanct . . . [as a result of] an inherent rule in literary production which compels a minimal element of substantive novelty" (*Tradition,* p. 45), literary tradition imposes itself nonetheless as a canonical model for the aspiration of subsequent writers and artists. I demonstrate how the culture-specific ideological circumstances of the Revolution turned the Cuban documentary novel into a state-sanctioned tradition whose basic tenets Arenas singularly subverted and called into question through his literary voice.

The characteristic subversive feature of Arenas's work is that it challenges and undermines all systems of power that attempt to establish themselves as absolute authority, discourses of the highest truth. Hence, we can see how the normative element in traditionalist ideology becomes for a writer such as Arenas an oppressive authority that must be undermined. However, this undermining of tradition, dogmatism, and authoritative rules—what I see as Arenas's insistence that the writer's voice be a cry for freedom challenging both the literary and social establishments—should not be considered pure anarchy. Arenas's subversion is creative and directed toward affirmative, positive, and humanistic action: the right of the individual to free expression. This profound sense of individual freedom and human dignity is present in all of his texts. Arenas's purposely exaggerated subversion, what might also be called his "carnival sense of the world" (much as the Russian critic Mikhail Bakhtin proposed in *Rabelais and His World*), was a direct challenge to the authoritative rhetoric and centralized discourse of power the Cuban writer witnessed around him. Like Rabelais, who confronted the medieval world's asceticism with excess and grotesque laughter, Arenas's subversion or carnival sense of the world was a result of having to confront a similarly powerful foe, the Cuban revolutionary government with its limited cultural policies and open hostility toward all those not projecting the revolutionary ideal. Although one might be inclined to see Arenas as an anarchist who proclaimed pure and total relativity in his works, I do not agree with such a judgment. Pure relativism could never produce true creativity or authentic artistic representation such as Arenas achieves in his novels.

I must clarify that when I speak of *tradition* I do not mean direct *influence,* a word that implies a regulated handing down of concepts and themes as if within a centralized authority. (Some critics have spoken of the influence of José Lezama Lima, Virgilio Piñera, Juan Rulfo, and others in Arenas's work.) In addition, I dismiss Harold Bloom's oedipal theory of the anxiety of influence, for it likewise attempts to establish a particular cause for a literary work. Perhaps Jonathan Culler has best advised us in his essay "Presupposition and Intertextuality" against designating any single significant precursor to a writer's work: "What makes possible reading and writing is not a single anterior action which serves as origin and moment of plenitude—but rather an open series of acts, both identifiable and lost which work together" (p. 110).

It is not my intention simply to equate Arenas's aesthetic work with his life. However, I also do not support the equally naive position that pretends that a work of art has no relationship whatsoever to the individual who produced it and the society in which it was created. My reading the novels of the pentalogy within the tradition of the Cuban documentary novel does not in any way pretend to limit or exhaust the profound singularity and possibilities of Arenas's novels, texts that are nonconformist and in themselves highly rebellious and contradictory to any type of underlying systematization. In short, studying Arenas's texts within the specific context of the Cuban documentary novel tradition allows me to illustrate better the writer's narrative strategies as well as his subversive attacks against the politicizing of the artistic media in revolutionary Cuba.

Finally, in the appendix to *Reinaldo Arenas: The Pentagonía,* there appears a conversation I had with Arenas, translated into English, in which he talks at length about the novels of the pentalogy and their genesis. This conversation, which took place in 1987, and the text of which Arenas revised and expanded shortly before his death, first appeared in Spanish in 1990 as *Conversación con Reinaldo Arenas.*

PART ONE

The Pentagonía within the Context
of the Cuban Documentary Novel

ONE

The Emergence of the Cuban Documentary Novel

This chapter contains an overview of the cultural policies that were instituted in Cuba after the triumph of the Revolution and that actively promoted the publication of documentary texts. In it, I will demonstrate how the explicit emphasis laid on the documentary-testimonial function of the artistic media in revolutionary Cuba clearly led to the flourishing of the documentary novel, a specific vein within the larger documentary genre. It will also uncover how the cultural policy makers of the Cuban Revolution—individuals who defined the function of literature as political and of immediate utility—actively encouraged the publication of documentary texts in building a revolutionary consciousness for its citizenry. Historical information will show how the documentary novel first emerged in Cuba and how it was immediately sanctioned and promoted thereafter. This historical foundation will allow me to illustrate in subsequent chapters how Arenas's *Celestino antes del alba, El palacio de las blanquísimas mofetas, Otra vez el mar, El color del verano,* and *El asalto,* texts conceived during this particular period in Cuban revolutionary letters, expand the general outlining principle of this popular narrative form to include marginal members of the revolutionary society while simultaneously engaging in a subversive dialogue from within the genre's specific characteristics.

Post-Revolutionary Cuban Literature

When the Cuban Revolution triumphed in January of 1959 most Cuban writers eagerly took part in the common effort to promote the new social, economic, and political order that was being instituted in the country. The Revolution called on the writer to take on a new sense of social responsibility; he or she was to be an exemplary member of society, working and living within the Revolution, contributing to building and defending Cuban sovereignty and liberty. Cuba needed the support of its intellectuals, and as a result, the cultural policies of the nascent revolutionary government favored all classes of literary production that served the cause of the Revolution. Fidel Castro's oft-quoted "Palabras a los intelectuales" (Words to the Intellectuals), perhaps the first semi-official document in which Cuba defines revolutionary art, was delivered before the first Congress of Cuban Writers and Artists in 1961. It clearly states the role of the Cuban artist (p. 147): "Creo que esto es bien claro. ¿Cuáles son los derechos de los escritores y artistas revolucionarios o no revolucionarios? Dentro de la Revolución, todo; contra la Revolución, ningún derecho" (I think this is very clear. What are the rights of revolutionary or nonrevolutionary writers and artists? Within the Revolution, everything; against the Revolution, nothing).

Cuban literature of the 1960s, as well as governmental policies toward the arts, mirrored the rapid changes that were occurring in the new revolutionary government. The renovating spirit of the Revolution initiated a fecund period of literary production unknown on the island until then; at the same time intellectuals received support and status, something they previously had not enjoyed. In 1959 Casa de las Américas was founded in Havana as a cultural institution to help foster creativity, communication, and understanding among writers of the Americas. In 1961 the official UNEAC (*Unión Nacional de Escritores y Artistas de Cuba* or National Union of Writers and Artists of Cuba) was formed; its purpose was the recognition of the new status of Cuban writers and their role in Cuban society. This new spirit of cooperation between the government and intellectuals is clearly echoed in Alberto Baeza Flores's assertion that "Never, in the history of Cuba, had writers and artists been so praised and offered so much as under the regime of Castro, who needed them. Never were so many books published. Never were they given such publicity, never was so much importance attached to them."[1] Cuban governmental policies toward the arts, however, were to pass through a series of crucial changes in the years ahead that would end this early tolerance and openness.

Perhaps Seymour Menton (*Prose Fiction of the Cuban Revolution*) has done the most extensive job of surveying the evolution of prose fiction during the first three decades of revolutionary Cuba.[2] Although Menton's book at times merely presents a synopsis of narrative plots, it nonetheless provides a valuable inventory of Cuban revolutionary novelistic production up to 1981. Menton takes on the monumental task of analyzing and recording over two hundred novels and short story collections that appeared in Cuba between 1959 and 1981. Half of his book is devoted to the Cuban novel's development, which he divides into four chronological periods spanning three decades of narrative production. Each period reflects certain decisive moments of the revolutionary process with its evolving attitude toward the arts: 1959–60, 1961–65, 1966–70, and 1971–81. It is within the political and cultural juncture of Cuban reality (1959–81) that Menton studies that Arenas first conceived of the novels of the *pentagonía*.

Menton entitles his first period "The Struggle against Tyranny: 1959–1960." The seven novels that belong to this first division reflect the enthusiasm and fervor generated by the overthrow of the dictatorial government of Fulgencio Batista. Menton proposes that these novels, published after the triumph of the Revolution, provide an important testimonial function, for they give witness to the insurrectionary struggle while emphasizing the enthusiasm of the young revolutionary soldiers. Yet as a whole, according to Menton, these novels are of "relatively poor quality . . . [because of] the authors' inexperience and by the fact that they were written hurriedly during the height of the enthusiasm for the Revolution" (p. 7). Menton identifies *El sol a plomo* (1959) by Humberto Arenal, *La novena estación* (1959) by José Becerra Ortega, *Bertillón 166* (1960) by José Soler Puig, and *Mañana es 26* (1960) by Hilda Perera Soto as the most significant novels published during this period. All written without any claim to formal literary experimentation, they were intended to document the historical overthrow of the Batista regime.

Menton's second category is "Exorcism and Existentialism: 1961–1965." This period was characterized by the strong desire of many Cuban artists to expiate the guilt of their bourgeois past in order to focus on the work of the Revolution (what José Rodríquez Feo termed *exorcismo*).[3] The self-criticism and sense of guilt felt by many writers made them avoid polemical issues that would be considered counterrevolutionary. In addition, Menton sees Jean-Paul Sartre's visit to Cuba in March 1960 as having had a profound effect on the novels that subsequently emerged. Indeed, French existentialist literature, with its insistence that the writer be *engagé* or committed to sociohistorical action and that his or her writings should reflect that commitment, became widely read in Cuba. But the event that had the most profound effect on the development of the Cuban novel during this period was Fidel Castro's declaration on April 16, 1961, that the Revolution was Marxist-Leninist. The writers of this second period now became aware that the Revolution's main goal was not the overthrow of Batista, but rather the establishment of a socialist state that required a Marxist-Leninist perspective in addressing the problems of creating a revolutionary consciousness. Menton explains, "Between 1961 and 1965, with the aid of more sophisticated literary techniques, most of the novelists sought to justify this turn to the left" (p. 11).

The 1961–65 period also marked the beginning of an ideological debate in Cuban letters over the role of the writer and intellectual in the Revolution. Dissatisfaction over the quality of literature being produced, the sterility of social realism, the search for formal experimentation that did not compromise the Revolution, the lack of profundity in the novel, inhibition and self-censorship for the good of the Revolution were all issues causing confusion for the Cuban writer. Ernesto "Che" Guevara, an important voice of the Revolution, spoke out on this matter. His celebrated essay "El socialismo y el hombre en Cuba" (Socialism and Man in Cuba) appeared in 1965. In it he examined the Cuban artists' desire for experimentation along with the Cuban aesthetic "problem" in general. Although he concluded that placing mere formal experimentation over the writer's service to humanity was at odds with the principles of the Revolution, he acknowledged that social realism was an obsolete form that would only stymie the writer. Che Guevara advised writers to find an authentic revolutionary expression without falling into the trap of imitating foreign models that would merely express the decadence of the capitalist world. Che Guevara, despite understanding the writer's desire to break away from the colonial past and catch up with contemporary trends, emphasized that this new attention to aesthetic expression should be viewed critically. However, this willingness to debate the role of the writer within the Revolution would soon change. The coming years ushered in an era of stricter governmental control of the arts that concluded with the imposition of a definitive and rigid revolutionary cultural policy by the First National Congress on Education and Culture in 1971.[4]

Menton's third period, "Epos, Experimentation, and Escapism: 1966–1970," finds the Cuban novel catching up with and joining the ranks of the Latin American novelistic "Boom."[5] Menton chooses 1967 as a critical year for the Latin American novel as well as for the Cuban novel. (The year marked the immediate success of Gabriel García Márquez's *Cien años de soledad,* award of the Rómulo Gallegos prize to Mario Vargas Llosa's

La casa verde, and the Nobel Prize for literature to the Guatemalan Miguel Angel Asturias.) In 1967 fifteen novels were published in Cuba, a significant increase from the previous years when only five appeared. This intensity of novelistic production, according to Menton, was the result of literary and political events that started to develop in 1966. In literature, 1966 marked both the appearance of José Lezama Lima's *Paradiso* and the awarding of the Casa de las Américas prize to Jesús Díaz Rodríguez's book of short stories *Los años duros,* a collection of stories featuring explicit sexual practices and obscenities that surprisingly did not produce governmental censorship. In the political arena, 1966 marked a strong determination by Cuba to maintain a distinct identity and group consciousness apart from the essentially conservative brand of Soviet-style communism. Cuban-Soviet relations reached an all-time low with Cuba's founding of the Organization for Latin American Solidarity (OLAS) in August 1967. However, this goal of national self-determination and freedom from external control was only to last until 1968, when the island's sagging economy and problems abroad pushed Cuba back into a dependent relationship with the Soviet Union. In August 1968, Castro's official approval of Soviet intervention in Czechoslovakia established a reconciliation with the Kremlin. Curiously, 1968 saw a drop in the publication of novels from the previous year (only eight were published). In 1969 only three appeared.

The Cuban writers who achieved international prominence during this 1966–70 period were José Lezama Lima, Guillermo Cabrera Infante, and Severo Sarduy. Their works were disseminated through the journal *Mundo Nuevo* under the direction of Emir Rodríguez Monegal. Menton maintains that the strength of literary production of this third period was the result of the absorption of four distinct generations, each represented by its most important writer: Alejo Carpentier (b. 1904), José Lezama Lima (b. 1912), Virgilio Piñera (b. 1912), Guillermo Cabrera Infante (b. 1929), Severo Sarduy (b. 1937), and Reinaldo Arenas (b. 1943) (*Prose Fiction,* p. 43).

In 1970 Lourdes Casal published a compendium of Cuban revolutionary literature, "La novela en Cuba 1959–1967: una introducción" (An Introduction to the Cuban Novel: 1959–1967). This was the first important overview of the new literature produced by the writers of the Revolution. Casal set up, rather awkwardly, a number of tables and charts to assist in classifying the literary production of these early years. In one such table, she attempted a classification of novels by themes: "Lucha insurreccional" (Insurrectional Struggle), "Cambios durante la época revolucionaria" (Changes during the Revolutionary Era), "Anatomía de la época revolucionaria" (Anatomy of the Revolutionary Era), "Tema fantástico" (Fantastic Themes), and "Ambiente extranjero" (Foreign Settings). Under these thematic headings she placed over forty novels. Still, she found it necessary to include an additional heading, "No encajan en las categorías anteriores" (Novels Not Fitting into the Previous Categories), under which she placed José Lezama Lima's *Paradiso,* Guillermo Cabrera Infante's *Tres tristes tigres,* Severo Sarduy's *De donde son los cantantes,* and Reinaldo Arenas's *Celestino antes del alba.* It is evident that the Revolution did not know what to make of these unorthodox literary expressions.

Menton proposes that with the publication in 1966 of Lezama Lima's celebrated *Paradiso* there appeared to be a relaxation of official restraints on Cuban writers.[6] He concludes that the novels of this period can all be characterized by an exuberance of linguistic experimentation and freedom of expression. In these experimental texts (such as Guillermo Cabrera Infante's *Tres tristes tigres* or Severo Sarduy's *De donde son los cantantes*), reality is not conceived as something separate from language. This new fiction demonstrates how language is as much a reality in and of itself as it is the substance out of which fiction is created. It is precisely within this moment of literary experimentation that Arenas's *Celestino antes del alba, El mundo alucinante,* and the stories of *Con los ojos cerrados* first appeared.[7]

The period 1966–70 also saw the publication in Cuba of two works by Miguel Barnet (*Biografía de un cimarrón* in 1966 and *Canción de Rachel* in 1969) that achieved instant popularity and received immediate governmental support. Both works introduced a new form of narrative fiction, the documentary novel, that claimed to articulate the collective memory of the Cuban people.[8] Menton dedicates only a few pages to Barnet and the emergence of documentary literature in Cuba. Still, he identifies the documentary novel's wide appeal and dissemination on the island.

The difficulty in classifying *Biografía de un cimarrón* when it first emerged attested to the singularity of its new narrative form. Barnet himself referred to it as *socio-literatura,* claiming that it was part sociology, part history, and part fictional novel. *Biografía de un cimarrón* displayed a strong effort to reconcile scientific material (documentary) with artistic form (novel). Esteban Montejo, both protagonist and narrator of the text, was a 104-year-old black Cuban who had lived through slavery, abolition, and the War of Independence. Thus, he served the purpose of documenting, for the first time, Cuban history from a black man's point of view. Barnet, a student at the Institute of Ethnography and

Folklore of the Academy of Sciences, was immediately attracted by the rich personal history of this unusual survivor of Cuba's past and began recording his stories.[9] While *Biografía de un cimarrón* was based on tape-recorded interviews, in *Canción de Rachel* Barnet seemed to renegotiate his role as *compilador* (compiler) and writer in order to take advantage of the novelist's privilege to create freely.

In December 1969 Barnet published the essay "La novela-testimonio: socio-literatura" in an attempt to provide a poetics for this new genre.[10] Barnet wished to establish credibility for the documentary novel by attesting to its validity, while arguing the need for its publication to be further promoted in Cuba. In addition, Barnet underscored that the documentary novel's main objective was not aesthetic, but rather utilitarian: to shape a collective revolutionary consciousness:

> El superobjetivo del artista gestor de la novela-testimonio no es meramente el estético, . . . es más funcional, más práctico. Debe servir como eslabón de una larga cadena en la tradición de su país. Debe contribuir a articular la memoria colectiva, el nosotros y no el yo. ("La novela-testimonio: socio-literatura," p. 142)

> The overriding objective of the artist who promotes the documentary novel is not simply aesthetic, . . . it is more functional and practical. The artist should be the link in a long chain in his or her country's tradition. He or she should help to articulate the collective memory, the *we* and not simply the *I*.

Barnet went on to propose how the documentary novel could serve as a tool for better understanding Latin America's complex reality:

> América necesita conocerse, sustentarse. Junto a la corriente rica de ficción, las obras de testimonio deben ir de la mano, rescatando, escudriñando, la enmarañada realidad latinoamericana. (p. 150)

> Latin America needs to know itself, to build itself up. The documentary novel should go hand in hand with a rich current of fiction, both claiming for, searching for, and unraveling the tangled web of Latin American reality.

As it was, revolutionary Cuba of the 1970s did see an increased production of this new type of writing. Since this topic will be elaborated on later, let us now move on to consider Menton's final category.

Menton's fourth period, "The Ideological Novel: 1971–1981," marks a distinct break with the preceding era in Cuban literary policy. While 1966–70 marked the publication of highly experimental novels, government policies during this last period were characterized by careful circumspection of the writer's freedom of expression. The diverse surge of literary production and apparent freedom of the previous period came into question with the "Padilla affair," beginning as early as 1968 and coming to a head in 1971.[11]

While the period 1966–70 featured the publication of over thirty experimental novels, 1971 saw the publication of only six novels, and the years 1972–73 saw none. In the appendix to the Spanish-language edition of *La narrativa de la Revolución cubana* (1982), Menton attests to "la gran escasez de novelas cubanas publicadas en Cuba en el último lustro" (p. 327) (the drastic shortage of novels published in Cuba in the last five years). In short, a sharp drop in novelistic production was the earmark of this era. Since literary production in Cuba is closely linked to governmental policies, Menton proposes that one only has to look to certain historical events to explain this drastic drop.

In December 1967 a highly commented article, "Situación del escritor en América Latina" (The Situation of the Writer in Latin America), by the Uruguayan critic Mario Benedetti appeared in *Casa de las Américas*. It stressed the responsibility of the Cuban artist, above all, to the revolutionary community:

> [P]ero no estoy dispuesto a que, en mérito a esa excelencia artística, eximamos a ese mismo escritor de su responsabilidad como simple ser humano. . . . El hecho de que reconozcamos que una obra es genial, no exime de ningún modo a su autor de su responsabilidad como miembro de una comunidad, como integrante de una época. (p. 35)

> But I am not prepared, in light of that artistic excellence, to exempt that writer from his or her responsibility as a simple human being. . . . The fact that we recognize that a work is brilliant does not excuse a writer in any way from his or her responsibility as a member of a community, and as an integral part of an era.

There is no doubt that the era Benedetti referred to is the revolutionary era that Cuba had initiated and hoped to inculcate in the rest of Latin America. Hence, it was clear that the so-called committed or responsible writer was to adhere, for the benefit of the new society or community, to the revolutionary message.

In 1968, as the commotion over the Padilla case was beginning to escalate, the declaration was made at a meeting of the UNEAC in Cienfuegos that "The writer must contribute to the Revolution through his or her work and this involves conceiving of literature as a means of struggle, a weapon against weaknesses and problems that, directly or indirectly, could hinder this advance."[12] Echoed above is Fidel Castro's "Palabras a los intelectuales" (Words to the Intellectuals) of 1961, a cry for a committed literature and the writer's responsibility, above all, to the Revolution. In 1969 this message was again voiced, more vehemently, by Juan Marinello, then chancellor of the University of Havana: "a committed historical period demands a committed literature . . . [and] the writer should wisely adopt a clarity accessible to everyone."[13] Two years later, on April 27, 1971, the most dramatic phase of the Padilla case took place with the writer's meeting and subsequent confession before the UNEAC.[14] The case ushered in a new era of conservatism and vigilance on the part of the government, which was determined to prevent attacks against the Revolution.

In 1970 an unsuccessful attempt to produce a record ten-million-ton sugar crop contributed much to Cuba's protectionist attitude and subsequent turn to the Soviet Union for economic assistance. Moreover, the already tense situation was aggravated in early 1970 by the publication of René Dumont's *Cuba, est-il socialiste?* (*Cuba, Is It Socialist?*) and K. S. Karol's *Les Guérrilleros au Pouvoir* (*Guerrillas in Power*)—both critical of Cuba and embarrassing to Fidel, for it was by his request that both French writers were invited to the island. In his book *Cuba Libre, Breaking the Chains?* Peter Marshall informs us that both Dumont and Karol were censored in Cuba as a result of their criticism of the Castro regime: "After another visit, René Dumont left the country critical of the growing bureaucratic centralism and militarization of the regime. He entitled his book *Cuba, est-il socialiste?* (1970); and to this question, gave a resounding "no." Even the sympathetic K. S. Karol in his *Guerrillas in Power* (1970) accused Castro of abandoning Guevara's ideals and returning to the Soviet-style Communism of the 1930s. Henceforth, customs officers in Cuba were to confiscate these books from visitors who brought them in" (pp. 3–4).

The year 1970 also saw the closing down of *Project Cuba*: "a study of the impact of a revolution-in-progress upon the daily lives of individuals and families representing different socio-economic levels in both rural and urban settings."[15] This project, under the direction of the renowned North American anthropologist Oscar Lewis, who had previously been hailed in Cuba for his work, was terminated for fear that it also might bring negative criticism to the Revolution.[16] As we have already seen, the entire issue of intellectual freedom finally came to a head in 1971 with the arrest and subsequent confession of Heberto Padilla before the Cuban Writers' Union, an incident that was to create a deep and lasting breach in the world literary community; from this moment on it was split between those who pledged their unwavering alliance to the Revolution and those who refused to compromise on the principle of artistic freedom of expression.[17] All these incidents provoked Fidel Castro to deliver a caustic closing speech before the First National Congress on Education and Culture (April 23–30, 1971) in which he excoriated the "liberal bourgeois artists" who placed artistic freedom over the Revolution as "agents of cultural colonialism," "good-for-nothing pseudo-leftist intellectuals who only want to earn laurels living in Paris, London, and Rome," "intellectual rats," "agents of the CIA," and so forth. According to Castro:

> ¿Concursitos aquí para venir a hacer el papel de jueces? ¡No! ¡Para hacer el papel de jueces hay que ser aquí revolucionarios de verdad, intelectuales de verdad, combatientes de verdad, poeta de verdad, revolucionario de verdad! Esto está claro. Y más claro que el agua. ("Discurso de clausura," p. 27)

> Little literary contests in Cuba so they can come and play the role of judges? No! In order to be a judge in Cuba one has to be a true revolutionary, a true intellectual, a true soldier, a true poet, a true revolutionary. This is quite clear. Clearer than water.

Castro continued his attack, this time against writers not committed to the Revolution:

> Para nosotros, un pueblo revolucionario en un proceso revolucionario, valoramos las creaciones culturales y artísticas en función de la utilidad para el pueblo. . . . No puede haber valor estético sin contenido humano, no puede haber valor estético contra el hombre. No puede haber valor estético contra la justicia, contra el bienestar, contra la liberación, contra la felicidad del hombre. ¡No puede haberlo! ("Discurso de clausura," p. 28)

> We as revolutionaries in the process of a revolution value artistic and cultural creations that serve a useful function for the people. . . . There can be no aesthetic value without human content, there can be no aesthetic value that goes against mankind. There can be no

aesthetic value that goes against justice, against well-being, against freedom, against man's happiness. There cannot be!

The message was quite clear. In Cuba all art would be valued in terms of its service to the Revolution; the reality described by works of art would have legitimacy only in terms of the Revolution; all reality would receive its meaning within the context of the revolutionary struggle.

Castro's speech was printed in full in the March–June issue of *Casa de las Américas* (nos. 65–66). More telling, the "Comité de Colaboración" (Advisory Board) of the magazine, which had previously included such prominent literary figures as Julio Cortázar and Mario Vargas Llosa, was dissolved. From this moment on Cuba began to revise its criteria for international literary contests and for the selection of judges for these events. The resolutions of the 1971 congress defined the new course of cultural management for the decade ahead.[18]

Menton's final observation concerning the 1971–81 period pertains to the cultivation of the historical novel and the detective novel and story. Since 1959 there has been an ongoing effort to rewrite national history as a way of legitimating Cuba's new social order. In such a highly politicized culture, historiography, with its institutionalized discourse of power, has become one of the dominant discourses, playing a key role in shaping social consciousness. In this light, it is not surprising that the historical novel would be cultivated, given its emphasis on documentary realism and its unsuitability to the empty formal artistry of modernist aesthetics. Later I shall study closely how the documentary novel, in essence an offshoot of the historical novel, flourished in Cuba.

The cultivation of the detective genre, as much in the novel as in the short story, is at first rather puzzling. In *Cuba: The Shaping of Revolutionary Consciousness* (1990), Tzvi Medin examines some of the more important channels of expression (for example, education, film, poetry, and so forth) that the Castro regime has used to convey the revolutionary message in its attempt to structure social consciousness in Cuba. According to Medin, detective fiction, which projects the monolithic revolutionary message in its own characteristic way, has been one of these channels:

Detective fiction is a genre that has been scarcely developed in Latin America as a whole, but in Cuba it has been flourishing since 1971. The wide popularity of this type of literature is indicated by the fact that best-seller lists are generally headed by detective novels. Very significantly, the thriving condition of Cuban detective fiction is due to the initiative and encouragement of the Dirección Política (Political Directorate) of the Ministerio de Asuntos Internos (MININT), which is in charge of internal security forces. It was the directorate that instituted the annual Anniversary of the Triumph of the Revolution competition for detective fiction. (p. 101)

Cuban detective fiction is contained by the revolutionary perspective that determines its objectives and modalities. Upon reading a Cuban detective novel or story one immediately discovers that the criminal is not the enemy of a single character but rather of the entire revolutionary enterprise. Also, the detective is not a brilliant individual, but an ordinary member of society with whom the reader can identify. He or she is an individual who works with an efficient revolutionary police force that is assisted by concerned and responsible Cuban citizens. It is the collective nature of the investigation, the individual collaborating with the legal apparatus of the socialist state, that gives the Cuban detective genre a distinctive character. Cuban detective fiction reinforces the normative code that defines behavior as appropriate or inappropriate within the revolutionary judicial system.[19]

Another important channel of expression that the Cuban government has used to shape social consciousness, according to Medin, is documentary literature. Tzvi Medin underscores the popularity of this artistic genre, whose overt and unmistakable revolutionary message is very much alive in Cuba: "Each of the different media projects the monolithic revolutionary message in its own characteristic way, and some lend themselves to this more easily than others. For example, the entire raison d'être of both the testimonial [documentary] and the detective novel is the transmission of the revolutionary message; they were created for that specific purpose, and they achieve it" (p. 170).

Documentary literature, in its desire to give testimony of revolutionary reality, has been promoted by the cultural practices of the Revolution. When the Batista regime collapsed in 1959, the revolutionary leaders that took power were not interested in merely reinstating a democratic regime conforming to the Cuban constitution of 1940. The intention was to reshape the Cubans' conceptual world through a revolutionary consciousness that would completely break with twentieth-century Cuban history. This break called for an immediate revision of history that would legitimate the new social order in light of the first independence movements of the previous century. The documentary genre, which uses both historiographic discourse and literary realism to reflect Cuban revolutionary reality, has been vigorously supported by the state, for it provides a revision of Cuban history from an official revolutionary perspective.

Government Support for the Cuban Documentary Novel

Cuba's post-revolutionary record of novelistic production makes it impossible to ignore the sociopolitical impact of the Revolution on the Cuban literary community. In the appendix to the 1982 Spanish-language edition of *La narrativa de la Revolución cubana* (p. 327), Seymour Menton observes: "Uno de los factores que más ha influido en la producción literaria, y, sobre todo, novelística, de la Cuba revolucionaria ha sido la política oficial del Gobierno hacia las artes" (One of the factors that has most influenced literary production, and especially the novel, in Revolutionary Cuba has been the official policy of the government toward the arts).

When the Revolution triumphed in 1959 the Cuban government immediately initiated active support for all types of literary production that fostered revolutionary consciousness. As we have seen, in 1971, as a result of the declarations made at the First National Congress on Education and Culture, governmental policies toward the arts were officially instated. Henceforth, art had to be created in terms of the new social order. Cuban officials began to judge works according to their usefulness to the society, considering apolitical attitudes toward culture unacceptable and counter-revolutionary. Moreover, the government discouraged the infiltration into Cuba of bourgeois intellectuals whose work and ideology conflicted with the interests of the Revolution. Hence, it was with government sanction that the *narrativa de testimonio* (documentary narrative), a literary form that through its immediacy and zeal for communication supported the Revolution's cultural policies, began to flourish in Cuba during the 1970s.[20]

The documentary-testimonial genre in Cuban revolutionary literature can in fact be traced to 1962 and the publication of Daura Olema García's *Maestra voluntaria,* a work that won the Casa de las Américas novelistic prize that same year.[21] *Maestra voluntaria* relates, in documentary fashion, the experiences of a volunteer teacher during the Revolution's early campaign to eliminate illiteracy on the island. In this book, which resembles a journalistic account of the literacy campaign more than a work of fiction, the protagonist converts to communism as a result of her training and subsequent dedication to the teaching of Cuba's illiterates. This novel clearly illustrates the type of literature that contributed to the shaping of a revolutionary consciousness.

In 1963 the publication of Che Guevara's autobiographical *Pasajes de la guerra revolucionaria* (*Reminiscences of the Cuban Revolutionary War*), a personal memoir of the early revolutionary struggle against Batista, continued the documentary vein in Cuban letters.[22] According to John Beverley, the success of Che Guevara's account "inspired in Cuba a series of direct-participant *testimonios* by combatants in the 26 of July Movement and later in the campaigns against the counter-revolutionary bands in the Escambray mountains and at the Bay of Pigs."[23] This literature of personal witness represented precisely the type of revolutionary artistic expression welcomed by the regime.

Although both *Maestra voluntaria* and *Pasajes de la guerra revolucionaria* are not true documentary novels, they nonetheless paved the way for the popular support that Miguel Barnet's *Biografía de un cimarrón* (1966) and *Canción de Rachel* (1969) brought to this new narrative form. In 1970, Barnet stated: "Para mí la novela testimonio como yo la veo es un canal de expresión extraordinario, útil, necesario—casi diría yo inevitable—para un país como el nuestro, que aún no puede definirse porque se conoce muy poco"[24] (For me the documentary novel, as I see it, is an extraordinary, useful, necessary channel of expression—I would almost say inevitable—for a country like ours that still cannot define itself, for it knows little of itself).

After the publication and wide success of *Biografía de un cimarrón* and *Canción de Rachel,* Barnet wrote his critical poetics for this new genre, "La novela testimonio: socio-literatura." Here Barnet attempted to explain the hybrid nature of the documentary novel—part history, part sociology, part novel—by elaborating its most salient features and characteristics. Well aware of the limitations of his study, for Barnet saw himself more as *un gestor* (a writer-promoter) of this literary form than as a theoretician, he hoped that his essay would be a first step for other critics to build upon. Yet, Barnet was certain that the documentary novel would continue to proliferate: "La novela-testimonio va a crecer en nuestro continente, estoy seguro. La necesidad, como dicen los negros viejos, obliga" (p. 150) (I for one am certain that the documentary novel will prosper in Latin America. As the old blacks say, necessity requires it).

In 1970 Casa de las Américas decided to include "el género literario de testimonio" (the documentary genre) among the categories for their annual prize. Raúl González de Cascorro, winner of the 1975 prize for documentary writing for his *Aquí se habla de combatientes y de bandidos*, a book that uses the direct testimonies of more than sixty people who fought on either side of the Escambray struggle, stated in 1978:

> En el año 1970 la Casa de las Américas decide incluir en las bases de su concurso anual el género literario de testimonio. . . . Y se hace necesario prorrogar el plazo de admisión de este género y hasta dar información a los escritores de las características que deben observar los trabajos a concursar.[25]

> In 1970 Casa de las Américas decides to include the documentary genre in its annual competition. . . . And it becomes necessary to extend the deadline for admission and to even give the writers information concerning the characteristics that they should conform to in their submissions.

On account of this change, on February 28, 1970, there appeared in *Granma*, the official newspaper of the revolutionary government, precise information concerning this new category in the Casa de las Américas prizes. Stated briefly, the *testimonio* was to deal with "un libro donde se documente, de fuente directa, un aspecto de la realidad latinoamericana actual" (*Granma*, p. 2) (a book that documents, using direct sources, an aspect of present Latin American reality).

As it turned out, the winner of the 1970 prize for documentary writing was not a Cuban, but the Uruguayan María Ester Gilio for her work *La guerrilla tupamara*, which chronicled the Tupamaro liberation movement's fight against dictatorial oppression in Uruguay. However, the committee unanimously granted a first-place honorable mention to *Girón en la memoria* by the Cuban writer Víctor Casaus, a book that "atestigua la gran victoria obtenida por el pueblo de Cuba contra el imperialismo norteamericano; . . . la técnica de investigación y narrativa utilizada constituye un modo capaz de fijar pautas en el género" (documents the great victory of the Cuban people over North American imperialism; . . . the investigative and narrative techniques used provide a way of establishing useful guidelines for this genre).[26] The jury also granted, again unanimously, a second-place honorary mention to another Cuban writer's work, Jorge Calderón González's *Amparo: millo y azucenas*. In addition, *Mi isla es un cocodrilo verde* by Cuban writers Elena Díaz and Germán Sánchez, together with *Por llanos y montañas* by Aracely de Aguililla (also Cuban), were recommended for publication. Although the first prize was not awarded to a Cuban writer, four prizes were given *por unanimidad* (unanimously) to Cuban writers whose works were subsequently published.

Although the competition of Casa de las Américas was perhaps the most important annual literary event in Latin America during the 1960s and 1970s, it was by no means the only literary contest open to Cubans. As Lourdes Casal states in her essay on the Cuban novel: "Además de los concursos de la Casa de las Américas, que tanta importancia han tenido como estímulo a los novelistas y cuentistas, se han creado otros muchos" (In addition to the competitions of Casa de las Américas, which have provided such an important incentive for novelists and short story writers, many other competitions have been created).[27]

On February 3, 1971, *Granma* announced the literary contest "26 de julio" (26th of July) as a way to pay homage to those who had died in the assault on the Moncada barracks. The *testimonio* was established as a category in this contest. When the awards were announced on July 30, 1971, the documentary prize went to Commander José Quevedo Pérez's *La batalla de Jigüe,* a book that describes how the writer, who had commanded a battalion in Batista's army, reconsidered his moral and political position after the battle of Jigüe. At the awards ceremony it was stated: "[T]enemos el propósito de continuar promoviendo este género [testimonial] en forma constante, por el elevado valor científico y educativo del conocimiento de una historia, que como la nuestra, es tan aleccionadora"[28] (It is our intention constantly to continue promoting this [documentary genre] because of the highly valuable scientific and educational understanding it provides of an instructive history such as ours).

A significant change in the prizes of Casa de las Américas occurred in 1975. For that year's competition, the novel, short story, poetry, and theater were placed together in a single category. A second category consisted of the essay and the *testimonios,* leaving the third category earmarked for children's literature.[29] The importance placed on documentary literature as a result of these changes is apparent. The winner of the 1975 prize for *testimonio* was the previously mentioned *Aquí se habla de combatientes y de bandidos* by Raúl González de Cascorro, a novel later published in the *Colección Premio* of the Casa de las Américas publishing house. On February 8, 1975, Raúl González de Cascorro, in an interview with *Granma,* stated that his novel derived from three years of investigations he had performed concerning the "lucha contra bandidos en la provincia agramontina" (struggle against bandits in Agramonte [in Cuba's Matanzas Province]). Previously in 1974 González de Cascorro had won the UNEAC prize for theater for his *El hijo de Arturo Estévez* that treated the same theme. In his 1975 interview with *Granma* he added:

> La riqueza del tema y el querer apresar en distintos géneros literarios esa gesta heroica de nuestro pueblo, me llevó a escribir un libro testimonio. . . . Evadirnos mediante otro tipo de literatura que no esté de acuerdo con nuestro tiempo, no es la posición adecuada para un escritor que se considere comprometido.[30]

> The richness of the subject and the desire to capture that heroic moment in a different literary genre made me write a documentary book. . . . To lose ourselves in another type of literature that is not in tune with our times is not the proper position for a writer that considers him- or herself committed.

On January 24, 1975, there appeared an interview in *Granma* with Héctor P. Agosti, one of the judges for the 1975 Premio Casa de las Américas in the *testimonio* category. In his remarks Agosti maintained that the documentary was a relatively new but important genre:

> Ante todo creo que toda literatura es testimonial, incluso la poesía que se presume como la más pura, pero refiriéndonos a él como género nuevo, que acaso tenga su modelo en *Los diez días que estremecieron al mundo* de John Reed, el testimonio se emparenta con las formas más altas del periodismo. Es un género que a mí se me ocurre apasionante, con posibilidades extraordinarias en nuestra América Latina, donde hay infinitos temas que pueden ser abordados y esclarecidos por esta literatura testimonial.[31]

> First of all, I believe that all literature is documentary, even poetry, which considers itself the most pure. But the documentary, a new genre which perhaps might have its model in *Ten Days That Shook the World* by John Reed, has much in common with the most elevated forms of journalism. It is a genre that I consider passionate, with extraordinary possibilities for Latin America, where there are an infinite number of themes that can be examined and illuminated by documentary literature.

To date the documentary genre still enjoys a position of importance within Cuban letters; the best-seller lists published regularly in *Bohemia* reflect its popularity. In addition, the *testimonio* is still one of the chief prize categories for Casa de las Américas.

Miguel Barnet: Novel, Documentary, or Documentary Novel?

In her study "Novela-testimonio: historia y literatura," Nubya C. Casas establishes the documentary as a genre that expresses itself in five forms: (1) chronicles and reporting, (2) memoirs, (3) professional investigations, (4) diaries, and (5) documentary novels. It is this last that has produced the most interest and debate. The difficulties in providing a generic definition for *testimonio* become twofold when one attempts to define the more protean *novela testimonio* (documentary novel). According to John Beverley, *testimonio* is the general category for narrative texts "told in the first person by a narrator who is also the real protagonist or witness of the events he or she recounts, and whose unit of narration is usually a 'life' or a significant life experience."[32] The documentary novel, on the other hand, is a specific literary manifestation within the general *testimonio* category. Barbara Foley (*Telling the Truth: The Theory and Practice of Documentary Fiction*) claims that the documentary novel "locates itself near the border between factual discourse and fictive discourse, but does not propose an eradication of that border. Rather, it purports to represent reality by means of agreed-upon conceptions of fictionality, while grafting onto its fictive pact some kind of additional claim to empirical validation" (p. 25). This integration of fact and fiction, according to Foley, creates a so-called mimetic contract that persuades the reader to trust the legitimacy of the writer's words.

The hybrid nature of the documentary genre, which appropriates conventions of ethnography, history, and literature, has caused much debate. My intention, however, is not to continue debating its generic definition—a futile enterprise in light of contemporary literary efforts at erasing the traditional boundaries of genre—but rather to show how the genre was widely promoted and disseminated in Cuba from the early years of the Revolution and, consequently, to describe its impact on Cuban writers in general and on Reinaldo Arenas specifically. It is evident that the explicit emphasis on the documentary function of the artistic media (cinema, popular music, and theater, among others) by Cuba's revolutionary cultural policies has influenced literary forms. Miguel Barnet's documentary novels are a clear example of how the Revolution's ideological coordinates were integrated into the novel form. Barnet has always insisted that his texts, starting with *Biografía de un cimarrón*, are all documentary novels, a combination, fusion, or synthesis of true life experiences with the writer's artistic contributions. However, after *Biografía de un cimarrón*, Barnet renegotiated this synthesis of fact and fiction in his documentary novels.

According to Nubya C. Casas's study, based on close observations of both Miguel Barnet's novels and his critical texts, all documentary novels have a common textual structure:

> [T]odos los testimonios que hemos estudiado se ajustan a esta estructura textual. . . . Hay un informante—testigo o *testimonialista*—que revela un hecho ignorado, o un aspecto de éste, en el que ha estado envuelto directa o indirectamente. Se esfuerza, además, porque esta información se conserve—por escrito—en la opinión de que es un valioso documento histórico.[33]

> [A]ll the documentary texts that we have studied conform to this textual structure. . . . There is an informant—witness or *testifier*—who reveals an unknown event, or an aspect of one, in which he or she has been involved directly or indirectly. Moreover, he or she struggles to preserve this information—in writing—believing it is a valuable historical document.

By examining Miguel Barnet's documentary novels we immediately see how this general textual structure (which I shall designate as *testigo-testar-testamento*) is indeed evident in *Biografía de un cimarrón* (1966), *Canción de Rachel* (1969), *Gallego* (1981), and *La vida real* (1984). All four novels give voice to a *testigo* or witness (Esteban Montejo, Rachel, Manuel Ruiz, Julián Mesa) who discloses (*testar* 'to state') ignored events (concerning slavery in Cuba and the War of Independence, the first republican era, immigration, emigration) by leaving a valuable document or *testamento* (will) that rescues important facts that otherwise would be lost. (These include an account of slave conditions, republican corruption, immigrant exploitation, and the misery of prerevolutionary life that forced thousands to emigrate to the United States.) Furthermore, all four witnesses are marginal members of society who, before the Revolution, suffered discrimination because of their race, class, or sex.[34] Esteban Montejo, Rachel, Manuel Ruiz, and Julián Mesa are what Barnet calls *la gente sin historia* (people without a history) who would lack a voice in society if it were not for documentary narratives: "Tenemos que ser la conciencia de nuestra cultura, el alma y la voz de los *hombres sin historia*" (We have to be the conscience of our culture, the soul and voice of *people without a history*).[35]

Barnet's documentary novels are built on two separate acts of enunciation that must renegotiate authority in order to produce literary representation: the voice of the narrator-investigator and the voice of the narrator-informer. The question then arises, Who really "speaks" in the documentary text? In Barnet's *Biografía de un cimarrón*, for example, is it Esteban Montejo (the narrator-informer-interviewee) or Barnet (the narrator-investigator-interviewer)? The answer is not simple and the issue has produced much debate.[36] Regardless of the controversies we can say that the double act of enunciation on which the documentary novel is based produces a text that, in order to communicate, must erase differences and accentuate affinities. Thus, in the documentary novel to narrate is to present a common front that is grounded in the uniformity of the revolutionary message. According to Barnet ("Testimonio y comunicación: una vía hacia la identidad," p. 137): "La política cubana, en perfecta armonía con la intención del investigador social o del escritor, está encaminada al rescate de los valores culturales plenos, así como a su identificación y divulgación" (Cuban politics, in perfect harmony with the social investigator or writer's intentions, is moving to preserve the genuine cultural values, as well as to identify and disseminate them).

The narrative pact between narrator-investigator and narrator-informer requires the narrator-investigator (writer) to select, organize, and polish the oral interviews of his or her witness and then present these to the reader as the experiences of an individual who was alienated from society before the advent of the Revolution, but who, since its triumph, has been welcomed into (or given a voice in) society. In the documentary novel there is a fundamental struggle between aesthetics and the accurate representation of fact. This is a struggle that Barnet himself constantly had to renegotiate, as for example in *Canción de Rachel, Gallego,* and *La vida real,* in which fictionalization acquires a more significant position, although never a more important position, than accurate documentary representation.

Specific Characteristics and Features
of the Documentary Novel

Below is a list of the characteristics and features that are displayed in documentary novels. I have taken these from Miguel Barnet's critical writings concerning the genre. First the characteristic or feature is presented; then it is substantiated by Barnet's own words.

(1) *In documentary novels a witness, who is representative of a group and not atypical or sensational, is chosen to give voice to a people without a history. Consequently, a first-person narrative voice is used to establish authenticity and verisimilitude.*

La primera característica que debe poseer toda novela-testimonio [es] un desentrañamiento de la realidad, tomando los hechos principales, los que más han afectado la sensibilidad de un pueblo y describiéndolos por boca de uno de sus protagonistas más idóneos. ("La novela testimonio: socio-literatura," p. 135)

The first characteristic I think every documentary novel should have [is] that it should disentangle reality, focusing on those key historical events that have most affected the sensibilities of a people and presenting them in the words of one of its most suitable protagonists.

(2) *The use of "real" witnesses.*

Cimarrón o Rachel, sin proponérselo, son testigos . . . reales, en la medida sociológica y no en la literaria porque a pesar de que están recreados por mí, manejados por medio de algunas cuerdas de ficción, son seres de carne y hueso, reales y convincentes. ("La novela testimonio: socio-literatura," p. 135)

Cimarrón [Esteban Montejo] or Rachel, without asking to be, are . . . real witnesses, in a sociological rather than a literary sense. Despite the fact that I have recreated them by pulling a few literary strings, they are made of flesh-and-blood, they are real and convincing.

(3) *Events are presented chronologically; there is a respect for sequential order.*

Las secuencias cronológicas, sobre todo cuando la obra se basa en la contrapuntística [como *Canción de Rachel*], es fundamental. . . . [T]odo ha de estar supeditado a un orden de conjunto. Para lograr este fin una cronología es indispensable porque fija la orientación histórica. No se trata de convertir la obra en un rompecabezas. ("La novela testimonio: socio-literatura," p. 147)

Chronology is fundamental, above all when the work is based on a counterpoint structure [like *Canción de Rachel*]. . . . [E]verything has to be reduced to an organizing principle. Chronology is indispensable to achieving this because it establishes a historical orientation. The point isn't to turn the book into a jigsaw puzzle.

(4) *Documents, papers, photographs, and memoirs are included in order to authenticate the testimony given.*

Junto a las gavetas con las fichas del fruto de las entrevistas, deben estar las copias de los documentos, fotografías, recortes de periódicos, impresos en general, libros de consulta . . . ("La novela testimonio: socio-literatura," p. 147)

Along with drawers filled with records of interviews, one must have copies of documents, photographs, press clippings, general printed matter, reference books . . .

(5) *As a result of the emphasis placed on the oral nature of the testimony, there is a mistrust of literary forms.*

Sabemos que poner a un informante es, en cierta medida, hacer literatura. Pero no intentamos nosotros crear un documento literario, una novela. (*Biografía de un cimarrón*, p. 18)

We know that to allow an informer to speak is, in a certain way, to create literature. However, we are not trying to create a literary document, a novel.

(6) *The documentary novel reinterprets and rewrites recorded history from the perspective of an official revolutionary historiography to reveal events not known and to rescue the past from conventional or distorted accounts.*

El fenómeno histórico también engaña. Generalmente nos da la cara más diáfana, o lo más sobresaliente de su composición. Y lo otro queda velado. Como envuelto por un realismo dominante. Lo difícil es quitarle a ese hecho histórico la máscara con que ha sido cubierto por la visión prejuiciada y clasista. . . . El gestor de la novela-testimonio tiene una sagrada misión y es la de revelar la otra cara de la medalla, . . . descubrir lo intrínseco del fenómeno, sus verdaderas causales y sus verdaderos efectos. ("La novela testimonio: socio-literatura," p. 138)

The historical phenomenon can also be misleading since it can present its most diaphanous face, or its most outstanding elements. The "other" remains veiled, as if draped by a dominant realism. What is difficult, is to remove from that historical event the mask of prejudiced class outlook with which it has been covered. . . . The writer-promoter of the documentary novel has a sacred mission to reveal the other side of the coin, . . . to discover the intrinsic elements, the real causes and effects.

Time has been taken to establish the general structure and specific characteristics and features common to documentary fiction in order to demonstrate how the novels of Reinaldo Arenas's *pentagonía* indeed fit the general textual structure of *testigo-testar-testamento* while simultaneously subverting and deviating from the aspects of the genre that place more emphasis on the documentary elements of the text than on its aesthetics. Whether Arenas subverted the tradition of the Cuban documentary novel consciously or unconsciously is not germane to this study. By now it is accepted that no writer works in a literary vacuum. We will see that Arenas, like all Cuban writers quite aware of the type of literary expression expected by the revolutionary regime, appears to have assimilated and subverted the documentary function of Cuba's artistic media in *Celestino antes del alba, El palacio de las blanquísimas mofetas, Otra vez el mar, El color del verano,* and *El asalto,* texts conceived in a highly politicized atmosphere in which literature was perceived as a vehicle for shaping revolutionary consciousness.[37] How Arenas specifically incorporated the general textual structure and organizing principle of the documentary novel is the subject of the next chapter.

TWO

The Pentagonía: Giving Voice to the Voiceless

Arenas in Cuba

During the late 1960s and the early part of 1970, before falling into disfavor with the revolutionary regime, Reinaldo Arenas contributed articles to *La Gaceta de Cuba* and *Unión,* two periodicals published by UNEAC. In 1968 he published a review in *Unión* of Antonio Benítez Rojo's collection of short stories *Tute de Reyes* (1967). He wrote:

> Un libro al que se le haya otorgado algún premio literario debe leerse siempre con recelo. Las lecturas de casi todas las obras premiadas nos han creado el prejuicio, muy justificado, de que dichas obras son, generalmente, panfletos de escaso valor literario o libros insignificantes y simplistas, sin puntos misteriosos u oscuros; sin atrevidas innovaciones que los jurados, en un plazo siempre limitado, no podrían descubrir ni detenerse a discutirlas. Con la mayoría de las obras premiadas en Cuba (y en cualquier sitio) se podría escribir otra *Historia universal de la infamia* más extensa, desde luego, que la ya comenzada por el gran poeta argentino Jorge Luis Borges. Obras como *Cualquiercosario, Maestra voluntaria, Gente de playa Girón, Los hombres de a caballo* y otros *horrores,* son testimonio desgraciadamente irrebatibles de que *el premio* muchas veces no es el premio. ("Benítez entra en el juego," pp. 146–47)

A book that has been awarded a literary prize should always be read with suspicion. Our readings of almost all the works that have been awarded prizes have prejudiced us, and very justifiably so, since these works are, generally speaking, propaganda of little literary worth, insignificant and simplistic books, without mysterious or dark moments; books without daring innovations that juries, always with a limited amount of time, could not discover or stop to discuss. With the majority of works that have been awarded prizes in Cuba (and in any place) one could very well write another, yet more extensive, *Universal History of Infamy* than the one already started by the great Argentine poet Jorge Luis Borges. Books like *Cualquiercosario, Maestra voluntaria, Gente de playa Girón, Los hombres de a caballo* and other *horrors,* unfortunately give indisputable testimony that *the prize* many times is not the prize.

The texts mentioned above all won prizes in the annual Casa de las Américas literary competition. Arenas's suggestion that one could well write another *Universal History of Infamy*—the title of Jorge Luis Borges's bizarre 1935 collection of fictionalized histories of unsavory individuals—makes clear his contempt for these winning texts. The short story collection *Cualquiercosario* by Jorge Onetti, the son of the celebrated Uruguayan writer Juan Carlos Onetti, won the short story prize in 1965. Daura Olema García's *Maestra voluntaria* won for best novel in 1962, while *Gente de playa Girón* by Raúl González de Cascorro was judged best short story collection in that same year. The Argentine David Viñas, an ardent Marxist, won the prize for best novel in 1967 for his *Los hombres de a caballo.* Although these are not, strictly speaking, documentary novels, they nonetheless reflect a revolutionary conceptual perspective and strive to inculcate in their readers a revolutionary consciousness.[1] It is clear that Arenas was well aware of the type of literary expression that enjoyed governmental sanction in Cuba. Ironically, he underscores that the awarding of prizes to mediocre and simplistic (propagandistic) works only attests to the (revolutionary) politics behind literary production in Cuba. The review was published at a time when criticism was still tolerated by the Revolution, and Arenas goes on sarcastically to express his amazement that a prize was awarded to Antonio Benítez Rojo's book by Casa de las Américas—"El libro no solamente merece el premio, sino que asombra que se le haya otorgado" (p. 147) (The book not only deserves the prize, but it is amazing that it received it)—for this is a complex and varied book of imagination and fantasy that erases traditional boundaries, a book intended for a sophisticated reader willing to tackle the challenges it presents. Arenas continues:

Es además un libro variado donde sorprenden tanto los aciertos como los defectos, y donde la verdadera unidad—la médula del libro—lo forman, más que las anécdotas que se cuentan y el contenido de las mismas, el propio estilo del autor, el mundo que él inventa o recrea; su imaginación. Libro a veces fantástico y por lo tanto verdaderamente realista . . . (p. 147)

Moreover, it is a diverse book where the finer points, as well as its defects, are surprising, and where the true unity—the essence of the book—is shaped by the author's style, the world he invents or recreates, by his imagination, more than by any anecdote or theme he narrates. A book that is at times fantastic and, therefore, truly realistic . . .

In essence, what Arenas has done in this review (and we should keep in mind that at the time this review was written *Celestino antes del alba* had just appeared and was the target of unfavorable criticism for its lack of documentary realism) is to describe and defend his own aesthetic position: the literary text as a limitless space where the writer's imagination and fantasy are free to soar. With *Celestino antes del alba*—published when Arenas was only twenty-two years old—it was already clear that he had no intentions of writing a closed, linear text that presented a coherent, objective representation of empirical reality. In the novels that were to follow Arenas would become progressively more daring in his compositional experimentation and subversion of authoritarian and reductionist attitudes toward literature and life. It was this refusal to establish a clear revolutionary consciousness in his writings that forced the Revolution finally to censor and designate Arenas's texts as counterrevolutionary.

The strong government support given to documentary literature in Cuba is evident in the large print runs for certain first-edition novels: *Maestra voluntaria* (10,000 copies), *La guerrilla Tupamara* (20,000), *Biografía de un cimarrón* (20,000), *La batalla de Jigüe* (20,000), and *Canción de Rachel* (25,000). If one compares these figures to the 2,000 copies issued of the first edition of Arenas's *Celestino antes del alba* (1967) and the 4,000 copies for the first edition of Lezama Lima's *Paradiso* (1966) the discrepancy is apparent. It was obviously a question of what type of literature the Cuban state chose to support, since the new editorial houses could easily have published a greater number of copies. As Pamela María Smorkaloff writes in *Literatura y edición de libros*: "De 1962 a 1966, la nueva organización del sistema editorial posibilita el perfeccionamiento de lo aprendido en la etapa anterior con respecto al quehacer editorial. . . .

Las novelas tienen ahora tiradas más armónicas, de quince a veinte mil ejemplares" (From 1962 to 1966, the new organization of the editorial system brings about the consolidation of what was learned in the previous stage with respect to editorial work. . . . Novels now begin to be published more consistently in editions of fifteen to twenty thousand copies).[2] This revolutionary support for and monitoring of what was considered acceptable literature—that is, literature that reflected revolutionary reality and projected the revolutionary message in an attempt to help build social consciousness—was the literary atmosphere in which Arenas found himself writing until his escape from Cuba in 1980 through the Mariel boatlift.

The Pentagonía: Testigo-Testar-Testamento

While living in Cuba Reinaldo Arenas published only *Celestino antes del alba* and a few short stories. After his fall from favor with the revolutionary government, his books were no longer published on the island.[3] As a result, he secretly began to send his manuscripts abroad, many of which were printed in pirated editions. When he arrived in the United States in 1980, Arenas saw the need for definitive editions of his works. Thus, in 1982 an authorized edition of *Celestino antes del alba*, retitled *Cantando en el pozo*, appeared.[4] In the preliminary note to this revised edition, Arenas mentions for the first time a projected *pentagonía* (pentagony) about Cuban society that would consist of *Celestino antes del alba* (*Cantando en el pozo*), *El palacio de las blanquísimas mofetas*, *Otra vez el mar*, *El color del verano*, and *El asalto*. Well aware of the emphasis laid on the documentary-testimonial function of the artistic media in Cuba, Arenas appears intentionally to play off the words *testigo* (witness) and *testimonio* (testimony) in the preliminary note to this new edition:

En todo este ciclo furioso, monumental y único, narrado por un autor-*testigo*, aunque el protagonista perece en cada obra, vuelve a renacer en la siguiente con distinto nombre pero con igual objetivo y rebeldía: cantar el horror y la vida de la gente. Permanece así en medio de una época convulsionada y terrible, como tabla de salvación y esperanza, la intransigencia del hombre—creador, poeta, rebelde— contra todos los postulados represivos que intentan fulminarlo. Aunque el poeta perezca, *el testimonio* de la escritura que deja es *testimonio* de su triunfo ante la represión y el crimen. Triunfo que ennoblece y a la vez es patrimonio del género humano (emphasis added).

In all this feverish cycle, monumental and unique, narrated by an au-
thor-*witness*, although the protagonist perishes in each work, he is reborn in the following ones with a different name, but with the same
rebellion and objective: to sing of the horror and the life of the people. In this way he endures in a turbulent and terrible era, like
a life raft of hope, the intransigence of man—creator, poet, rebel—
against all the axiomatic truths that would censure him. Although
the poet might perish, the *testimony* of writing he leaves behind is
a *testimony* of his triumph in the face of repression and legal persecution. His triumph ennobles him and is at the same time patrimony of
the human condition (emphasis added).

With this statement, Arenas proposes that although *Celestino antes del
alba, El palacio de las blanquísimas mofetas, Otra vez el mar, El color del
verano,* and *El asalto* are works of fiction, they nonetheless are valid testimonies of human dignity in the face of oppression. The testimonial or
documentary structure of these texts is clearly outlined by Arenas's words:
"un autor-testigo" (a writer-witness) who testifies to "el horror y la vida
de la gente" (the horror and life of the people) by leaving a valuable
"testimonio" (testimony) of his triumph over "la represión" (repression).[5]
Arenas positions the pentalogy within the general textual structure of
testigo-testar-testamento. Each of the five works features a witness (the
child-narrator/Celestino; Fortunato; Héctor; the trinity that unites Gabriel, Reinaldo, and the Tétrica Mofeta; the nameless narrator of the final
novel) with an urgent need to give testimony about his particular world.
Their worlds range from the child-narrator/Celestino's rural existence of
deprivation and violence; to Fortunato's frustration, extreme poverty, and
tortured family existence; Héctor's personal and sexual angst; the struggle
of Gabriel/Reinaldo/the Tétrica Mofeta to survive within a homosexual
subculture while being persecuted by a homophobic and hostile military
regime; and the nameless narrator's impressions of a tyrannical and abominable future society in which individual rights are sacrificed for the good
of the state. Moreover, each witness (with the exception of the nameless
protagonist of *El asalto,* who inhabits a world where citizens have virtually
forgotten how to speak and are only allowed to recite the party's official
dialogues) attempts to leave a written document of these events: the
incessant writing of Celestino on tree trunks and Fortunato on stolen
reams of paper, Héctor's anguished cantos, Gabriel/Reinaldo/the Tétrica
Mofeta's determination to write and rewrite his lost novel, *El color del*

verano. The testimony in each novel progressively struggles to articulate, expanding from presignification (Celestino's scribbling on trees) to signification (Héctor's cantos and Gabriel/Reinaldo/the Tétrica Mofeta's anecdotes and stories of survival). In addition, each witness dies in order to be reborn to new realities that affirm the power of the poetic spirit over repression and destruction. The only novel in which the protagonist does not die is *El asalto*. Ironically, the final novel of the pentalogy leaves the reader with a glimmer of hope. The decrepit tyrant el Reprimerísimo Reprimero (the Represident) is destroyed, and the protagonist, who has suffered countless persecutions throughout the five-book cycle, can finally stretch out on the beach and rest.

The characters-witnesses of the five novels clearly and honestly intone the persecution and anguish they experience. Indeed, the aesthetic distance of fiction in no way diminishes the authenticity of these voices, whose marginal perspectives are precisely those that the documentary novel was designed to give voice to. Not all marginal informers, however, have enjoyed the same recognition in Cuban revolutionary society; those individuals who value the imaginative over the historical or who do not represent the ideal *hombre nuevo* (new man) of the Revolution have not been given a voice within the state for they represent a threat to the established order. Cuban documentary writers give voice to witnesses who provide information about their personal lives, but nevertheless do so to emphasize how in the past certain members of society (for example, blacks, women, immigrants) were left out and alienated. These are *la gente sin historia* (people without a history) whom the writers of documentary novels wish to incorporate into the new revolutionary society. Arenas's characters-witnesses—dissidents, "extravagants," dreamers, freethinkers, homosexuals—are also people without a history. They represent those individuals not welcomed into the new revolutionary regime, for they fail to contribute, in the government's eyes, to the political and sociohistorical legitimacy of a revolutionary consciousness.[6] It is precisely these marginal voices, these social outcasts, these victims of totalitarian utopianism, these so-called people without a history whom Arenas allows to speak and welcomes into his novels.

These texts never propose a narrow or specific historical definition; they never give an oversimplified historical explanation for a character's existential dilemmas, nor do they try to rewrite history from an official point of view in the attempt to help build a revolutionary consciousness. Nonetheless, historical realities are not ignored, as each novel is embedded in a specific sociohistorical context: *Celestino antes del alba,* the prerevolutionary years; *El palacio de las blanquísimas mofetas,* the last years of the Batista regime; *Otra vez el mar,* the first decade of the Revolution; *El color del verano,* the 1960s and 1970s in Cuba; *El asalto,* an imaginary future Cuban society that the writer allows himself to invent and examine. In 1983 Arenas stated: "En todo país, y especialmente en los países totalitarios, hay una historia oficial que es la que generalmente se publica, pero la historia real, la que se padece, solamente pueden contarla sus víctimas. . . . [A] mí me interesa más la historia contada por sus intérpretes que por los historiadores"[7] (In every country, and especially in totalitarian countries, there exists an official history, which is generally what gets published, but the real history that people suffer through can only be told by its victims. . . . I prefer history told by its interpreters rather than by the historians).

In the above statement the word *intérpretes* (interpreters) could well be replaced by the word *testigos* (witnesses). While historians claim to record and faithfully reconstruct the "facts" and "truth" of the past, interpreters (witnesses) of history provide their own versions and personal accounts of events often forgotten and overlooked by historiography. Arenas makes known his distrust of history's legitimating discourse of power, for it is subject to the changing ideological constructions of whatever group finds itself in control. Still, he does support the documentary novel's basic principle of giving voice to the voiceless, those who have been forgotten by history. Arenas proclaims his affinity with the victims of totalitarian oppression who are banished to the lower levels of the social pyramid simply because they fail to legitimate the ideology of the group in power.

El color del verano: The End of a Cycle

In his autobiography, Arenas informs us that although *El color del verano* is the fourth novel of the *pentagonía,* it was in fact the last novel he wrote (*Antes que anochezca,* pp. 12–13). He also tells of his determination, despite his precarious health, to complete the novel. In this respect *El color del verano* is a significant text, for with it Arenas was finally able to bring to a close a cycle of novels he began writing three decades earlier. In the prologue to *El color del verano,* which playfully appears halfway through the text (pp. 246–50) and purposely erases the lines between fiction and metafiction, the documentary nature of this fourth novel of the quintet is underscored:

De alguna forma esta obra pretende reflejar, sin zalamerías ni altiso-
nantes principios, la vida entre picaresca y desgarrada de gran parte
de la juventud cubana, sus deseos de ser jóvenes, de existir como
tales. Predomina aquí la visión subterránea de un mundo homosexual
que seguramente nunca aparecerá en ningún periódico del mundo y
mucho menos en Cuba. Esta novela está intrínsicamente arraigada a
una de las épocas más vitales de mi vida y de la mayoría de los que
fuimos jóvenes durante las décadas del sesenta y del setenta. *El color
del verano* es un mundo que si no lo escribo se perderá fragmentado
en la memoria de los que lo conocieron. (p. 249)

To a certain extent this work pretends to reflect, without flattery
or high-sounding principles, the life of a great portion of Cuban
youths—somewhere between the picaresque and dissolute—their desires to be young and to exist as such. The underground vision of a
homosexual world, which surely will never appear anywhere in news-
papers, and much less in Cuba, predominates here in these pages.
This novel is intrinsically tied to one of the most vital eras of my life
and that of a great majority of us who were young during the sixties
and seventies. If I don't write about it, *El color del verano* is a world
that will be lost and fragmented in the memory of those who knew
and lived it.

Who writes this prologue? The willfully ambiguous but provocative
answer lies in the fact that both Reinaldo Arenas (the flesh-and-blood
writer) and Gabriel/Reinaldo/the Tétrica Mofeta (the fictitious writer)
are the writers of a novel entitled *El color del verano*. This *mise-en-abyme*
undermines the authority of traditional authorship that is central to the
documentary novel; the writer-narrator-investigator presumes to control
the work and convey precisely what he or she wishes. Yet, more important, in keeping with the general organizing principle of the genre, the
writer(s) of the prologue to *El color del verano* carefully underscore(s) the
importance of recording this particular era in Cuban history that would
be lost forever if not preserved in writing.

The prologue also reveals how the novel, originally conceived and started
in Cuba, fell victim to revolutionary censorship on the island. The distinc-
tions between reality and fiction are blurred, instead of being carefully
kept separate as in the documentary novel. The Tétrica Mofeta, Arenas's
fictitious alter ego, is forever rewriting his novel because it has been either
confiscated, stolen, lost, or destroyed (for example, see pages 66, 108–9,

122, 202, 441); while Arenas, the extra-literary writer, recounts how he had to memorize certain chapters of *El color del verano*—for example, "El hueco de Clara" (Clara's Hole)—and the thirty tongue twisters in order to guarantee the survival of these portions of the manuscript.[8]

The prologue also underscores both the personal importance of the *pentagonía* in the writer's life and the societal significance of metaphorically representing twentieth-century Cuban history. Still, the writer confesses his contradictory feelings of grief and tenderness over what he refers to as the malady of Cuban history:

> Siento una desolación sin término, una pena inalcanzable por todo ese mal y hasta una furiosa ternura ante mi pasado y mi presente. Esa desolación y ese amor de alguna forma me han conminado a escribir esta pentagonía que además de ser la historia de mi furia y de mi amor es una metáfora de mi país. (pp. 248–49)

> I feel an interminable anguish, an unreachable pain as a result of all that wrong. Yet, I also feel a raging tenderness for my past and present life. In some way, that anguish and that love have driven me to write this pentagony, which in addition to being the story of my fury and my love is also a metaphor for my country.

The driving force behind the writer's desire to write this cycle of novels is revealed as a complicated combination of love and pain, a fusion of conflicting emotions that requires a metaphorical (literary) language to articulate and suggest. While the documentary novel is presented as a tightly woven network of determined significations, a set of so-called real affirmations in which reference is guaranteed by the correspondence of language to some objective reality existing before being called forth in language, the novels of the *pentagonía* make no attempt to establish such a correspondence. Arenas's texts do not presume to be anything but what they are, pure fiction. And as fiction, they delight in the deployment of a poetic and metaphorical language that alludes, suggests, and evokes, touching the reader and drawing him or her into a dazzling and provocative literary space of multiple possibilities.

Toward the end of the prologue, the reader is given a summary of each novel of the cycle and the role each text plays in the total *pentagonía*. In effect, the preliminary note to *Cantando en el pozo* (1982) is here rewritten with minor but significant additions. The fact that the note reappears only underscores its importance, especially in this, the last novel Arenas wrote.

It is clear that for Arenas the *pentagonía* was a living and vital testimony of his "desolación y amor" (anguish and love) for his country. It is important to reproduce the following paragraph in its entirety to better appreciate the changes from the statement in *Cantando en el pozo*. I have highlighted in the text the most significant passages added to the 1990 note:

En todas estas novelas, el personaje central es un autor testigo que perece (*en las primeras cuatro obras*) y vuelve a renacer en las siguientes con diferente nombre pero con la misma airada rebeldía: cantar o contar el horror y la vida de la gente, *incluyendo la suya*. Permanece así, en medio de una época conmocionada y terrible (*que en estas novelas abarca más de cien años*), como tabla de salvación o de esperanza, la intransigencia del hombre—creador, poeta, rebelde—ante todos los postulados represivos que intentan fulminarlo, *incluyendo el espanto que él mismo pueda exhalar*. Aunque el poeta perezca, el testimonio de la escritura que deja, es testimonio de su triunfo ante la represión, la violencia y el crimen. Triunfo que ennoblece y a la vez es patrimonio del género humano *que además, de una u otra forma (ahora lo vemos otra vez) proseguirá su guerra contra la barbarie muchas veces disfrazada de humanismo*. (*El color del verano*, p. 250)

In all these novels, the main character is an author-witness who perishes (*in the first four works*) and is reborn in the following ones with a different name, but with the same angry rebelliousness: to sing or tell of the horror and the life of the people, *including his own*. In this way, he endures in the middle of a turbulent and terrible era (*which in these novels spans one hundred years*) like a life raft of hope, the intransigence of man—creator, poet, rebel—before all the axiomatic truths that would censure him, *including the horror that he himself is capable of emitting*. Although the poet might perish, the testimony of writing he leaves behind is a testimony of his triumph in the face of repression, violence, and legal persecution. His triumph ennobles him and is at the same time patrimony of the human condition *that in one way or another (today we see it again) continues its war against barbarity, often disguised as humanism*.

I would like to comment briefly on three of the additions in the revised note. The first is the insistence that the witness should provide a personal account of his experiences, not solely for the purpose of representing a specific group, like in the Cuban documentary novel, but also as an independent and authentic act of individual expression ("to sing or tell of the horror and the life of the people, including his own"). The responsibility of each character for creating his own "horror" is underscored by the phrase "including the horror that he himself is capable of emitting." This added revelation is significant in that it puts aside blaming a particular political group or government for the characters' vicissitudes while placing responsibility on the protagonist-witness, who in the final analysis is responsible for creating his own reality, be it a world of imaginative fantasies or an anguished hell. This final point is evident, for example, in *El asalto*, a novel in which the nameless protagonist, who in the previous four novels of the quintet emerges as a likeable character, is represented as an iniquitous and selfish individual who ultimately is responsible for the anguished hell he has created.

Secondly, the idea that barbarity (that is, exploitation, oppression, totalitarianism, intolerance, and so forth) can disguise itself as humanism comments on the sinister ambiguities, the devious and insidious nature of barbarity that can resurface and assert itself under different forms and guises. An example is a government's decision to round up so-called deviants and lock them up (as was the case in Cuba's infamous UMAP camps), at the same time presenting itself to the world as the champion of the underdogs and the downtrodden.[9] In 1984 Arenas dedicated an entire novel to this period in Cuban revolutionary history, *Arturo, la estrella más brillante*. First published in Barcelona in 1984, it is a fictitious account of one man's experiences in one of the many UMAP work camps that existed in Cuba in the late 1960s. In it the desire to document the conditions of the camps is focused from a literary perspective. It is interesting to note, however, that Arenas's text, presented as pure fiction, was born out of a desire to remember his friend Nelson Rodríguez Leyva, whose unpublished book of stories about his own experiences in an UMAP camp was confiscated and destroyed by the Cuban authorities. Far from being political propaganda, *Arturo, la estrella más brillante* is simply a defense of the individual right to dream, to rise above the oppression that threatens existence. In *El color del verano* Arenas ironically recalls the UMAP camps in a passage in which the dictator Fifo first denounces his minister of education and later has him killed for referring to these camps as "concentration camps for homosexuals" when in fact, according to Fifo, they are only "rehabilitation camps": "Nosotros lo que hacemos es educar o reducar, jamás concentramos a nadie a la fuerza. Esos jóvenes están ahí voluntariamente porque quieren reducarse" (p. 147) (What we do is edu-cate or reeducate, we never concentrate anyone by force. Those youths are there voluntarily because they want to be reeducated).

Finally, the observation that all of the novels of the pentalogy represent "a turbulent and terrible era (which in these novels spans one hundred years) like a life raft of hope" can be read as a parodic allusion to Gabriel García Márquez's novel *Cien años de soledad,* the story of the founding of Macondo by the Buendía family and of the town's progressive decay and final apocalyptic destruction over the course of a century. Many critics have seen García Márquez's fictional world of Macondo specifically as a history of Colombia and by extension a microcosm of Latin American history from colonialism to the present. Here Arenas suggests that the *pentagonía* likewise provides for the reader a history of twentieth-century Cuban society, and by extension a microcosm of Latin American total-itarianism, be it from the political right or left.[10]

One final aspect of *El color del verano* is relevant to our discussion of the Cuban documentary novel. Early in the novel (pp. 64–68), in a chapter entitled *Del bugarrón* (About the Bugger), the reader is introduced to a character identified simply as *el viejo bugarrón* (the old bugger). This old bugger, disillusioned by the fact that he considers himself to be one of the last of a disappearing breed on the island, decides to visit his grandfather, "un anciano de más de 130 años llamado Esteban Montejo" (p. 66) (an old man of more than 130 years called Esteban Montejo).[11] Believing his grand-father to also be a true bugger—and by definition a true bugger does not allow himself to be passive and is repelled by effeminate homosexuals and their extravagant behavior—he is disillusioned to find Montejo dressed in women's clothing and getting ready for the carnival. The appearance of Miguel Barnet's famous protagonist (recall ex-slave Esteban Montejo from Barnet's *Biografía de un cimarrón*) dressed in women's clothing—and Barnet himself is also fictionalized and ridiculed in the text as *Miguel Barniz,* "un pájaro de la peor catadura" (p. 360) (a faggot of the worst kind)—is a parodic undermining not only of Hispanic patriarchal ma-chismo but also of the seriousness and prominence of Barnet and his famous protagonist within the canon of Cuban revolutionary letters.[12] Significantly, the old bugger of *El color del verano* and Barnet's Esteban Montejo are both survivor-witnesses. As we recall, Barnet, a student at the Institute of Ethnography and Folklore of the Academy of Sciences, had discovered Montejo in the early 1960s and immediately began to record the stories of this unusual survivor of Cuba's past. The old man served the purpose of documenting, for the first time, Cuban history from a black man's point of view. Likewise, but on a more literarily subversive level, the old bugger of *El color del verano,* "el bugarrón número uno de la Isla de Cuba, . . . el único que se templó a Mella, a Grau San Martín y a Batista (todos ellos notables bugarrones), y después ay, a Fifo" (p. 64) (the number one bugger in Cuba, . . . the only one that fucked Mella, Grau San Martín and Batista [all prominent buggers themselves], and later alas!, Fifo), is also a survivor who has witnessed Cuba's governmental blunders and political mismanagement from the right (Fulgencio Batista) and the left (Julio Antonio Mella, Ramón Grau San Martín, and Fifo/ Fidel Castro). Arenas's old bugger is indeed a witness who gives "testimony" of the ineffectiveness of Cuban politics of the twentieth century, of the political polarization that has divided the Cuban people and failed to produce a fair and just system of government.

As we shall see in part 2 of this book, to enter the fictive universe of the novels of the *pentagonía* is to enter a precarious space that asserts its freedom from the rigid and banal set of narrative responses of orthodox Cuban socialist realism to which the documentary novel remains faithful. Arenas's novels belong to contemporary postmodern literature's unmasking of the inherent naïveté in the realistic novel's claim to veracity; to the belief that the literary text can indeed be a guarantor of fixed meaning, a repository of irrefutable truth. *Celestino antes del alba, El palacio de las blanquísimas mofetas, Otra vez el mar, El color del verano,* and *El asalto* are self-conscious texts that present a plurality of voices that dismantle all hierarchical discourses. The *pentagonía* shatters all expected generic boundaries and limitations in an attempt to provide the reader with a literary space of multiple possibilities. For Arenas, writing as a literary creative act was a necessity, a liberating act of self-expression, an emotional act of fury in which he challenged, undermined, and subverted all types of ideological dogmatism, all forms of absolute truths. This liberating energy, which takes on its own singular meaning and particular artistic goal in each text in the writer's oeuvre, is the single most salient feature of Arenas's writing.

In *The Art of the Novel* Czechoslovakian writer Milan Kundera suggests that perhaps all writers write a kind of single theme in their first work and variations thereafter. I believe that this observation is valid in speaking of Arenas's work. If one carefully examines his entire literary production, one finds an argumentative center that persistently resurfaces: a staunch defense of our imaginative capabilities and our right of self-expression in a world beset by barbarity, intolerance, and persecution.

PART TWO

The Pentagonía: Subversion
of the Cuban Documentary Novel's
Specific Characteristics

THREE

The First-Person Narrative Voice

In Miguel Barnet's documentary novels, as well as in other documentary texts, the presentation of a competent witness who tells the story of his or her life in the first person is a narrative strategy that aims to establish an immediate and trusting relationship with the reader. The witness is presented as an observer of history who remembers and informs the reader of past events in his or her own words. John Beverley ("The Margin at the Center: On *Testimonio* [Testimonial Narrative]") observes: "The dominant formal aspect of the *testimonio* is the voice that speaks to the reader in the form of an 'I' that demands to be recognized, that wants to or needs to stake a claim on our attention" (p. 16).

This type of narrative strategy, providing well-established and recognizable order and meaning for the reader, fits well within Linda Hutcheon's definition of *mimesis of product*. In an attempt to redefine mimesis and return it to its original Platonic and Aristotelian meaning, Linda Hutcheon (*Narcissistic Narrative: The Metafictional Paradox*) elaborates a distinction between what she calls *mimesis of process* and *mimesis of product*.[1] According to Hutcheon, the theoretical basis of traditional realism (as characterized, for example, by the nineteenth-century European novel with its system of conventions producing a lifelike illusion of some "real" world outside the text) could well be called a *mimesis of product*. The reader is asked to concentrate on the product being imitated, that is, the characters, settings, situations, language, and so forth, and to recognize how these are similar to those in empirical reality; thus literary worth is determined in part by how accurately a text refers directly to outside "reality" and to experience immediately recognized by the reader. According to Hutcheon, this type of reading is characterized by a passive acceptance of the product since no codes, no new procedures, are presented. On the other hand, *mimesis of process* reforges the life-art connection on the level of the imaginative process (the storytelling) instead of on the level of the product (the story told). Explicit demand is placed on the reader as co-producer of the text, for "he must self-consciously establish new codes in order to come to terms with new literary phenomena" (p. 39). While the documentary novel operates within Linda Hutcheon's definition of *mimesis of product,* measuring literary worth by how accurately and faithfully a text records, reconstructs, and is consistent with "reality," the novels of Reinaldo Arenas's *pentagonía* are structured, to varying degrees, on the type of textual self-awareness (*mimesis of process*) that Linda Hutcheon proposes.

Like documentary novels, *Celestino antes del alba, El palacio de las blanquísimas mofetas, Otra vez el mar, El color del verano,* and *El asalto* rely predominantly on the use of a first-person narrative voice (the child-narrator/Celestino, Fortunato, Héctor, Gabriel/Reinaldo/the Tétrica Mofeta, and the nameless narrator of *El asalto*) to recount the situations and events in the story or *diégèse*.[2] Yet at the same time these novels break open the homogeneity of traditional one-sided or dogmatic singular points of view by denying exclusive authority to any one voice. In Arenas's novels no single character's words are granted more importance or authority than any others, and often the statements made by one character are contradicted or challenged by another. Moreover, as a result of their constant mutations, splittings, and metamorphoses the characters of the pentalogy are never presented as whole and autonomous. It is for this reason that the five novels are ideally read together, for each is progressively developed from traces of the previous text. (This of course does not invalidate the reading of each novel for its own singularity.) The interrelationship or intratextuality of the works gives rise to a reconceptualization of the traditionally closed vehicle of the realistic novel, for the ending of one novel is but a new beginning. In this way each character is presented as a protean consciousness that can never be fully defined or exhausted.

Celestino antes del alba (*Cantando en el pozo*)

In *Celestino antes del alba* (retitled *Cantando en el pozo* in the 1982 edition) there is an intentional undermining of the representation of a stable and closed monologic consciousness unfolding within itself.[3] In this novel the construction of subjectivity is deprived of any power to define or finalize characters as indisputably individualistic. Not pinning down or reducing characters to the relative or the limited requires from the reader a more active role insofar as he or she is asked to establish meaning on a poetic-symbolic-allegorical level, rather than a referential level.

From the very first sentence of *Celestino antes del alba,* the narrative discourse is focused through the voice of a child-narrator who remains nameless throughout the entire *diégèse* and whose unrestrained and whimsical imagination subjugates any respect for accuracy or objectivity. This choice of focalization is best suited in presenting the character's world of imagination and limitless possibilities. The child-narrator's narrative voice, unable to cope with the desolate conditions of the pre-Revolution Cuban countryside as well as the ignorance and conventionalism of his family, splits itself in order to create an alter-ego, a more pure being, an imaginary cousin (Celestino) who is also a poet. In this way the child-narrator— *el buen creador* (the good creator), as the Cuban poet Eliseo Diego referred to him—duplicates the creative capacity of the extraliterary writer (Arenas).[4] Unlike the documentary novel, in which the writer-investigator takes great pains to maintain a voice separate from that of the witness-investigatee, in *Celestino antes del alba* the boundaries between writer, narrator, and character are blurred. This blurring will continue in Arenas's subsequent novels, in which characters create other characters, doubles that complement them or show other aspects of their personality. This mirroring or doubling of the creative process within the texts makes Arenas's characters extremely rich and complex.

In Barnet's *Canción de Rachel* the narrator-witness is already announced in the title. This naming establishes the authenticity of the informer, a specific individual with a real, proper name.[5] While in the documentary novel, which incorporates the conventions of ethnographical and historiographical writings, to name is to establish referential constancy, in *Celestino antes del alba* the child-narrator remains nameless throughout the entire text. (In the last novel of the pentalogy the narrator also remains nameless.) It is striking how in *Celestino antes del alba* it is not the creator, but rather the narrator's creation, Celestino, the imaginary cousin or doppelgänger, who is named and identified. By naming the creation instead of the creator, fictionalization is valued over, and given more significance than, so-called empirical objectivity and referentiality.

In his study of the menippean satire tradition—a form of intellectually humorous work characterized by comical discussions on philosophical topics, dating to antiquity—the Russian critic Mikhail Bakhtin observed that the use of a split personality in the menippea was a common device to proliferate the subject, thus making it cease to coincide with itself. In this fashion, doubles continually reflect aspects of one another rather than existing as isolated, self-enclosed psyches: "[The] destruction of the wholeness and finalized quality of a man is facilitated by the appearance, in the menippea, of a dialogic relationship to one's own self (fraught with the possibility of split personality)" (*Problems of Dostoevsky's Poetics*, p. 117). This decentering or dismantling of a unified subject, embryonic in the menippea, creates a psychic interweaving in *Celestino antes del alba*, making it difficult to clearly differentiate the various fragments and furthermore challenging the reader's notion of the representability of individual wholeness through language. In this novel the reader is required to participate actively in the child-narrator's act of creation. The dialogic relationship proposed by Bakhtin, inherent in the split personality of the menippea, is an important aspect of the relationship between the child-narrator and Celestino. Early in the text we see the significance placed on this dialogic relationship as the child-narrator is overcome with excitement when Celestino speaks to him for the first time:

> De pronto me acuerdo que por primera vez Celestino me ha hablado. Sí: ¡me habló cuando yo traté de arrancarle la estaca del pecho! ¡Me habló! ¡Me habló! Y se me han quitado las ganas de dar gritos. (*Celestino*, p. 40)

> All of a sudden I remember that for the very first time Celestino has spoken to me. Uh-huh, he spoke to me when I tried to pull the stake out of his heart! He spoke to me! He spoke to me! And now that urge to bawl I had has gone away. (*Singing*, p. 30)

The child-narrator's feelings of sadness are temporarily arrested through his relationship with Celestino. On the level of the *diégèse* the creation of a split self serves the child-narrator as a type of emotional escape valve, another recourse of expression in a world of brutality. As a textual strategy, the creation of the double enriches the possibilities of characterization, allowing for the articulation of a young child's feelings, fantasies, dreams, flights of fancy, and so forth, that otherwise would be difficult to express in a conventional *mimesis of product* (such as documentary novels), in which subjects are represented as stable, whole, and coinciding with themselves.[6]

The possibility of comic elements in split personalities is illustrated in

Bakhtin's discussion of Marcus Terentius Varro's menippea *Bimarcus* (The Double Marcus).[7] Bakhtin goes on to observe that in Dostoevsky's novels the phenomenon of the double always preserved an element of the comic alongside its tragic element—for example, Ivan Karamazov's conversation with the devil in *The Brothers Karamazov* is a carry-over from the menippean tradition. In *Celestino antes del alba* this comic element is likewise present. It is interesting to note, however, that comedy—rarely displayed in documentary novels, in which seriousness is the norm[8]—is not to be found in the presentation of the double, that is, the second being (Celestino), but rather in the presentation of the child-narrator's world view. The child-narrator's ingenuous (humorous) remarks go beyond monologic seriousness to create an open dialogue with his world. In the following monologue, for example, the religious hypocrisies of the adult world are not attacked directly, but simply questioned through the creative potential of laughter:

> Padre Nuestro que estás en los cielos que estás en los cielos que . . . ¿qué palabra vendrá después de ésa? Ya no sé rezar. Pero, bueno, de todos modos, moveré los labios, como hace la mayoría de la gente que no sabe rezar y se las dan de médium.
> Moveré los labios.
> Moveré los labios . . .
> ¡Qué se salve!
> —mmmmmmmmmmmmmmmmmmmmmmmmmmmmmmmmmmmmmmmmm mmmmmmmmmmmmmmmmmmmmmmmmmmmmmmmmmmmmmmmmmmmmm mmm . . . (*Celestino*, p. 64)

Our Father which art in heaven hallowed which art in heaven hallowed which art in heaven hallowed which . . . I wonder what the next word is after that. I don't know how to pray anymore. But—well—anyway I'll move my lips like almost everybody that doesn't know how to pray does when they make themselves be holy. I'll move my lips. Let him be saved! Mmmmmmmmmmmmmmmmmmm mmmmmmmmmmmmmmmmmmmmmmmmmmmmmm . . . (*Singing*, p. 54)

While the character of the child-narrator is presented with humor, Celestino is presented as a fragile and delicate creature who cannot be ridiculed for he is the only authentic object of value in this world of violence and brutality. At one moment in the text the chorus of dead cousins warns the child-narrator: "Celestino es el único que queda aún vivo y nosotros tenemos que protegerlo. Tú eres el elegido: Sálvalo" (*Ce-lestino*, p. 43); "Celestino is the only one that's still alive and it's up to us to protect him. You're It—save him" (*Singing*, p. 33). As a reflection of his own hopes and aspirations the child-narrator must protect Celestino's delicate spirit, the only true living creature in his asphyxiating world.

What I have taken as obvious, that Celestino is the creation of the child-narrator, has not always been fully seen by the critics who have studied the novel.[9] The mistaken view that both subjects are separate characters can be attributed to the fact that not only the child-narrator but all the other characters in the text react to Celestino's presence. Celestino is introduced as the son of Carmelina, who after being abandoned by her husband hanged and set herself afire.[10] But in various interviews that Arenas gave during his life he always made it quite clear that the child-narrator was the creator of Celestino. Even if Arenas had not revealed this, their fusion is suggested in the text. I will take just one of the more revealing episodes as an example. Near the end of the novel Celestino, who has metamorphosed into a bird, is revealed to be dying.[11] The child-narrator, here identified as *tú* (you), speaks to his grandfather concerning the fragile bird:

> TU. —Enséñeme el pájaro. ¡Enséñeme el pájaro!
> ABUELO. —(*Muy alegre.*) ¡Aquí está! ¡Míralo!
> TU. —¡Celestino!
> ABUELO. —Sí, ¡Tú! (*Celestino*, p. 174)

> YOU. Show me the bird! Show me the bird!
> GRANDFATHER (*very cheerfully*). Here it is! Look at it!
> YOU. Celestino!
> GRANDFATHER. Yes, you! (*Singing*, p. 166)

In the above passage we can see how individual subjectivity is decentered by the use of a technical device that turns the other ("You") into a reflection of the "I." This devaluing of the defining properties of personal pronouns will reappear in Arenas's second novel, *El mundo alucinante*, in which a juxtaposition of first, second, and third-person points of view will be utilized to undermine and parody the notion of a reliable speaking subject.

El palacio de las blanquísimas mofetas

Like the phoenix ensured its progeny, the child-narrator/Celestino is destroyed in Arenas's first novel to reincarnate as the adolescent Fortunato in *El palacio de las blanquísimas mofetas*. This novel covers the adolescent stage of the protean main character of the quintet. Fortunato, a sensitive and restless young man living through a turbulent political period in Cuban history (the insurrectional struggle against the Batista regime), is desperate to escape the cruelties of his family—he refers to them as "bestias" (wild beasts)—as well as to escape from Holguín, a conservative, small rural town "de calles simétricas y gente invariablemente práctica" (*El palacio*, p. 37); "of symmetrical streets and townfolks inalterably practical" (*The Palace*, p. 36). The other characters in the novel, all members of the same family, live brutally agonizing lives expecting to find solace only in death. But death brings no relief, as is evident in the sections entitled "Vida de los muertos" (The Life of the Dead).

The story of *El palacio de las blanquísimas mofetas* is not just the story of Fortunato, it is also the story of Fortunato's eccentrically cruel and obsessive family: Polo, the grandfather who considers himself cursed for having engendered only daughters; the superstitious and blasphemous grandmother, Jacinta, who spends her days compulsively going to the bathroom; Aunt Celia, who is driven to madness after her only daughter, Ester, commits suicide; Aunt Digna, abandoned by her husband, Moisés, and left to raise the mischievous Tico and Anisia; Aunt Adolfina, a spinster desperate to lose her virginity; and Onérica, Fortunato's mother, who abandons him and goes to the United States in search of her own "fortune." These characters, or rather voices (for the text is constructed as a cacophony of voices), are given the opportunity to recount their own obsessive stories of despair. In this Tower of Babel in which no one understands anyone else, personal agonies are fated to echo within the chambers of the novel. That the characters, prisoners of their own suffering, yearn desperately to find a receptive listener only underscores their alienation.

Perhaps it is *El palacio de las blanquísimas mofetas* that challenges most the notion of a single reliable voice that can faithfully telegraph reality to the reader, for the audibility of Fortunato's testimony, a testimony that wishes to see itself as the authentic voice of the family, is incessantly suppressed by the multiplicity of voices of other family members eager to tell their own sides of the story. Although the first, second, and third-person narrative voices are utilized in *El palacio de las blanquísimas mofetas*, the first-person predominates. This narrative "I" is shared by all the family members who speak in the first person. The proliferation of a first-person focalization produces a cacophony of voices in which each individual—

at times unrecognizable—struggles in vain to be heard. Multiple narrative "I's" contradict each other, in this way not granting referential stability to any speaking subject. Thus, the text is reduced to a crisscrossing of affirmations and contradictions that totally refuse the concentration of veracity into a single authoritative voice.

This chorus of voices is not the case of a collective subject working to establish a unified ideology, as it occurs, for instance, in *Canción de Rachel* and other documentary novels composed of accounts by different participants in the same event. Barnet's presentation of a chorus of voices in *Canción de Rachel* only served to emphasize the protagonist's racial prejudices. In 1969 Barnet revealed that "En Rachel he utilizado la técnica contrapuntística o sistema Rashomón . . . con el propósito de que el público se identifique en el libro, ya sea a favor o en contra de Rachel" ("La novela testimonio: socio-literatura," p. 137) (In [*Canción de Rachel*] I used the counterpoint method or Rashomon system . . . with the intention that the public would identify itself in the book either in favor or against Rachel). But in fact, the racial prejudices that Rachel incorporates are so stereotyped that any reader, given the smallest amount of social consciousness, would never identify with the character. In "La novela testimonio: socio-literatura" (p. 135), Barnet criticizes Truman Capote for siding with his main character, Perry, from *In Cold Blood*. It is interesting to note, however, that Barnet himself was guilty of partiality; in *Canción de Rachel* he takes sides *against* his main character, Rachel. By opposing the voices of stronger members of society representing a higher level of social consciousness, Barnet underscores the extremity of Rachel's racism within the novel, thus eliminating any ambiguity as to the accepted ideology.

El palacio de las blanquísimas mofetas is divided into three parts: "Prólogo y epílogo" (Prologue and Epilogue), "Hablan las criaturas de queja" (The Creatures Utter Their Complaints), and "Función" (The Play). In the first part, "Prólogo y epílogo," the crisscrossing of voices is so entangled that it is extremely difficult for the reader to decipher the narrative during a first reading. (These fragments of voices will be contextualized and expanded in the second and third parts of the novel.) With the (con)fusion of what is traditionally the first word (prologue) and last word (epilogue) of the traditional novel, the suggestion is made that there is no first or final word on any given matter; rather, discourse is open-ended, without a finalizing period. In the end, the supremacy of any narrative continuity is undermined as words appear to be but muffled echoes reverberating within the pages of the text.

The second part of the novel, "Hablan las criaturas de queja," constitutes the major portion of the text. This part is subdivided into *agonías* (agonies) instead of chapters. Each family member attempts in monologue to present his or her most intimate suffering. These spoken accounts are presented as a rambling hodgepodge of voices that often conceal the identity of the speaking subject. The gallery of voices is reminiscent of the divided spoken sections by different characters in Guillermo Cabrera Infantes's *Tres tristes tigres,* a work in which it is similarly difficult to delineate the individual voices that present themselves in the first person.[12] While the characters of *Tres tristes tigres* do engage in dialogues (for example, in the section "Bachata" Silvestre and Cué converse as they drive around Havana in a convertible), the characters of *El palacio de las blanquísimas mofetas,* in contrast, are reduced to mere diatribe. At times the typography of a single page is literally adjusted to accommodate two or more voices whose speech crisscrosses but never intersects. In 1981 Arenas stated:

> [*El palacio de las blanquísimas mofetas*] está estructurada por monólogos completamente aislados; aun cuando en un momento determinado parece que están hablando, a cada uno lo que le interesa es contar su propia tragedia. Están tan enajenados por su propio dolor que toda posibilidad de diálogo queda excluida.[13]

> [*El palacio de las blanquísimas mofetas*] is structured around completely isolated monologues; even when it appears at certain moments that the characters are talking, they are only concerned with telling their own tragic story. They are so alienated by their own pain that all possibility of dialogue is out of the question.

Fortunato, like the witness in the documentary novel, wishes for his words to represent the other's (his family's) experiences. However, Fortunato must pay a price for his identification with other individuals who are equally oppressed. The following excerpt, presented in the third person, begins to reveal Fortunato in the role of victim and martyr. The adolescent wishes to bear the cross for his family's pain, a cross that will lead to the destruction and fragmentation of his vision of *self*:

> Y fue entonces cuando comenzó a interpretar a toda su familia, y padeció más que todos ellos sus propias tragedias. . . . Fue entonces cuando se pegó candela, cuando se exiló voluntariamente, cuando se convirtió en un viejo gruñón, cuando enloqueció, cuando, transfor-

mado en una solterona, se lanzó a la calle en busca de un hombre.
(*El palacio*, p. 90)

And that was when he started to look at, and try to understand,
his family, and he began to suffer for their tragedies even more than
they themselves did. . . . That was when he set himself afire, when
he went voluntarily into exile, when he became a grouchy old coot,
when he went mad, when, transformed into an old maid, he ran out
into the streets to try to find a man. (*The Palace*, p. 104)

Previous to this passage the reader learns that Fortunato begins to steal
reams of paper from his grandfather's store and begins to write "en forma
interminable" (incessantly) his constant "sensaciones" (sensations)—a word
that is repeated throughout the text to express the ineffable in regards to
the boy's feelings. Fortunato's sensibility and capacity for empathy is in
total contradiction to the egoism of his family, each member only concerned with his or her suffering. This desire to bear his family's suffering,
to understand (to feel) their intimate pain and frustrations, places Fortunato on the path to *self*-destruction. The adolescent-poet, whose existence is already marked by total isolation and hopelessness, begins to
fragment under the weight of all this misfortune. In the following passage
we see the final outcome of this direct identification with his family:

Muchas veces había sido Adolfina, y había padecido como ella, o
quizá más, la urgencia de ser abrazada, penetrada, degollada, as-
fixiada, aniquilada de amor por alguien. Muchas veces había sido
Celia. . . . Muchas veces fue Digna. . . . Muchas veces fue Polo y
Jacinta. . . . Muchas veces fue Tico y Anisia. . . . Muchas veces fue
Ester. . . . Muchas veces, siempre, seguramente, sí, había sido todos
ellos, y había padecido por ellos y quizá—porque él tenía más imaginación, porque él iba más allá—al ser ellos había sufrido más que
ellos mismos dentro de su propio terror, invariable, y les había
otorgado una voz, un modo de expresar el estupor, una dimensión
del espanto que quizá, seguramente, ellos mismos jamás llegarían a
conocer ni a padecer. (*El palacio*, p. 193)

Many times he had been Adolfina—he had suffered as she had (or
perhaps more) the urgent need to be embraced, penetrated, to have
his throat cut, to be strangled and asphyxiated, to be annihilated in
the name of love. Many times he had been Celia. . . . Many times he
was Digna. . . . Many times he had been Polo and Jacinta. . . . Many

times he had been Tico and Anisia. . . . Many times he had been Esther. . . . Many times—all the time, really—he had been all of them, and he had suffered for them, and perhaps when he had been them (for he had more imagination than they did, he could go beyond the mere here-and-now) he had even suffered more than they, deep within himself, deep within his own, invariable terror. And he had given them a voice, a way of expressing the stupor, the dull horror, the fear, the blind terror which they, surely, would never be fully able to know or to suffer. (*The Palace*, p. 234)

Fortunato's desire to become the authentic interpreter of his family's pain erases the boundaries between *self* and *other*, leaving the adolescent overwhelmed by the frustration and destitute existence of his family. Like the writer-informer of the documentary novel, Fortunato wishes to give voice to his family's agonies, but this close identification with the *other* produces a loss of *self* that results in confusion and ambiguity, as the following passage demonstrates: "Son ideas tuyas. Son ideas mías. Son ideas *tuyas mías*" (*El palacio*, p. 150); "Those are just 'those ideas' of yours. Those are just 'those ideas' of mine. Those are just 'those ideas' of myours" (*The Palace*, p. 183). Fortunato is not the only character who suffers from an inability to establish limits. Celia's symbiotic relationship with her dead daughter, Ester, likewise prevents her from distinguishing clearly between *self* and *other*: "Pero no duró mucho tiempo su sueño, mi sueño, nuestro sueño" (*El palacio*, p. 122); "But her dream, my dream, our dream did not last long" (*The Palace*, p. 147).

In *El palacio de las blanquísimas mofetas* the use of the doubling pair Fortunato/Adolfina or Adolfina/Fortunato goes further than the use of the split personality in *Celestino antes del alba*. Adolfina is as much the feminine double of Fortunato as he is her masculine counterpart; neither character's story or emotional struggles is presented as more important or consequential than the other's. Let us recall that although Fortunato is the adolescent reincarnate of the child-narrator of *Celestino antes del alba*, who furthermore wishes to see himself as the authentic voice within the family, his voice is never granted a position of supremacy over the other characters. The presentation of the doubling pair Fortunato/Adolfina or Adolfina/Fortunato undermines the integrity of the sex of the subject.[14] By erasing the boundaries of gender that have so easily defined characters in the realistic literary tradition, Arenas reveals the intricate complexities of the human subject that will not allow itself to be pinned down to a singular identity. This very notion will be reintroduced and further explored in *Otra vez el mar* in which the subject of the enunciation of the first part (the nameless wife) at the end of the novel is revealed to be the feminine side of Héctor's personality.

In *El palacio de las blanquísimas mofetas* Fortunato and Adolfina share similar sensibilities. Both experience feelings of extreme loneliness, dissatisfaction, and helplessness because of their respective situations: Fortunato's spiritual isolation in a small repressive town, and Adolfina's emotional isolation in not having found a man. In the following passage Adolfina identifies herself directly with Fortunato:

> Algunas veces yo dejo de ser Adolfina y me vuelvo Fortunato. Y Fortunato soy. Y me siento sobre la cumbrera de la casa y empiezo a conversar con las palomas de castilla y cojo dos o tres alacranes y me los como de un solo bocado, o dejo que me piquen en los ojos. Algunas veces yo soy Fortunato. (*El palacio,* p. 169)

> Sometimes I stop being Adolfina and turn into Fortunato. And I *am* Fortunato. I sit up on the ridgepole of the house and I have long conversations with the pigeons and I pick up two or three scorpions and pop them in my mouth and swallow them just like *that*, or maybe I let them sting me in the eyes. Sometimes I am Fortunato. (*The Palace,* p. 203)

Adolfina identifies with Fortunato's liberating spirit, his ability to express himself freely. She finds in the dreaming and sensitive Fortunato who spends his hours having "long conversations with the pigeons" a spiritual kinship. Yet, while Fortunato expresses himself openly she, by contrast, must bury her emotions. As the oldest daughter and sister in a traditional Hispanic family, Adolfina takes on the role of the responsible caretaker who must abandon her dreams and hopes and sacrifice herself for her family.

In the following passage we see how Fortunato finds in Adolfina's deep frustration and emotional pain an equally reciprocal counterpart:

> Fue entonces cuando comenzó a celebrar sus primeras sesiones privadas de llanto. Fue entonces cuando, escondido tras de la prensa de maíz, comenzó a imitar a Adolfina. . . . Un día cogió un palillo de guano y se lo metió en el culo tan sólo, quizá, para experimentar una nueva sensación de dolor. Esa vez lloró como Adolfina . . . (*El palacio,* p. 39)

It was at those times that he began to celebrate his first private sessions of weeping. It was at those times that he would hide behind the cornpress and imitate Adolfina. . . . One day he picked up a withe of dried palm and put it up his ass just, perhaps, to feel a new kind of pain. That time he cried like Adolfina . . . (*The Palace*, pp. 38–39)

Like Adolfina, Fortunato is unfulfilled and desperate for emotional and physical contact with another individual. This is represented in the above passage by the (homo)sexual act of inserting the "withe of dried palm" into himself. This sexual stimulation establishes a special identification with Adolfina.

Throughout the novel Fortunato is seen in the bathroom, "his only refuge since they had moved to town" (*The Palace*, p. 100), masturbating. The bathroom is likewise presented in the novel as Adolfina's only refuge. It is here, in private, where she can express her anger and dissatisfaction in long monologues of bitter resentment:

Yo lo que quisiera, coño, fuera que Dios se me presentara. Que fuera hombre y se me acercara, para caerle a trompadas. Para decirle: Dios maricón, por qué, por qué. Para decirle eso y caerle a bofetadas, para matarlo y rematarlo. Por qué no te presentas, hijo de La Gran Puta. (*El palacio*, p. 111)

What *I'd* give good money to see is God showing His face around here. Let Him be a man and come in here, I'd show Him. I'd bust His face for Him. Listen, you old faggot, I'd say to Him—Why? Why? . . . I'd first say to Him and then I'd jump all over Him and then I'd kill Him again. Why don't you just come down here, You son of the biggest bitch that ever lived. (*The Palace*, p. 131)

The grandmother's pleading "¡Adolfina! ¡Hasta cuándo vas a estar metida en el baño!" (*El palacio*, p. 67) ("Adolfina! How long are you going to stay in the bathroom!" *The Palace*, p. 76) becomes a constant refrain throughout the entire text. In the end, both Fortunato and Adolfina reach such a state of frustration that even these momentary self-gratifying fantasies (Fortunato's masturbation and Adolfina's monologues of anger) are no longer sufficient. Action (or rather *interaction*) must be taken. Hence, Fortunato decides to join the rebel army and Adolfina makes one last attempt to find a man. In the following passage Fortunato, who has just finished masturbating, is overcome by a sense of futility; the "sensations" of this act, of his fantasies (also note how the "magic cousin" [Celestino] is mentioned), of his dreams, are no longer satisfying to him:

> Sensaciones, sensaciones. Otra vez las terribles sensaciones . . . el viaje a lugares soñados, . . . el encuentro con el personaje ideal, . . . el recinto de las babosas, la mata de zarzarosas, el primo-mágico. . . . Inventos. Inventos. . . . Pero la vida no puede tolerarse cuando sólo la habitan cosas figuradas, irreales. La vida necesita de la aventura, de lo diverso. El intercambiado choque de los cuerpos, el correr por sitios verdaderos. . . . Inútil era ya volver a masturbarse, inútil danzar, . . . inútil gesticular, llorar como Adolfina . . . (*El palacio,* pp. 88–89)

> Sensation, sensation. Once again the awesome sensations . . . the voyage to dreamed-of places, . . . the fantasy of an encounter with that dreamed-of ideal person. . . . The place where all the slugs came out, the dog-rose bush, the magic cousin. . . . Pure invention. . . . But life is not to be borne when it is filled with only made-up people and unreal things. Life needs adventure, change, diversity—. . . the collisions of bodies, the running through real, and different, places. . . . It was futile to masturbate again, futile to dance, . . . futile to gesture, cry like Adolfina . . . (*The Palace,* pp. 101–3)

In a similar, yet more delirious tone, Adolfina is moved to action. She must do something, she must stop complaining and act. She decides to go out on the town and lose her virginity:

> Hoy mismo voy a salir a la calle y me voy a acostar con el primero que encuentre. Me da igual un caballo que un hombre, una lagartija que un perro. Lo que sea. . . . Haz lo que te parezca. Acuéstate con quien te lo proponga. Pero haz algo. Haz algo. Haz algo. Ay, yo quiero hacer algo. (*El palacio,* p. 186)

> This very day I'm going to leave this house and go out and go to bed with the first man I find. Or a horse, for all I care, or a lizard, or a dog. Anything. . . . Do anything you feel like doing. Go to bed with any man that comes along. But do something. Do something. Do something. Ay, I want to do something. (*The Palace,* p. 225)

Both Fortunato and Adolfina are moved to action by their isolation and frustration. In the "fifth agony," characterized by a tremendous amount of crisscrossing of voices, there appears on the same page Fortunato's decision, "Creo que lo mejor que puedo hacer es alzarme" (*El palacio*, p. 203) ("I think the best thing I can do now is go off and join the rebels," *The Palace*, p. 248), as well as Adolfina's, "Esta misma noche voy a salir" (*El palacio*, p. 203) ("I'm going out this very night," *The Palace*, p. 248). According to Jorge Olivares, the fifth agony "consists of the pendular narration of these characters' respective quests; and, although aware that Fortunato left home some days before Adolfina's special evening, the reader is deceived by this narrative strategy and senses a feeling of simultaneity ("Carnival and the Novel," p. 474). The drawing together of Fortunato and Adolfina's attempts to change their existing situations is of interest for one method of change or "revolution" is not favored or valorized over the other. Fortunato's political engagement is not presented as a superior or nobler act than Adolfina's quest for physical and emotional contact. Still, in the end both quests fail; Fortunato's flight for freedom tragically ends when he is arrested, tortured, and executed by the Batista police, and Adolfina returns home defeated, still a virgin, and sets herself afire.

In *El palacio de las blanquísimas mofetas* Arenas provides the reader with a disturbing portrait of the poverty and misery that were present in rural Cuba shortly before the triumph of the Revolution. Ironically, however, while many Cuban novelists during the 1970s were writing documentary works presenting the Revolution as the decisive moment that radically transformed Cuban society for the better, Arenas, undermining this rather utopian vision of history, portrays the Revolution as the catalyst responsible for the death of his protagonist and the emotional destruction of a family.

Otra vez el mar

Fortunato is destroyed in *El palacio de las blanquísimas mofetas* to reappear in *Otra vez el mar* as the adult Héctor. With an entire history behind him (childhood and adolescence) Héctor, now living under an institutionalized revolution, continues questioning his tortured existence and marginality. Structurally, *Otra vez el mar* is an interplay of two monologues of personal frustration that work as a duo. Part 1 (the wife's discourse) and part 2 (Héctor's discourse) present the histories, dreams, memories, and hallucinations of this Cuban couple as they drive home to Havana after a six-day vacation at the beach. Part 1 is a straightforward narration (in essence a *mimesis of product*) that divides itself into six chapters, each corresponding to the six days spent at the beach. Part 2, narrated by the poet-Héctor, is a dramatic meshing of poetry and prose (*mimesis of process*) divided into six cantos, each likewise corresponding to the six days of vacation. Furthermore, there exists an intertextual web that links both parts. Situations that occur in Part 1 are continued or resolved in the second.

The story of *Otra vez el mar* commences precisely when the six-day vacation has ended and the couple abandon the beach and begin their return trip home by car. It is at this moment when both characters—first the wife, then Héctor—begin to speak, to remember, to imagine, to dream, to sing of their personal frustrations and disenchantment. Although the wife relates the entire first part of the novel she remains nameless throughout the text. The dominance of her discourse within the textual linearity of the novel (part 1) sets up the reader to rely on the authenticity of her voice. However, her discourse, and very existence, is challenged in the last sentences of the novel, when it is revealed that she is only an invention, a ghost or obsession of Héctor's imagination: "Aún tengo tiempo de volverme para mirar el asiento vacío, a mi lado. Allá voy yo solo—como siempre—en el auto. Hasta última hora la fantasía y el ritmo . . ." (*Otra vez,* p. 418); "There I go alone—like always—in the car. To the last second equanimity and rhythm—fantasy . . ." (*Farewell to the Sea,* p. 412).[15] The traditional separation between creator and creation and the instance of narrating the fictional account is erased and called into question. Like the child-narrator of *Celestino antes del alba,* Héctor has created a double, an alter ego, in order to survive in a repressive environment that, in his particular case, excludes and condemns him on two counts: for being a political dissident, and for being a homosexual. While in the documentary novel the witness insists on the authenticity and verisimilitude of his or her story and takes the time and trouble to establish his or her concrete presence in the text, in *Otra vez el mar* the autonomy and integrity of the character of the wife is totally discredited when it is revealed that she does not exist. Yet it is precisely through the negation of this developed and complex character, who narrates her memories, dreams, hallucinations, and fears over 193 pages of the text, that attention is called to Héctor's need to invent, create, compose as a way to defend himself from a rigid and intolerant society that is extremely hostile toward transgressions from the norm and believes that order is to be found in the preservation of an exemplary revolutionary social consciousness.

In my analysis of *El palacio de las blanquísimas mofetas* I established how Adolfina is presented as the feminine double of the adolescent Fortunato. This doubling pair reemerges not only in Héctor/the nameless wife, but also in the figure of Tedevoro from canto 6 of *Otra vez el mar*, a character who will also reappear in *El color del verano*. (I will use the original Spanish name Tedevoro instead of the English translation, Eachurbod.) Tedevoro serves as a symbolic synthesis of the three main pairing doubles we have examined so far: child-narrator/Celestino, Fortunato/Adolfina, and Héctor/the nameless wife. Tedevoro's "constant yearning, . . . his perpetual need (never sated or appeased) . . ." (*Farewell*, p. 357) is present in all three pairs. Furthermore, Tedevoro's sexual inversion echoes the masculine/feminine doubles of Fortunato/Adolfina and Héctor/the nameless wife. In the text both masculine and feminine pronouns and past participles are used to refer to Tedevoro. When Tedevoro reappears in *El color del verano* he (she) is described as carrying around a pistol and a little bottle of gasoline to kill himself (herself), just in case "estaba condenada a la virginidad" ("*she* was condemned to remaining a virgin," *El color del verano*, p. 70). This passage is fraught with meaning given the fact that these are the objects responsible for Fortunato's and Adolfina's deaths in *El palacio de las blanquísimas mofetas*.

The Tedevoro story, as I shall call it, comes immediately after the frustrated meeting between the adolescent boy and Héctor at the beach. Therefore, it is composed by the poet-Héctor in the aftermath of unfulfilled desire. Tedevoro's inability to turn a trick is a reiteration of Adolfina's similar failure and of Héctor's refusal to consummate his desire with the boy. Tedevoro's name—literally translated as "I devour you"—although meant as a pun, exposes the yearning and unsatisfied desire of Arenas's characters. The Tedevoro story becomes the final anecdote that the reader encounters before the text literally breaks open into a bifurcation of nervous anxiety. (The Tedevoro story concludes with a parody of Hamlet's famous soliloquy in which the poet-Héctor questions his attempt even to continue speaking at all):

¿Seguir?
¿No seguir?
He aquí el dilema. (*Otra vez*, p. 385)

Go on?
Not go on?
That is the question. (*Farewell*, p. 375)

The Tedevoro story injects the cantos, which at times are marked by the seriousness of Héctor's tortured psyche, with a playfulness of camp laughter. Like other characters in Arenas's texts, Tedevoro creates an imaginary world populated by cartoon heroes and sexual fantasies that allow him to escape from his own cruel environment. In the end, the reader discovers that Tedevoro, alias José Martínez Mattos, is found dead one morning, killed by the members of his very own community, the other homosexuals that frequented the beach urinals. It is important to recognize that the death of Tedevoro is not blamed on the political system but on human cruelty. In *Arturo, la estrella más brillante,* written around the same time of *Otra vez el mar* but not published until 1984, Arenas again avoids simplistic political propaganda by suggesting that oppression is not solely the result of a repressive political system but of human cruelty. In *Arturo, la estrella más brillante* oppression is not only the result of a repressive government, but is also evident in the homosexual prisoners of the UMAP camp who create their own hierarchy of power, a *sistership,* as they call it, that does not tolerate homosexuals who do not assimilate.

El color del verano

> En aquella isla todo el mundo vivía por lo menos una doble vida: públicamente no dejaban ni un instante de alabar al tirano, secretamente lo aborrecían y ansiaban desesperadamente que reventase. (*El color del verano,* p. 123)

> On that island everyone led at least a double life: in public they would unceasingly praise the tyrant while secretly hating him and desperately hoping he would kick the bucket.

The island on which the story of *El color del verano* is played out is explicitly identified as Cuba (p. 124). It is the summer of 1999 and the dictator Fifo is celebrating "fifty" years in power: "cincuenta años que en realidad son cuarenta, aumentados por él en diez más, pues él ama . . . los números redondos y la publicidad" (p. 64) (fifty years which in fact are only forty, but he increased them because he loved . . . round numbers and publicity). Under Fifo's tyrannical rule the people on the island must shield their true feelings for fear of recrimination; they are forced to live double, even triple, lives in order to survive. In addition to creating an internal dialogism that enriches the resonances of characterization, the splitting of characters underscores the dishonesty and fear present within this totalitarian state in which individuals must fragment themselves into a multiplicity of selves, each fulfilling and meeting different social functions.

In *El color del verano* the first-person narrative voice is shared by Gabriel/ Reinaldo/the Tétrica Mofeta. This trinity, like the poet-Héctor in part 2 of *Otra vez el mar*, is responsible for writing the anecdotes, letters, tongue-twisters, stories, and so forth, that make up the novel and in turn give voice to Cuba's excluded and marginal homosexual subculture of the 1960s and 1970s. The splitting of the protagonist in three is explained early in the text. Gabriel, returning from the United States to visit his mother in the small Cuban town of Holguín, imagines himself confessing to her of his true self or selves:

> No soy una persona, sino dos y tres a la vez. Para ti sigo siendo Gabriel, para aquellos que leen lo que escribo y que casi nunca puedo publicar soy Reinaldo, para el resto de mis amigos con los cuales de vez en cuando me escapo para ser yo totalmente, soy la Tétrica Mofeta. (*El color del verano*, p. 101)

> I'm not one person, but two or three at the same time. For you I am Gabriel, for those who read what I write, which I'm rarely able to publish, I'm Reinaldo, for the rest of my friends with whom from time to time I can escape and be totally myself, I'm the Tétrica Mofeta [the Gloomy Skunk].

In addition to underscoring how society's rejection of homosexuality forces the homosexual to protect his true identity by hiding behind a mask to avoid suspicion, Arenas's poetic trinity is also a parodic, sullen, and blasphemous (sub)version of the Catholic trinity (Father, Son, and Holy Spirit in one divine godhead) that reflects and gives voice to the very complex and contradictory human facets of the protagonist's personality. Reinaldo is the writer-creator (God the Father) who gives life to his characters. The nostalgic recollections of Gabriel (a biblical name of one of the archangels who appears as a divine messenger) must be sacrificed, like the son Jesus Christ, in order for the Tétrica Mofeta (the protagonist's vital homosexual spirit) to exist. In one of the last interviews he granted shortly before his death Arenas declared: "The Gloomy Skunk [the Tétrica Mofeta] undergoes a metamorphosis so he can extend his existence through that of various characters. He is a homosexual who lives in Cuba, the victim of all sorts of persecution. In spite of it all, he's trying to write a novel which the government is trying to find and destroy. He's got a double in the United States, Gabriel, . . . [who] has a series of complexes he can't overcome . . . because he didn't fulfill his mother's dream.[16]

The splitting of the protagonist in three is also alluded to in the novel's subtitle, "El nuevo jardín de las delicias" (The New Garden of Delights). Hieronymus Bosch's famous and provocative triptych *The Garden of Delights*—a portion of which, incidentally, is reproduced on the cover of Arenas's collection of poems *Voluntad de vivir manifestándose* (1989)—is a combination of three panels that represent the Garden of Eden and the creation of Adam and Eve (left panel), the joy of the senses in the world of the flesh (center panel), and the anguish of hell (left panel). Each character of the trinity Gabriel/Reinaldo/the Tétrica Mofeta corresponds to one of the panels: Gabriel who reminisces about his childhood in Holguín, his personal beginning (right panel, the creation); the homosexual extravagance and carnal exploits of the Tétrica Mofeta (center panel, the carnal desires and sensual appeal of the world of the flesh); and Reinaldo, who as he writes is dying from AIDS (left panel, the nightmarish and pestilential scenes of hell).

There is one final allusion to a triad in *El color del verano*. The notion of trinity is also evoked in the divine Parcae, or Three Fates, "Clotos, Láquesis y Atropos," who have condemned "Arenas (alias Gabriel, alias la Tétrica Mofeta)" (p. 235) for not trusting them with the fate of his novel. The three Parcae or *Tria Fata*, who in Roman mythology were represented as spinners who presided over birth, marriage, and death, were identified by the Romans with the severe Greek Moirae. Originally a single divinity, the Moirae were three sisters: Clotho, whose turning distaff symbolized the course of existence; Lachesis, who distributed the lots received for each man; and Atropos, who without remorse cut the thread of life. As we can see, the sequence of birth (Gabriel), life (the Tétrica Mofeta), and death (Reinaldo) is again alluded to through the divine Parcae.

Of the novels of the pentalogy, *El palacio de las blanquísimas mofetas* and *El color del verano* make the most extensive use of the third-person narrative voice. In *El palacio de las blanquísimas mofetas* this voice is not that of the omniscient narrator or God's point of view in the traditional novel that claimed privileged inner views of the individual subjects. The third-person narrator who appears in this novel possesses no absolute vantage point that allows it to see events not already accessible to the other characters.[17] This third-person narrative voice distances itself from the narrated events only to repeat information that the reader has already acquired from the characters. The narrator offers the reader no definite explanation, only a share in the characters' confusion. Thus, the narrator does not retain any essential surplus of meaning, but is rather on an equal footing with the subjects. In a 1981 interview with Perla Rozencvaig, Arenas stated that in *El palacio de las blanquísimas mofetas*:

> [H]ay un narrador que trata de darle coherencia a todo ese descon-cierto de gritos y de dolor que es esta novela. Ese narrador es como una caricatura de ese narrador omnisciente, ese pequeño Dios que en la novela tradicional se situaba en un plano superior al de los per-sonajes y desde ahí los miraba de un modo indiferente. En mi caso, yo creo, que es un narrador que representa la voz de mi pueblo na-tal—Holguín—que se sube a la loma de la Cruz, que es la más alta de mi pueblo, y desde allí ve la calle, los puentes, la gente y le da cierta coherencia a un relato que es de por sí bastante delirante.[18]

> There is a narrator that tries to give coherence to the confusion of loud cries and pain that make up this novel. That narrator is like a caricature of that traditional omniscient narrator, that little god in the traditional novel that would situate himself in a plane superior to his characters and from high above would look at them indifferently. In my case, I believe, it is a narrator that represents the voice of my home town—Holguín—that goes up to the Hill of the Cross, which is the highest in my town, and from there sees the street, the bridges, the people and gives certain coherence to a story that is by itself quite delirious.

This traditional omniscient or heterodiegetic narrator is but one more voice striving to usurp a position of dominance and authority within the Tower of Babel that is *El palacio de las blanquísimas mofetas*. Yet, this is an unreliable narrator whose voice should not be trusted. In the "fifth agony," for example, the omniscient narrator denies that Fortunato ever joined the rebel forces, a claim that the heterodiegetic narrator had previ-ously affirmed.

Unlike the heterodiegetic narrator of *El palacio de las blanquísimas mofetas,* who is not a character in the events and situations recounted, the third-person voice of *El color del verano* (Gabriel/Reinaldo/the Tétrica Mofeta) is a homodiegetic narrator who is also part of the *diégèse*. Still, in *El color del verano* the statements made, and stories told, by Gabriel/Reinaldo/the Tétrica Mofeta are frequently contradicted or challenged, as for example in the following passage:

Hace tiempo que te veo trabajar y no te interrumpo porque lo que dices es más o menos cierto, aunque metes tus puyas y tus venenos. Pero venirme ahora con esas de que *Halisia bailaba*, cuando la última vez que la vi andaba en una silla de ruedas y sólo daba unos pasitos con unas muletas . . . ¡Bailaba! Decirme eso a mí, Daniel Sakuntala la Mala (sí, la mala porque siempre digo la verdad); eso es el colmo, canalla . . . (*El color del verano*, p. 227)

I've been watching you work for quite a while now and I haven't interrupted you because what you say is more or less true, although you do throw in your digs and poison. But to say to me that *Halisia was dancing*, when the last time I saw her she was in a wheel chair and could only walk a little on crutches . . . She was dancing! To tell me that, me Daniel Sakuntala the Bad One (yes, the bad one because I always tell the truth); that's going too far, you swine . . .

Daniel Sakuntala, a character who also appears in Arenas's story "Mona" (*Viaje a La Habana*, 1990) correcting and challenging the narrator's declarations, ironically undermines the authorial voice of Gabriel/Reinaldo/the Tétrica Mofeta. This passage attacks the traditional concept of authorship, demystifying the creator's aura with which traditional criticism endowed the writer. The passage also recalls the Spanish literary tradition of the reversibility of writer and work as found in Miguel de Unamuno's famous novel *Niebla* (1914). In chapter 31 of *Niebla* the main character, Augusto Pérez, emerges from the story to confront the writer (Unamuno) and protest the things he is being made to do; creator and creation clash, undermining the traditional literary convention in which characters relate to one another and not to the writer. In *Niebla* the intention behind this passage is philosophical, to question the meaning of human existence, a recurrent theme in Unamuno's work. In Arenas's *El color del verano* the clash between creator (Gabriel/Reinaldo/the Tétrica Mofeta) and creation (Daniel Sakuntala) is a carnivalesque inversion of the traditional hierarchy between author and character in which the authorial narrative discourse, traditionally possessing sovereign authority, is leveled.

As I have previously established, in the documentary novel the writer-investigator functions as a medium through which the witness-investigatee's words are supposed to *pass* undisturbed and be recorded with only slight literary modifications by the writer. The illusion is created that the writer-investigator disappears behind the authentic voice of the character-witness. In *El color del verano* this peaceful and harmonious coexistence between writer and character is transgressed and undermined. The writer does not disappear behind his characters, and the clash or competition between creator and creation over who indeed is telling the "truth" uncovers the ideological intent behind all discourse. On the one hand, Gabriel/ Reinaldo/the Tétrica Mofeta labels Daniel Sakuntala with the epithet "la mala" (the Bad One, feminine form) to cast doubt on the validity of his words as well as on his sexual interests. On the other hand, Sakuntala's refusal to believe that "*Halisia was dancing*" (a parodic allusion to the aging Cuban ballerina Alicia Alonso) discredits Gabriel/Reinaldo/the Tétrica Mofeta. In the end, neither the voice of the writer-narrator nor the character's voice is presented as completely reliable to the reader.

El asalto

In the final novel of the pentalogy we return once again to a first-person narrator who remains nameless throughout the entire *diégèse*. Still, there is a major difference. While the child-narrator of *Celestino antes del alba* is a likeable character, the nameless narrator of *El asalto* is not. The innocence and naïveté of the child-narrator of the first novel is diametrically opposite to the viciousness and cynicism of the nameless narrator of the final novel. The first paragraph of each novel establishes the character's antipodal personalities. In the first paragraph of *Celestino antes del alba* the child-narrator desperately recounts his worry over the fact that his mother had threatened to throw herself in the well and tells of his desperate search to find her. In the opening paragraph of *El asalto* the first-person narrative voice is also in search of his mother; this time, however, the search is driven by hostility, anger, and a desire to destroy the woman who gave him life:

> La última vez que vi a mi madre . . . [no] perdí tiempo y me le aba-lancé para matarla. La cabrona, parece que me miraba con el ojo del culo, pues antes de que yo pudiese reventarla se volvió asustada. (*El asalto*, p. 7)

> The last time I saw my mother . . . I knew I must not waste a sec-ond. I ran straight for her, and I would have killed her, too, but the old bitch must have an eye where her asshole ought to be, because before I could get to the old woman and knock her down and kill her, she whirled around to meet me. (Hurley trans.)

Unlike the other novels of the *pentagonía* in which the first-person narrative voice is contradictory, unreliable, split and permutated, the narrative voice in *El asalto* appears at first glance to be quite reliable. Yet, as the reader begins to sense the extreme anger and hostility of the nameless protagonist, the question no longer becomes whether the reader can rely on his voice, but what reader would take sides or identify with such a vile and repulsive individual whose verbal onslaughts and vilifications directly assault him or her: "váyase usted a la mierda" (p. 46) (*You* go to hell); "váyase usted al carajo" (p. 49) (*You* go to fucking hell); "qué coño sé yo" (p. 114) (What the fuck do I know). These tirades, as well as the nameless narrator's outspoken hate for his mother, do little to help establish an immediate and trusting relationship with the reader, a key and essential feature of the documentary novel. *El asalto* transgressively challenges one of the most revered images of Cuban society, the mother as symbol of goodness, selflessness, and virtue.[19] In addition, the taboo of incest is brought to light when the mother—in the end discovered to be the dictator—is assaulted by the nameless narrator, who penetrates her with his enlarged penis and finally destroys her. This aberrant and unorthodox image intentionally thwarts the securing of any intimacy with the reader or gaining his or her confidence. With this, the last novel of the pentalogy, Arenas has written perhaps one of the most dark and inhuman novels in Spanish American literature. Yet, through the excessive negativity and malevolence of the protagonist and his dystopian vision of society, the reader is given access to the sinister and pervasive brutality of totalitarianism run amok.

FOUR

"Real" Witnesses

The presentation of a "real" witness, a person with a more or less verifiable history who can guarantee the authenticity of what is being told, is at the foundation of the documentary text: "[E]l protagonista del testimonial tiene que ser una persona de carne y hueso. Se supone que el lector oye la voz auténtica de un hombre real"[1] ([T]he protagonist of the documentary text has to be an individual of flesh-and- blood. One assumes that the reader hears the authentic voice of a real individual).

The notion that witnesses must be "real" in order for their testimony to be valid is flat and simplistic when one considers Reinaldo Arenas's narrative worlds. Arenas's characters are witnesses who testify of their marginal existence within Cuban (prerevolutionary and revolutionary) society. Their fictitious nature does not minimize in any way the strength of their testimony. The life-art connection is neither severed nor destroyed, but rather is imaginatively reforged and reaches the reader on a cognitive, aesthetic, and human level. The characters or witnesses of *Celestino antes del alba, El palacio de las blanquísimas mofetas, Otra vez el mar, El color del verano,* and *El asalto* clearly and honestly intone the persecution and anguish they experience. Indeed, the aesthetic distance of fiction in no way diminishes the authenticity of these voices, whose marginal perspectives are precisely what the documentary novel was designed to give voice to.

It should be noted that Esteban Montejo of *Biografía de un cimarrón* is the only true flesh-and-blood witness in Miguel Barnet's documentary novels. In *Canción de Rachel,* for example, Rachel is not a witness *de carne y hueso* (of flesh-and-blood) but the work of Barnet, who made her a composite of the experiences and anecdotes of *vedettes* of the era that typified her. In 1979 Barnet stated: "Rachel es la síntesis de todas esas coristas. Yo entrevisté también a Luz Gil, a Blanca Becerra, a todas esas otras mujeres"[2] (Rachel is the synthesis of all those chorus singers. I also interviewed others like Luz Gil and Blanca Becerra). Like Rachel, Manuel Ruiz, the Galician immigrant of *Gallego,* and Julián Mesa, the Cuban who emigrated to New York in *La vida real,* are the result of the gathering and editing function of the compiler-investigator, Miguel Barnet, who gathered testimonies from various witnesses to give life to these characters. It is precisely Barnet's poetic license in recreating these characters that has been the subject of controversy within the revolutionary literary establishment. While *Biografía de un cimarrón* was unanimously applauded in Cuba for its fidelity in representing its subject matter, *Canción de Rachel* met criticism when it first appeared for its over-reliance on literary techniques. In his review of *Canción de Rachel,* Ramón López criticized the text for being "más novela que testimonio de una época"[3] (more novel than a document of an era).

In response to his critics, Barnet has always maintained that his documentary novels are "life histories" that are recreated through the writer's imaginative contributions. For the most part, after *Biografía de cimarrón* Barnet's documentary novels have been read and accepted as representing "real" periods in Cuban history—*Canción de Rachel,* the Cuban Republic through Gerardo Machado's dictatorship (1925–33); *Gallego,* the twentieth century up to the 1959 Revolution; *La vida real,* Cuban migration to New York in the 1940s and 1950s—rather than as representing "real" people. Given this fact, why haven't Reinaldo Arenas's novels, regardless of their fanciful flights of the imagination, been equally accepted by the revolutionary regime as representing Cuban society? Aside from differences of political ideology, I believe the answer lies in the fact that Miguel Barnet's novels present the personal lives of individual characters only to highlight the public and historical life of the period. Arenas's characters, on the other hand, meditate on their own existential problems and the issues shaping individual existence, a practice that runs counter to the accepted revolutionary consciousness, which places class struggle over individual experience. Thus, in Cuba the question is not whether a given character in a documentary novel is "real" or not, but whether a given character adheres to and supports the accepted revolutionary consciousness.

In *Celestino antes del alba, El palacio de las blanquísimas mofetas, Otra vez el mar, El color del verano,* and *El asalto* Arenas's characters-witnesses are the complex synthesis of his personal experiences, creative imagination, and artistic inspiration. They are not limited, like the characters in

Barnet's documentary novels, to representing a given ideology, and for this reason they are perhaps more "real" and complex than Rachel, Manuel Ruiz, and Julián Mesa. In a 1988 interview with Nedda G. de Anhalt, Arenas makes clear the extent to which he felt that the characters he created were indeed "real":

> En cuanto al personaje, para mí es algo tan importante en la construcción de la obra que recuerdo en la época en que escribía *Celestino antes del alba,* yo estaba con un amigo mío y de pronto apareció Celestino y le grité el nombre. O sea, vivo con esos personajes, son fundamentales, son parte mía; son una realidad que hasta cierto punto se sobrepone a la otra realidad.⁴

> For me characters are very important in the construction of the work. I remember the time when I was writing *Celestino antes del alba,* I was with a friend of mine and suddenly Celestino appeared and I yelled out his name. That is to say, I live with my characters, they are fundamental, they are a part of me; they are a reality that to a certain extent overpowers the other reality.

After the publication of *Celestino antes del alba* Miguel Barnet interviewed Arenas for *La Gaceta de Cuba*. Significantly, although Barnet was well aware that Arenas's characters were not of flesh-and-blood, he felt that they nevertheless cried out the truth of their anguish. In an introduction to the interview Barnet emphasized the overwhelming anguish present in what he called Arenas's "phantasmagorical reality": "El mundo imaginativo de Arenas, su fantasmagórica realidad, la vida en el campo, el acoso familiar, ¡ah la eterna familia!, nutren esa corriente de angustia que atraviesa la obra"⁵ (Arenas's imaginative world, his phantasmagorical reality, life in the countryside, the family persecution, oh the eternal family!, nourish that current of anguish that runs through the novel).

At one point in the interview Barnet asked Arenas if his novel was "*rigurosamente* autobiográfica" (*rigorously* autobiographical). Arenas, somewhat playfully, but rather revealingly, answered:

> Sí, en lo que respeta a la aparición de las brujas y los duendes, los primos muertos, el coro de tías infernales, el acoso de infatigables hachas, los desplazamientos del personaje hacia la luna (las huidas) sin obtener resultados ventajosos. Es autobiográfico también el ambiente, la brutal inocencia con que se expresan los personajes; pero lo más rigurosamente autobiográfico en esta novela es el estilo, enmar-

cado bajo una esquizofrenia incontrolable que me impedirá siempre escribir una novela "normal". Pero también puedo decir, no, no es una novela autobiográfica, no es más que un juego de la imaginación, pero, ¿acaso lo imaginado no es un reflejo de la vida misma? (p. 21)

In respect to the witches, hobgoblins, dead cousins, chorus of infernal aunts, the endless persecution of the hatchets, the displacements (the escapes) of the main character toward the moon without obtaining advantageous results, as far as all these are concerned, yes. The novel is also autobiographical in its atmosphere, the brutal innocence with which the characters express themselves; but the most strictly autobiographical part of this novel is the style, framed by an uncontrollable schizophrenia that will stop me from ever writing a "normal" novel. But I can also say no, this is not an autobiographical novel, it is no more than a game of my imagination, but isn't what one imagines perhaps a reflection of life itself?

Arenas fuses personal biography (personal history) and imagination and in the process informs us that literary characters can indeed be "real"; although they might not be made of flesh-and-blood, they nonetheless reflect life in all its vitality. By not assigning privileged or hierarchical modes of being Arenas's novels propose a nonrestrictive code of reality; "real" experience, as manifested in the way most people attempt to secure an univocal meaning of experience and of themselves, is *not* opposed to other forms of personal experiences, such as dreams, hallucinations, and fantasy. What most people call reality is never presented as one-dimensional or strictly univalenced in Arenas's novels but rather as multifaceted and even magical. In an interview that Arenas gave shortly after falling into disfavor with the revolutionary regime, later published in the limited edition of *La Vieja Rosa,* he reaffirmed his nonexclusive position concerning reality:

Para mí el realismo no es solamente decir: se levantó, cogió la guagua. . . . Para mí eso es real, pero cuando el hombre se acuesta y empieza a soñar, también eso, de alguna forma es real. ¿Es real o no es real? Todo cuanto imagino es real. (p. 108)

For me realism is not just saying: he got up, he took the bus. . . . For me that is real, but when a man goes to bed and begins to dream, that also, to a certain extent, is real. Is it real or isn't it real? Everything I imagine is real.

In his essay "Magia y persecución en José Martí" Arenas insists that the tradition of the Americas is based on magic, a magic that refuses to be controlled or dominated by logic. Magic in Arenas's lexicon becomes synonymous with the poetic imagination (freedom) struggling against persecution: "La opresión resulta intolerable para el poeta porque la imaginación es la expresión más absoluta de la libertad. El poeta que no conoce la libertad, la imagina"[6] (Oppression is intolerable for the poet because imagination is the most absolute expression of freedom. A poet who doesn't have freedom imagines it). Arenas cites as an example the magic of Sor Juana Inés de la Cruz's *Primero Sueño* (1692), which allowed her to see beyond her Cartesian rationalism in order to perceive "la gran realidad americana" (the great American reality). Arenas adds: "el concepto mágico no puede separarse de la realidad americana" (p. 14) (the concept of magic cannot be separated from the American reality). In short, the novels of the pentalogy question the revolutionary literary establishment's restrictive concept as to the accepted (expected) "reality" that must be represented in literary texts.

Celestino antes del alba (*Cantando en el pozo*)

Near the end of *Celestino antes del alba*, the child-narrator finds himself talking with a goblin, who reproaches him for not believing in his existence:

> Nunca me hiciste caso, y cada vez que me acercaba a ti, tú tratabas de imaginar que estabas soñando. ¡Tan increíble te resulta que alguien que no se justifique pueda brindarte ayuda! ¿Es que solamente confías en lo que palpan tus manos que en definitiva son más irreales que cualquiera de mis leyendas? (*Celestino,* p. 213)

> You never paid any mind to me, and every time I got close to you, you tried to imagine you were dreaming. It was so incredible to you that somebody could just for no reason try to give you a helping hand! Is it that you don't trust anything you can't put your hands on?—and your hands, I'll tell you, are a lot less real than any of my legends. (*Singing,* p. 205)

Soon after, as the goblin begins to disappear, the child-narrator asks him his name; the answer, "Mi nombre es Celestino" (My name is Celestino). The novel has come full cycle: the creation (Celestino) has usurped the child-narrator's position of dominance thereby calling into question his very existence. Much the same as in Borges's masterful piece "Borges y yo" ("Borges and I"), the creator/child-narrator's identity is fragmented and finally usurped by his very creation. Ironically, however, at the same time that the character's stability is undermined, the power of the human imagination as a defense against life's brutality is underscored.

In a review of his own *Celestino antes del alba,* published in *Unión* in 1967, Arenas emphasized the ambiguity of this first work: "que no sé si es novela, que no sé si es mía, y que no sé, en definitiva, qué cosa es" ("Celestino y yo," p. 118) (which I'm not sure is a novel, which I'm not sure is mine, and which I'm definitely not sure of what it is). In this review Arenas goes on to defend reality as multiple; he also defends the power of the imagination, a key feature permeating every part of the work:

> Porque no creo que exista una sola realidad, sino que la realidad es múltiple, es infinita, y además varía de acuerdo con la interpretación que queramos darle. . . . Pero lo triste de todo esto es que cuando alguien se preocupa por expresar las demás realidades, se molestan, o lo tachan a uno de poco realista, como si la realidad se [pudiese limitar]. (pp. 118–19)

> Because I don't believe that there is only one reality. Reality is multiple, infinite, and furthermore varies according to the interpretation we choose to give it. . . . But what is sad about all this is that when one tries to express the other realities, other people get bothered, or they label one as unrealistic, as if reality could be limited.

The *diégèse* of *Celestino antes del alba* is filtered through the child-narrator's imagination, as we have previously noted. Hence, reality is portrayed as a state of mind, a psychic interweaving or intercrossing that appears more conceptualized than concrete. This conceptualization totally disregards the notion of any stable and unambiguous state that coincides with itself outside of the perceiving subject. In *Celestino antes del alba* there is a (con)fusion of what I shall term *wakefulness* and *dream state* in which there is no valorization of one over the other; that is, one state is not presented as more real than another. Both appear as plural and unfixed.

Although this tension between wakefulness and dream state is present throughout the entire novel, I will study where it is first suggested in the text, or rather pre-text: the three epigraphs at the beginning of the book. By analyzing the three (quotes from Oscar Wilde, Jorge Luis Borges, and

Federico García Lorca), we will better be able to comprehend the function of this wakefulness/dream state in the dazzling world of Celestino, as well as in the subsequent novels of the pentalogy, for the source of each epigraph proposes an intertextual game that breaks down the hierarchical logocentrism of the wakeful state over the dream state.

The first epigraph is a Spanish translation of a quote from Oscar Wilde's story "The Young King": "Pero ninguno se atrevía a mirarlo a la cara, porque era semejante a la de los ángeles" (But no man dared look upon his face, for it was like the face of an angel). Central to this tale is the notion that dreams can indeed contain states of consciousness that are more worthy than the hypocrisies that humans are capable of committing in life. The story is about a country lad who recoups the inheritance that is rightfully his as the legitimate heir to his kingdom's throne. The night prior to his coronation the young prince, who demonstrates a poetic sensibility to his surroundings from the time of his arrival at the palace, has three dreams in which he sees represented the injustices of those who labor to finish his royal robe, crown, and scepter. Awakening on the day of the coronation and affected by what he has witnessed, the lad instead of dressing in his regal attire decides to wear the leathern tunic in which he had come to claim the throne. When the courtiers discover that the lad refuses to wear the royal raiment simply because of the dreams he has had, they suspect that he has gone mad. When the lad arrives at the cathedral dressed like a pauper, the attacks and criticism begin; no one wishes to see the king dressed like a humble shepherd. The protest quickly becomes menacing with the arrival of nobles prepared to assassinate he who has brought disgrace to the kingdom. However, at that precise moment, the lad is transfigured by a celestial light that comes accompanied by a divine music; in the end, "no man dared look upon his face, for it was like the face of an angel."

In this story Wilde fuses the referential space of the kingdom with an oneiric or imaginative space (the protagonist's three dreams) in order to question human motives. The oneiric space, typically considered inverisimilar, contains elements from the referential space that are transformed to display a phantasmagorical reality.[7] In this story, as in *Celestino antes del alba,* what is imagined or dreamt is valued as much as what is normally considered "real."

The second epigraph to *Celestino antes del alba* is the last line of the poem "Insomnio," the first poem of the collection *El otro, el mismo* (1964) by Jorge Luis Borges: "Toscas nubes color borra de vino infamarán el cielo; amanecerá en mis párpados apretados" (Coarse clouds the color of wine sediment will disgrace the heavens; dawn will break on my tight-squeezed eyelids).[8] The problem of insomnia appears in many Borgesian texts as an abominable lucidity that does not allow the individual to escape the banalities of everyday existence. In "Insomnio" the poet, "el aborrecible centinela" (the abhorrent sentinel) of universal history, cannot relieve himself of the vigilance of reason, that is, his anguished present. The poet's reasonable mind does not allow him to separate from his body and for that he suffers, condemned to "una vigilia espantosa" (a frightful wakefulness). The poem ends with the arrival of the new day and the poet still yearning for the forgetfulness of the dream of imagination.

In Borges's poem the valorization of the wakeful state, traditionally seen as the only reality, is subverted by the oneiric activity. In Borges's poetic universe dreams are equivalent to creation, the possibility to achieve new realities in art. Hence, insomnia is the state of no creation. Thus for Borges, as for Arenas, the capability of dreaming is equivalent to the poetic expression. The creative impulse is like a dream, a directed dream, which grants the individual endless possibilities of expression. In the world of the child-narrator/Celestino, the boundary between what is real and what is dreamed or imagined is erased for the reader.[9] The reader's wish for clear limits is met by a multiplicity of realities that bifurcate and extend throughout the text.

The last epigraph is a section of the poem "Ritmo de otoño" (Rhythm of Autumn) from the first collection of poems by Federico García Lorca, *Libro de poemas* (1921). In this poem, the dream of the imagination is presented as the orchestrated dream of the poetic act. The "grito lírico" (lyrical cry) of the poet is presented as his only comfort against the frustrations of being unable to reach "el azul infinito" (the blue infinite), a metaphor for all that is denied to humanity. The poem suggests that when oppression becomes intolerable, the most absolute expression of freedom is the human imagination.

In *Celestino antes del alba* the child-narrator idealizes a pure being, a poet (Celestino), that cannot be destroyed by the violence of his surroundings. Celestino is a liberating force, an indomitable spirit that uncovers oppression and struggles against it. Celestino, who is always the same—"bravo, triste, alegre y todo al mismo tiempo" (*Celestino*, p. 69); "mad, sad, happy, and everything at the same time" (*Singing*, p. 59)—does not permit the violence that surrounds him to stop him from completing his poetic work. The paradoxical nature of the above statement underscores the child-narrator's need to integrate harmoniously the full gamut of human emotions in an ideal image of himself. Thus Celestino transcends, like the Lorquian poet, his surrounding brutality with an insatiable drive for self-expression that impels him to write even on the trunks of trees. Persecuted by the grandfather's hatchet, Celestino passionately writes a mysterious poetry that separates him and makes him different from the rest. According to Arenas:

> El niño no cuenta para defenderse más que con la imaginación; y esto le es suficiente para que no perezca, para que su mundo no sea destruido, porque, no podemos olvidarlo, la imaginación es maravillosa, es un formidable don, que en último caso sería el esencial y definitivo que diferenciaría al hombre del resto de las bestias. ("Celestino y yo," p. 118)

> The child only relies on his imagination for protection; and this is enough to assure that he will not perish, and that his world will not be destroyed. We cannot forget that the imagination is a marvelous thing, it is a formidable gift which in the end is perhaps the most essential and definitive thing that separates man from other animals.

Within the novel, in a moment of absolute rage, the young narrator defends the poetic activities of his cousin: "¡Salvajes!, cuando no entienden algo dicen en seguida que es una cosa fea y sucia. ¡Bestias! ¡Bestias! ¡Bestias!" (*Celestino,* p. 167); "They're a bunch of savages! If they don't understand something, they automatically hate it. They say it's ugly or it's dirty. Animals!" (*Singing,* p. 159). The child-narrator's cry reaffirms the infinite possibilities of expression in a world without reason. It is a cry of defense for all those whose unorthodox conduct, considered by the "superficiales" (superficial ones) as improper, represents the infinite game of difference that is life. The "superficiales," as Arenas calls them, are those who wish to domesticate plurality, those individuals who are bothered by any act—literary as well as individual—that is considered to be at variance with so-called normal social behavior:

> Ah, pero cuando tratamos de expresar las diferentes realidades que se esconden bajo una realidad aparente, los superficiales, que pululan en forma alarmante, los superficiales, a quienes hay que dárselo todo molido y masticado, [pegan] el grito en el cielo . . . ("Celestino y yo," p. 119)

> Ah, but when we try to express the different realities that are buried and hidden under an apparent reality, those superficial individuals,

who swarm in an alarming fashion and demand that everything that is presented to them be ground up and chewed for them beforehand, complain loudly.

It is evident that for Arenas characters in a literary work, just like human beings in life, are not logical and coherent beings anchored in an objective empirical reality, but complex and contradictory souls ceaselessly transforming themselves.

El palacio de las blanquísimas mofetas

El palacio de las blanquísimas mofetas is founded on genuine historical events, the fight of the Sierra Maestra rebel forces against the Batista regime. Nonetheless, the presentation of the characters' other levels of experience is never sacrificed for any type of accuracy or transparency, any hope to reproduce historical reality faithfully at a referential level of language. Arenas's concern here is not to rewrite history but to subordinate history's legitimating narratives to fiction, thus setting free all constraining boundaries that hinder further inquiry into the nature of human existence. In *El palacio de las blanquísimas mofetas* the laws of reality are not measured by fixed empirical standards but are constantly expanded and amplified. For example, early in the novel, describing Fortunato's turbulent existence, the heterodiegetic narrator states: "Porque lo cierto es que la realidad siempre era otra. Y [Fortunato] estaba siempre en otra realidad, en otra que no era precisamente aquélla, la que ellos llamaban *la verdadera*. La única que ellos conocían" (*El palacio*, p. 39); "Because the truth is that reality was always *other*. [Fortunato] was always in *another* reality, in another reality which was not precisely theirs, the one they called the *real* one. The only one they knew" (*The Palace*, p. 38).

Fortunato is a sensitive and restless adolescent desperate to escape from the closed social and familial circle in which he feels trapped. He must create and imagine other levels of reality to avoid the poverty, hunger, war, intolerance, and prejudices that those around him insist on seeing. With the image of death riding on a bicycle on the first page of this novel, the reader is asked to suspend his or her disbelief, not to look for overt messages but to find meaning on other levels. The reader is asked to make the text intelligible in spite of its violations and transgressions, to accommodate the shifting codes of a multifarious reality. Hence, the image of death riding on a bicycle around the family home is presented as being equally as "real" within the text as the protagonist's frustrated attempt to join the revolutionary struggle. Fortunato's walking on the roof while stabbing himself, Ester and Fortunato's chats beyond the grave, demons and spirits dancing in the living room, the extreme poverty of the rural town, the insurrectional struggle against Batista, the grandmother's blasphemies and insults, Adolfina's sexual frustrations, and so forth, are all presented side by side and contribute equally to the novel's textual validity.

Otra vez el mar

In part I of *Otra vez el mar* the wife's hallucinations, dreams, and flights of imagination all blend together, thus making it impossible for her, as a character, to distinguish between what is fantasy and what is "reality." Toward the end of part I, for example, the wife lying down next to Héctor at the beach wonders if her fears regarding her husband are perhaps unfounded:

> ¿Y si todo no hubiese sido más que un sueño? . . . Pero, oye, pero, oye: ¡Ya esto es el colmo! Tal cobardía no la podemos tolerar; estamos seguras de que sabes diferenciar tus pesadillas reales de las otras. Tus sueños ridículos, tus sueños grotescos y grandilocuentes. . . . Sí, sí, es cierto, digo, retomando yo misma el lenguaje de las voces; pero algunas veces, cuando me despierto palpo las sábanas, temiendo tropezarme con el hueso de algún animal prehistórico, con una tuerca gigantesca o con una especie rarísima de alacrán aún viva. Paso la mano por debajo del colchón, busco entre la almohada, pensando con terror, *aquí está*. (*Otra vez*, p. 171)

> And what if all this were only a dream? . . . But listen, listen, that does it! We cannot abide such cowardice, we are certain you know how to distinguish your real nightmares from the other ones. Your ridiculous dreams, those grotesque, grandiloquent dreams of yours. . . . Yes, yes, you're right, I say, using the same language as the voices; but sometimes when I wake up I feel the sheets, afraid I'll come across the bone of some prehistoric animal, or a gigantic nut and bolt, or some outlandish species of scorpion still alive in my bed. I run my hand under the mattress. I search through the pillow, thinking in terror, *Here it is.* (*Farewell*, pp. 148–49)

Although the wife wishes to believe that she can indeed distinguish between fact and fantasy, she wavers between different levels of experience (fantasies, dreams, hallucinations, memories) without being able to control them. Many of the wife's dream states are constructed around what Freud called wish fulfillments. This is evident in the representation of her first dream in which she identifies herself with Helen of Troy as a way to satisfy her unfulfilled sexual needs. Here a scene from the *Iliad* is turned into a display of battling phalluses over a flirtatious Helen of Troy, which ends, rather ironically, with the Trojans marching off behind the favorite of Aphrodite, Paris, who through his beauty provokes a homosexual orgy among the soldiers.

The wife's perceptions of what is real are challenged by a world that appears to permutate and transform itself capriciously around her. This emotional instability, which is expressed as a lack of self-governing, highlights how much the wife has been affected by a totalitarian society that denies the individual the freedom to express him- or herself without fear. Unlike the witness in the documentary novel who is asked to identify clearly the reality that shaped his or her experiences, a reality that is quite useful in recording revolutionary historiography, the wife in *Otra vez el mar* is unable to make such a clear and stable identification.

Similar to the patient's subconscious network of symbols that is uncovered and explained through the psychoanalytic procedure, the wife's hallucinations allow for the manifestation of certain hidden parts of her mental processes, with their own logic and order, that would be difficult to express in a conventional *mimesis of product*. In essence, through her hallucinations the wife dreams awake and is able to represent her innermost feelings. For example, through her hallucinations or visual images of the dinosaur that mockingly pursues her throughout part 1 of *Otra vez el mar*, erratically appearing and disappearing, her feelings of loneliness and isolation are symbolically revealed. As a child the wife had discovered a family trunk in which she had hoped to find some type of identification or comfort among the keepsakes and mementos of her family. Yet what she ended up being most fascinated with was a magazine containing a drawing of an unusual creature, a freakish monster with whose solitude she somehow identified. The fact that the wife picks an extinct creature whose destruction came about because of its inability to adapt to the harsh, changing conditions of the planet is rather telling in light of her own problems of assimilation.

El color del verano

In a late 1930s essay ("From the Prehistory of Novelistic Discourse"), Bakhtin first remarked on what he called the laughing truth of ancient parody, with its regenerating spirit of growth and change. In this essay Bakhtin praised ancient parody for its potential of liberating (creative) laughter. Bakhtin saw parody as an integral part of all carnivalesque literature for it creates a carnivalesque reversal, an intertextual game that destroys all privileged positions of authority. In *El color del verano* Arenas exploits the dialogic nature of parody that weakens seriousness and singular meaning, both characteristics of the documentary novel. *El color del verano* is a roman à clef which parodies a number of very real and prominent Cuban artists and intellectuals in order to undermine the seriousness and respectability associated with revolutionary Cuban letters. In *Antes que anochezca* Arenas points out:

> Una de las cosas más lamentables de la tiranías es que todo lo toman en serio y hacen desaparecer el sentido del humor. Históricamente Cuba había escapado siempre de la realidad gracias a la sátira y la burla. Sin embargo, con Fidel Castro, el sentido del humor fue desapareciendo hasta quedar prohibido; con eso el pueblo cubano perdió una de sus pocas posibilidades de supervivencia; al quitarle la risa le quitaron al pueblo el más profundo sentido de las cosas. (pp. 261–62)

> One of the most regrettable things about tyrannies is that they take everything very seriously and ultimately do away with humor. Historically Cuba has always escaped reality thanks to satire and mockery. However, with Fidel Castro, Cubans began to lose their sense of humor until it became prohibited; with that the Cuban people lost one of their few possibilities of survival; by taking away laughter they took away the most profound meaning of life from the Cuban people.[10]

El color del verano lampoons Cubans who remained faithful to the Revolution (for example, Retamal/Roberto Fernández Retamar, Halisia Jalonzo/Alicia Alonso, Odiseo Ruego/Eliseo Diego, Alejo Sholejov/Alejo Carpentier, among others) as well as those who went into exile (H. Puntilla/Heberto Padilla, Zebro Sardoya/Severo Sarduy, Kilo Abierto Montamier/Carlos Alberto Montaner), and finally Arenas also parodies himself in the trinity Gabriel/Reinaldo/the Tétrica Mofeta. By parodying members of both groups Arenas avoids the propagandistic attacks based on ideology that have polarized Cuban politics. In *El color del verano,* as in all Arenas's texts, no one subject, either literary or "real," is spared the full force of the writer's subversive attacks.

El asalto

The entire premise of this novel runs contrary to the basic notion of the documentary novel that states witnesses must have a verifiable history so that they can guarantee the authenticity of what they testify. *El asalto* presents a futuristic vision of Cuban society that the writer allowed himself to imagine and completely create. More than an accurate portrayal of a given historical period, the text functions as a literary forewarning of totalitarianism at its extreme.

El asalto can be read as a Spanish American (Cuban) version of the dystopian novel tradition as defined by such writers as Aldous Huxley (*Brave New World*) and George Orwell (*Nineteen Eighty-Four*). In fact, in one of Arenas's last interviews he stated that among the novels that affected him most when he was young were *Animal Farm* and *Nineteen Eighty-Four*: "Me acuerdo . . . que cuando terminé de leer *Rebelión en la granja* y *1984* estaba llorando" (I remember . . . that when I finished reading *Animal Farm* and *Nineteen Eighty-Four* I was crying).[11]

The theme of a utopian new world has persisted in Latin American literature, from Columbus's first description of his discovery of a new earthly paradise in *Diario de navegación,* through the accounts of Latin America's struggle for independence in the early nineteenth century that hoped to create a fresh new world in which to build a new polity (the most obvious literary example being Domingo Faustino Sarmiento's famous essay *Facundo,* which denied the validity of the colonial past and projected all goals toward a utopian future), to Cuban revolutionary literature with its utopian notion of a historical dialectic that progresses from darkness to a future enlightenment. *El asalto,* a cynical and dark novel, derides the notion of establishing an American utopia, much less a sane and caring world. While many Cuban novelists have written and continue to write realistic documentary works that idealize the Revolution as radically transforming Cuban society for the better, Arenas refused to subscribe to this utopian vision of history and portrayed the Revolution as the catalyst responsible for the persecution of certain members of Cuban society who simply failed, for whatever reason, to fit the revolutionary model.

FIVE

Chronology

In "La novela testimonio: socio-literatura" Miguel Barnet highlights chronology as a fundamental and indispensable feature of the documentary novel: "[La] cronología es indispensable porque fija la orientación histórica. No se trata de convertir la obra en un rompecabezas" (p. 147) (Chronology is indispensable because it establishes a historical orientation. The point isn't to turn the book into a jigsaw puzzle). Raúl González de Cascorro, winner of the Casa de las Américas prize for *testimonio* in 1975, confessed his own fear of losing the reader because of the unusual construction of his prize-winning *Aquí se habla de combatientes y de bandidos*: "Confesemos que lo más difícil para nosotros fue el ensamblaje, ya que se caía en el riesgo de confusión, de perder al lector en el laberinto de personajes y hechos" (I confess that what was most difficult was the construction of the text as a result of the constant risk of confusion, of losing the reader in a labyrinth of characters and events).[1]

The flagrant disregard for chronology in *Celestino antes del alba, El palacio de las blanquísimas mofetas, Otra vez el mar*, and *El color del verano* perhaps makes the label "jigsaw puzzle" the most appropriate. (*El asalto* will be studied separately, for it exploits and manipulates the thriller-detective format in which temporal succession corresponds to a gradation of intensity.) The undermining of chronology in Arenas's novels, however, is not an attempt to lose or confuse the reader, but rather a means of wrestling with the systematic absolutism of official (linear) history, which aspires to a truth-value grounded in the representation of a regulated, unfolding series of events. Chronology is fundamental in the Cuban documentary novel for it tells the reader in what direction to think about the events that are represented and charges those events with different emotional (revolutionary) values. The representation of a logical sequence and arrangement of events is a significant and authoritative "form" that imposes (revolutionary) meaning while camouflaging the actual conditions of production.

The ideological intention behind the spatio-temporal linearity of the documentary novel is challenged in Arenas's texts, which do not progress but incessantly move in all directions at the same time. Still, I must clarify that the writer does not and cannot refute linearity altogether, as is evident in the portrayal of certain individual and historical progressions in each of the novels (for example, the life stages of the protagonist—childhood, adolescence, and adulthood—in successive historical eras: the Batista regime, the early revolutionary years, the Castro regime). Yet, although there are certain general delineated sequences of progression, the field of discourse in these novels can best be defined as cyclic, reiterative; seeing events over and over from different perspectives. Arenas once maintained: "[En mis novelas] el lector puede adentrarse como se adentra en una sábana, por cualquier lugar. Puede empezar lo mismo por el principio del libro que por el final"[2] (The reader can enter [my novels] as one can enter a bed sheet, from any direction. It doesn't matter if one starts at the beginning or at the end of the book). This perhaps exaggerated declaration points to the writer's subversion of a traditional sequence of events with a clearly distinguishable beginning, middle, and end. The desire to challenge the limitations of linearity is likewise evident in the break with typographical conventions featured in many of the novels of the *pentagonía*. The use of different size letters and types, blank spaces, and even blank pages, off-centered, vertical, and slanted writing are all typographical transgressions that exploit the many possibilities of the blank page and promote the palpability of the texts, emphasizing them as *texts*, that is, linguistic artifices and not neutral transcriptions of reality. Also challenged is the notion of traditional realism—in one form or another the central model of Cuban revolutionary aesthetics—a notion based on a view of history as a sequential progression from backwardness to civilization. In essence, the violation of linearity in Arenas's novels impedes a passive reading (decoding) and thus gives the reader a more active role. While the writer of the documentary novel performs the task of *recopilador* (compiler), Arenas leaves this editorial job to his reader. The narrative power of these literary compositions derives from the decisive moment when the writer relinquishes the text to his reader; literary life is born from the act of reading.

Reception or reader-oriented theory sees the process of reading as a dynamic and complex activity in which each reader actualizes (concretizes) the text through a process of assumptions and revisions which initiates further inferences and modifications. As Wolfgang Iser has pointed out in *The Act of Reading: A Theory of Aesthetic Response*: "It is the reader who unfolds the network of possible connections, and it is the reader who then makes a selection from that network" (p. 126). In Arenas's novels the notion of a rigid, well-structured plot, providing the reader a sense of completeness, is subverted by the presentation of a cyclical narrative time-space of multiple possibilities that invites the reader to sort out the various narrative threads and thus to work out a larger meaning. These novels require an active reader who can make the text intelligible in spite of its violations and transgressions, a reader who can accommodate shifting codes in which everything is represented as possible and probable. Arenas's novels require a more flexible approach to reading, a *letting go* of traditional expectations and *going with* the creative detours and interruptions of the narrative discourse. Unlike the documentary novel, the experimental structures of the novels of the *pentagonía* demand the participation of the reader in the creative process. The reader must be extremely flexible in his or her approach to these novels, confronting, as do the characters, the chaos and non-sense of existence.

Celestino antes del alba (Cantando en el pozo)

In *Celestino antes del alba* there is no traditional plot; temporal sequences related to cause and effect, a before and after, are undermined. Story time (the period in which the situations and events occur, that is, the late 1940s and the early 1950s) is clouded and obscured by a magical and lyrical discourse time (the time of the enunciation, or actual narrating act). Furthermore, no attempt is made to distinguish between conventional intervals of time. In one moment of the novel the child-narrator states: "¡Y pensar que ya hace más de cien años que no probamos ni un bocado!" (*Celestino*, p. 115); "And to think it's been more than a hundred years since we had a bite to eat!" (*Singing*, p. 105). As we can see, conventional measurements of time are rendered useless by such hyperbolic expressions.

From its onset *Celestino antes del alba* is set in a concrete locality: the impoverished reality of the pre-Revolution Cuban countryside. From this spatial marker the fantastic and explosive imagination of the child-narrator is allowed to unfold. Yet beyond the presentation of this initial locality, steeped in historical time, it is impossible to distinguish among days, months, years, or any type of precise sequence of events. The most flagrant dismissal of chronology is seen in the use of three endings: "Fin" (The End), "Segundo Final" (The Second End), and "Ultimo Final" (The Last End) (*Celestino,* pp. 112, 144, 215). (In *El mundo alucinante,* which was written immediately after *Celestino antes del alba,* Arenas changes his subversive tactics and uses multiple beginnings; there are three separate chapter 1's.) The use of three separate endings supports the novel's devaluation of chronology and its emphasis on simultaneity. The text creates a literary tension or struggle as it repeatedly strives to escape from its condition of finitude, to stretch out from the limitations and confinement of a final determinacy.

Although Arenas works toward the elimination of time in *Celestino antes del alba,* the novel is still bound to the surface structure of the text, which itself is bound to the linearity (space) of words that move from left to right. The novel nevertheless transgresses time on a deeper, more abstract level through the elimination of death, deforming the logocentric concept of temporal action.[3] It is the coexistence of death alongside life, as another possibility and not as an end to a particular individual history, that most affects the presentation of time and space in this first novel. Death, seen as the end of a human chronology, is not respected and therefore the reader's notion of chronology appears suspended. But this absence of death does not eliminate tragedy and terror from the novel, as it does, according to Bakhtin, for example, in Rabelais's *Gargantua and Pantagruel*: "the most fearless book in world literature" (*Rabelais and His World,* p. 39). In *Celestino antes del alba* the possibility that death might not exist gives rise to a far greater fear and terror, that all the suffering and agony of life might last forever: "Será que nosotros no vamos a morirnos nunca. Ese es el miedo que yo tengo: que seamos eternos, porque entonces sí que no tenemos escapatoria" (*Celestino,* pp. 117–18); "Is it possible that we're never going to die? That's what I'm afraid of—that we might be eternal, because then there's really truly no way out" (*Singing,* p. 107).

El palacio de las blanquísimas mofetas

El palacio de las blanquísimas mofetas requires an active reader who can make the text intelligible in spite of its chronological violations and transgressions. The *diégèse* of this second novel of the pentalogy does not unfold as a regulated succession of events, but rather as an interrupted and temporally disconnected recording of conflicting voices. *El palacio de las blanquísimas mofetas* goes beyond the lack of a logical narrative progression as it jumps back and forth over the same material. This combinatorial game of discourses ignores the concept of sequence, as found typically in documentary novels, because events are told and retold through the voices of different family members. Throughout the text past and present are (con)fused while the future is condemned to be a repetition of the past. Bits and pieces of dialogues and ruminations recreate a bewildering collage that at first disorients the reader but later increases in symbolic significance. Only the fly—"un ser eterno" (an eternal creature)—appears to be free from the limitations of past, present, and future. In *El palacio de las blanquísimas mofetas* the heterodiegetic narrator, typically freed of chronological constraints, is also at the mercy of time as the following passage illustrates: "Fue entonces—o quizá antes, quizá siempre, quizá un poco después—cuando comprendió que ése era su sentido de estar" (*El palacio,* p. 193); "It was then—or perhaps before, perhaps forever, perhaps even a little while later—that he realized that that was his reason to live" (*The Palace,* p. 235).

The spatio-temporal coordinates of *El palacio de las blanquísimas mofetas* are quite ambiguous, although perhaps less so than in the first novel. In reading this second novel of the pentalogy, the reader experiences a greater sense of spatio-temporal detail. For example, the action of the novel—although initially set in an unnamed rural zone—predominantly occurs in a small interior town identified as Holguín. This presentation of an actual place attached to a particular historical time (the period prior to and including the overthrow of the Batista regime) serves as the starting point for the unfolding of the harrowing accounts of each family member. Moreover, there exist newspaper accounts scattered throughout the text that date certain events associated with the revolutionary struggle to overthrow Batista. These accounts enhance the notion of time-space.

Time-space is filtered through the turbulent ramblings of the family members, who do not concern themselves with providing an objective reference point. Each voice, agonizing over his or her particular perception of existence, finds itself at odds with objective empirical reality. The same state of instability and crisis that is described as assaulting the country already exists internally in each family member. As the title of part 2 of the novel clearly suggests, "Hablan las criaturas de queja" ("The Creatures Utter Their Complaints"), the characters are quite anxious to disclose their personal agonies. For this reason, it is virtually impossible to pin down specific spatio-temporal details of the world in which the subjects move. For example, time and distance are intangible in both Fortunato's undefined journey to join the revolutionary army and Adolfina's similar quest to find a man. Their respective wanderings lack precise spatio-temporal exactitude. Yet this lack of precision is irrelevant to the emotional intensity both characters disclose. Any reader searching for an objectified time-space will be at a loss and will consequently miss the artistic intensity of the novel. To appreciate *El palacio de las blanquísimas mofetas* the reader must surrender to the creative ramblings and digressions of the different voices.

The presentation of death in *El palacio de las blanquísimas mofetas* is different than in *Celestino antes del alba*. In Arenas's first novel the elimination of death was tied to a desire to eradicate time; for this reason the characters died, were reborn, died again, and were once again reborn. In *El palacio de las blanquísimas mofetas* the dead are not reborn but, significantly, inhabit a time-space that coexists alongside that of the living. The binary opposition of life and death is not exploited, but in true carnivalesque spirit both terms of the antithesis are embraced and united, intermixed and confused. Hence, life is not favored over death nor death over life. Life and death are simply two possible coexisting states, as in the prologue-epilogue in which the figure of death appears personified riding a bicycle around the family house. From this moment on, death will be physically present in this world of suffering and solitude.

Otra vez el mar

Otra vez el mar transgresses documentary-style linear progression by forcing the reader to decipher the intertextual web that links both of its parts. Arenas himself suggested (see the appendix, pp. 148–49) two possible ways of reading the text: (1) a straight linear reading and (2) an alternating of the first day of part 1 with the first canto of part 2, and so on. While part 1 introduces a clear presentation of events, it leaves certain gaps that are filled by Héctor's narration in part 2. The difficulties that the reader faces when reading the second part of the novel are more a result of a lack of chronology than a shift from a *mimesis of product* to a *mimesis of process*. *Otra vez el mar* demands active participation in manufacturing a literary universe that is as much the creation of the reader as it is of the novelist. Just as in *Celestino antes del alba,* in which the first and last image is that of the well—with the face of the child-narrator reflected in the water—in *Otra vez el mar* both parts 1 and 2 begin and end with the presence of the sea (*el mar*). In fact, "el mar" are literally both the first and last words of the novel. In *Otra vez el mar* the sea is a complex, contradictory symbol that is also a fundamental character, influencing in one way or another all the characters in the novel. The sea symbolizes freedom as well as imprisonment; it is a symbol for what we yearn for and desire, but it is also that which is unattainable and beyond our reach; it is both constant and changing.[4] The sea serves as a paradigm of the reiterative structure of the novel, an advancing, returning, ceaselessly transforming text.

Part 1 of *Otra vez el mar* has been classified by certain critics as prose while part 2 has been seen as poetry. However, this classification is an oversimplification, given the fact that the wife's discourse (part 1) is in itself highly poetic. Consequently, it would behoove the critic to refer to these two parts as two instances of writing, two different ways of intoning a discourse. What could be said is that while part 1 is more of an exploratory narrative that recounts experiences, memories, and dreams from a first-person point of view, part 2, likewise focalized through a first-person point of view, breaks beyond the issues of linearity and coherence in order to intone a multifaceted discourse whose artistic strength lies in its poetic charge.

Although *Otra vez el mar* continues within the novelistic experimentation of the Boom years, its curious construction makes it an anomaly within the Latin American novelistic tradition. Still, I see its immediate precursor in Julio Cortázar's *Rayuela* (1963). Cortázar's monumental novel, or anti-novel, with its breakdown of traditional genre boundary lines, paved the road for a collage novel such as *Otra vez el mar. Rayuela*'s "dispensable chapters" and "table of instructions" informing the reader how to interpolate these chapters can be seen as a spiritual progenitor to *Otra vez el mar.* The formal experimentation of *Otra vez el mar* makes clear once again the broadly encompassing, highly flexible, and ever changing generic definition of the novel. Arenas capriciously plays off traditional rules, subverting, exaggerating, and reinventing them.

In *Otra vez el mar* the introduction of an actual spatial marker (the car ride from Guanabacoa to Havana) attached to a particular time (more or less the first decade of the Revolution) serves as the starting point for the gradual unfolding of both Héctor's and his wife's stories. While part 1 of the novel provides for the reader a general sense of spatio-temporal coordinates, part 2 totally disregards such details, focusing rather on the inexorably increasing weight of Héctor's emotional cantos, in which an exterior chronological time-space is virtually unrecognizable. It is as if only the spatio-temporal coordinates of the cantos themselves, the ramblings of Héctor's tortured psyche, were of any importance. So it is that the textual surface of the second part of the novel is made palpable by Héctor's exasperating verse, printed sometimes vertically, sometimes diagonally or any which way. This playing with the typographical textual space indicates a desire to break free of the sequentiality that the printed word imposes on language.

Part 1 does provide general spatio-temporal reference points that allow the reader to situate many narrated events. For example, a reference is made to achieving the ten-million-ton sugar harvest the following year, establishing 1969 as the date of the events. However, part 1 is hardly anchored to any precise temporal chronology. The wife's 193-page narrative passage intermittently jumps back and forth, requiring the reader to make the necessary connections. The representation of time-space in part 1 is filtered through the memories, hallucinations, and dreams of the wife. The dream sequences are rather provoking for their poetic inquietude. They are represented, uninterrupted, side by side with the narrated events that occur during the six days at the beach.

In part 1 the reader finds the couple returning in their car to Havana after a short stay in a seaside cabin located in a northern part of Havana province. This initial returning-car spatial marker is the point from which all other time-spaces are recalled. Among the major chronotopes that have endured in the history of European prose,[5] Bakhtin identifies the chronotope of the road as one of the most used: "The chronotope of the road is both a point of new departures and a place for events to find their denouement. Time, as it were, fuses together with space and flows in it (forming the road); this is the source of the rich metaphorical expansion on the image of the road as a course: 'the course of life,' 'to set out on a new course,' 'the course of history' and so on; varied and multi-leveled are the ways in which the road is turned into a metaphor, but its fundamental pivot is the flow of time" (*The Dialogic Imagination*, pp. 243–44). In *Otra vez el mar* the chronotope of the road rather than dealing with beginnings or new departures, is involved with past events and with memories that have calloused sensibility and have made present life intolerable. Bakhtin's identification of the fundamental pivot of the chronotope of the road as "the flow of time" is evident in the epigraph to part 1, "La memoria es un presente que no termina nunca de pasar" ("Memory is a present which never stops going past"). This quote from Octavio Paz's "Poema," from *La estación violenta,* holds the key for the astute reader. For in fact everything in the text, from the very first page on, is the wife's (Héctor's) memory. Even though the sequence of events at the beach appears to the reader as occurring within a reading present, all is memory. So it is that the figure of the adolescent boy appears in the initial pages of the novel: "Héctor, y el muchacho, sin duda hermoso, tirado en la arena, quizás dormido. Haciéndose el dormido. Héctor, y el muchacho, flotando bocarriba, muy cerca de la costa" (*Otra vez,* p. 14); "Hector—and the boy, who really is beautiful, lying on the sand, perhaps asleep. Pretending to be asleep. Hector—and the boy, floating on his back, very near the shore" (*Farewell,* p. 7–8). Everything has happened and will now be relived *otra vez* (again), as the title suggests. Keeping this in mind, one can see the presentation of time in part 1 as follows: (1) a technical present that encompasses the duration of the car ride, from the moment of departure from the beach to the arrival at the tunnel that leads into the city of Havana; (2) the recent past, which consists of the six days spent at the beach and all that transpired there; and (3) a remote historical past in which family memories and personal experiences are related.

The six days at the beach, although providing for the reader a spatiotemporal reference point, also conceal a parodic intention, a decrowning of the story of Genesis. Each new morning the wife's first observations coincide with the first images that appear during the six days of the story of Genesis (the following pages are from the Spanish edition):

DAY 1 daylight (p. 42)
DAY 2 the sky and ocean (p. 75)
DAY 3 the green trees (p. 97)
DAY 4 moon and sun (p. 128)
DAY 5 gulls (birds) (p. 169)
DAY 6 Héctor (man) (p. 191)

The seventh day, when God rested and observed the goodness of his creation, is intentionally omitted. For Héctor, there is no rest and no evidence of God's goodness to be found. The human race, considered God's most perfect creation, is mocked and ridiculed throughout the novel for its selfishness and brutality. In *Canto tercero,* in a series of *"entremeses"* (interludes) that reveal the abominable and pathetic state of the human species, we read:

El hombre
es de todas las alimañas la más aborrecible,
pues convencido de que para todo
existe la irrevocable muerte,
mata.

El hombre
es de todas las calamidades la más lamentable,
pues habiendo inventado el amor se desen-
vuelve en el plano de la
hipocresía.
(*Otra vez*, p. 278)

∎∎∎∎∎

Man
is of all vermin the most loathsome,
for convinced that all things
go to irrevocable death,
he kills.

Man
is of all disasters the most lamentable,
for having invented love he only fully reveals
himself at the level of
hypocrisy.
(*Farewell*, p. 252)

The above passage challenges the notion of an original goodness present in the human species, an inherent innocence that humankind must
strive to unearth after its fall from God's grace. The Judeo-Christian
tradition, built on such metaphors as humankind's righteousness and vir-
tuousness, has been the foundation for society's value structures and
systems of hierarchical truths. Here the poet Héctor seriously transgresses
these sacred norms of society. The poet battles against the very fibers of
culture that have attempted to cage the individual's vital spirit. This
transgression is of course dangerous for the poet. His refusal to submit to
the law, that is, his transgression of society's limits, ostracizes him, marks
his solitude. Yet, ironically, this also is the poet's most profound moment
of freedom.

El color del verano

El color del verano is an ambitious novel that synthesizes many of Reinaldo Arenas's major themes: among others, the quest for freedom, the love/hate relationship with the mother, the writer's need for expression. The story, which takes place in 1999, contains hundreds of characters engaging in wildly transgressive adventures as they prepare to celebrate the dictator's official fiftieth (in reality fortieth) anniversary in power. The celebration ends in a homoerotic carnival that precipitates the fall of the state. The carnival celebration within the novel is reflected in the carnivalesque images and structure of the actual text. *El color del verano* delights in what Mikhail Bakhtin saw as carnivalesque literature's mingling of the sacred with the profane, the high and the low, the sublime and the ridiculous, for the purpose of attacking dogmatism, established authority, and narrow-minded seriousness.[6] In his seminal study *Rabelais and His World* Bakhtin explored the roots of carnivalesque folk humor and observed: "No dogma, no authoritarianism, no narrow-minded seriousness can coexist with Rabelaisian images; these images are opposed to all that is finished and polished, to all pomposity, to ever ready-made solutions in the sphere of thought and world outlook" (p. 3).

During the sixteenth century the world of the carnival was an opportunity to liberate society from all one-sided official seriousness through the inversion of hierarchy, of all so-called high culture. The topsy-turvy world view of the carnival revealed that established official authority was something relative that only led to dogmatism, a concept hostile to progressive ideas of change and evolution. What Bakhtin saw in the Rabelaisian text—a rebellion against dogma, authoritarianism, and all type of seriousness—is likewise present in Arenas's texts. Like Rabelais, who subverted with excess and grotesque laughter the ascetic medieval worldview, the carnivalesque transgressions in *El color del verano* propose a festive and parodic critique of "Fifoism" (read Castroism) with its insistence on Marxist thought (historical materialism) taken to its limits. Arenas undermines Marxism's systematic view of history (that is, the idea of continuous progress, perpetual evolution) with the assertion that *El color del verano* is circular in structure, with no clearly distinguishable beginning or end. In the prologue Arenas (Gabriel/Reinaldo/the Tétrica Mofeta) proposes:

> Dejo a la sagacidad de los críticos las posibilidades de descifrar la estructura de esta novela. Solamente quisiera apuntar que no se trata

de una obra lineal, sino circular y por lo mismo ciclónica, con un vértice o centro que es el carnaval, hacia donde parten todas las flechas. De modo que, dado su carácter de circunferencia, la obra en realidad no empieza ni termina en un punto específico y puede comenzar a leerse por cualquier parte hasta terminar la ronda. Sí, está usted, tal vez, ante la primera novela redonda hasta ahora conocida. Pero, por favor, no considere esto ni un mérito ni un defecto, es una necesidad intrínseca a la armazón de la obra. (p. 249)

I leave for the sagacity of the critics the possibilities of deciphering the structure of this novel. I would only like to point out that one is not dealing with a linear, but rather a circular work and for that very reason cyclonic, with a vertex or center which is the carnival, toward which all the coordinates radiate. And so, given its circumferential nature, the work really doesn't begin or end at a specific point and one can start to read it at any part going once around. Yes, you are perhaps holding the first known round novel. But please don't take this to be a sign of virtue or defect, but simply an intrinsic necessity in the framework of the work.

The insistence that the novel is circular challenges the idealistic (utopian) notion of historical materialism by underscoring the simultaneity of events and not their serialization. This is emphasized in *El color del verano* by the coexistence of famous Cuban historical and literary figures from different ages. In the end what is suggested is that the corruption, banishment, political foul play, and injustices that have plagued the Cuban people throughout their history have not been surmounted but senselessly repeated over and over.

El asalto

El asalto relies more heavily on the use of chronology as a result of the thriller-detective format that it utilizes. In chapter 1, I spoke of the cultivation and popularity of the detective genre in revolutionary Cuban letters. The detective story basically supports the idea that history can be reinterpreted and rescued from distorted accounts. The belief in causality, the complicity between the subject and his or her consciousness of a past, is very much the product of a belief that clues and vestiges of the past can be used to reveal the "truth" about the present. As we have seen, this tendency to revise or recover the past has been a fundamental concern of the official revolutionary historiography in Cuba.

Arenas's cultivation of the detective-thriller in no way follows the revolutionary model for the genre. In the latter the detective-protagonist is an ordinary member of society who works with an efficient revolutionary police force that is assisted by concerned and responsible Cuban citizens. In *El asalto* the thriller-detective structure describes a very specific milieu with unique characters and events: a vile and abominable Orwellian society where individuals have been so persecuted and browbeaten by the state that they have virtually lost their humanity.

Tzvetan Todorov dedicates a chapter of *The Poetics of Prose* to the detective fiction genre. He begins his essay by making a distinction between two subgenres of detective fiction: the whodunit and the thriller. I would like to focus on the two characteristics of the thriller subgenre as Todorov discusses them. First, in the thriller (unlike the whodunit, where the story of the crime ends before the [second] story of the investigation begins) there is no story told about a crime anterior to the moment of the narrative. The act or process of saying coincides and is simultaneous with the (chronological) action; the reader's interest is sustained by suspense, the expectation of what will happen. Second, according to Todorov, is the tendency to description. Todorov quotes Marcel Duhamel, the thriller's most active promoter in France, as saying that in the thriller the reader finds "violence—in all its forms, and especially the most shameful—, beatings, killings. . . . Immorality is as much at home here as noble feelings. . . . There [are] also . . . violent passions, implacable hatred" (p. 48). Todorov summarizes Duhamel's thoughts when he adds: "Indeed it is around these constants that the thriller is constituted: violence, generally sordid crimes, the amorality of the characters" (p. 48).

The thriller's two main characteristics are present in the last novel of the pentalogy. First, the narrative world of *El asalto* is indeed filled with sordid images and scenes of extreme violence, beatings, and general depravity. Secondly, chronology is respected and utilized to build suspense, also a necessary element of the thriller subgenre. Nonetheless, Arenas's thriller is anything but traditional in its subject matter, descriptions, or themes. The nameless narrator, fearing he is turning into his mother, spends the entire novel in search of her so that he can destroy her. This frantic search, creating suspense, intensifies throughout the novel until the moment when the nameless narrator is invited to the Gran Tribune, where he finally spots his mother, who in the end turns out to be the dictator himself. Perla Rozencvaig, in her last interview with Arenas, comments on the suspense in *El asalto*: "The tension really mounts when we find out who the hunted man is."7 Arenas's reply: "Sure, but that's like all my novels: masks and carnival, where the object of the chase reveals its double identity when captured. That's how the pentagony was supposed to end." Arenas's remark underscores the deliberate ambivalence of his novels, their duplicity (masks) and carnivalesque qualities. The dénouement of *El asalto*, which the writer professes to be the way the cycle "was supposed to end," can be read as a carnivalesque scene that indulges in the excess of the material body (grotesquerie) as a way of coming to terms with the (homo)sexual body image of the protean narrator of the pentalogy, who has struggled with his sexual feelings since the first novel of the five-book series.

Bakhtin saw in Rabelais's work a predominant place assigned to all corporeal functions. Inherited from the culture of folk humor, they created what Bakhtin termed a "grotesque realism." Grotesque realism uses material bodily functions, despite their vulgarity, as images of fertility and growth. According to Bakhtin, images of the human body as bulging and oversized are common in carnivalesque literature. The image of the carnival body is one of impure corporeal bulk, with its lower regions (buttocks and genitals) given priority over the upper ones (head, spirit, reason). All these grotesque qualities are seen as positive and cosmic forces in Bakhtin's analysis. In the final scene of *El asalto* the nameless narrator penetrates his mother with his enlarged penis and finally destroys her. This passage creates a scene of grotesque realism in which the protagonist finally defeats the mother (authoritarian symbol of power) by sexually possessing her. Through this act the protagonist accepts his own body image and is finally able to stretch out on the sand and rest. Clearly, the copulation with the mother, a societal taboo, can be read as a transcoding or displacement of the narrator's reaffirmation of his own (homo)sexuality.

SIX

Documentation

The use of evidence in the documentary novel purports to validate the testimony given. Presumably the reader is more inclined to believe a testimony if it is accompanied by photographs, newspaper articles, or any type of "official" information. Nubya Casas states:

> En cuanto a la urgencia documental, parece haber en el testigo una clara visión del efecto que conlleva la materialidad para convencer— "ver para creer". Así que recoge papeles, fotos, y primordialmente su recuerdo, y los registra en un texto para que pueda evidenciar—y persuadir—su relato de lo ocurrido. Esta función es común en todas las modalidades testimoniales. ("Novela-testimonio: historia y literatura," p. 47)

> In regard to the urgency to document, there appears to be in the witness a clear understanding of the effect of outward appearances to convince—"seeing is believing." Hence, the witness collects papers, photos, and primarily his or her memories, and then records them into the text in order to prove—and persuade—his or her account of the events. This function is common in all modalities of documentary texts.

Celestino antes del alba, El palacio de las blanquísimas mofetas, Otra vez el mar, El color del verano, and *El asalto* present subversive documentation that, rather than convincing or persuading the reader, opens itself to digressions that challenge and decenter the notion of an "official" account of an event. In the novels of the *pentagonía* the recording of events is relative; thus, documentation is (re)created or distorted much as Borges falsified and varied events according to his literary whims in *Historia universal de la infamia* (*A Universal History of Infamy*).

Celestino antes del alba (*Cantando en el pozo*)

Throughout *Celestino antes del alba*, the reader finds references to and quotations from important literary figures: Oscar Wilde, Jorge Luis Borges, Federico García Lorca, Arthur Rimbaud, Shakespeare, Sophocles, and others. Interspersed with these literary or "official" references, yet given equal status, are recorded "oral" testimonies (expressions and exclamations) by the child-narrator's family members: "mi abuela" (my grandmother), "mi madre" (my mother), "mi tío loco Faustino" (my crazy uncle Faustino), "mi tía Celia" (my aunt Celia). This mixture of literary and familial references creates a carnivalesque atmosphere that destroys all pretense to high (read official) and low (read unofficial) documentation. Moreover, these literary, nonliterary, and oral references multiply the allusions/illusions, thus intensifying the interpretational ambiguity of the novel.

In *Celestino antes del alba*, many of the references are not presented in the body of the text but on a single facing page with a blank verso. As a result, the flow of the base text is interrupted, forcing the reader somehow to accommodate this new information. The logic of a linear narrative is abrogated, and the reader as co-writer is given the opportunity to view things for him- or herself and discover how they fit, or even to decide if they fit, into the total *diégèse*. Hence, each reader will individually adapt these selections in his or her process of reading or (re)writing the text.[1] What needs to be underscored, however, is that the personal frustrations and destitution of prerevolutionary Cuban peasants are not any less convincing or any less authentic for the reader as a result of these lyrical and ambiguous "documents." Ironically, the reader intuits the harshness and wretched conditions of the Cuban countryside in the juxtaposition of literary passages and familial remarks. For example:

Deseo, cuando recibas esta carta te encuentres bien. Yo estoy bien.
Te mando una lata de jamoneta china. No dejes de comértela. Es de
la buena . . .

MI MADRE
(*Celestino*, p. 45)

I hope this letter finds you well. I am fine. I am sending you a can of
Chinese luncheon meat. Don't fail to eat it. It's the very best quality . . .

MY MOTHER

(*Singing*, p. 35)

■ ■ ■ ■ ■

No le preguntéis de dónde viene. Su historia es trivial. En la miseria,
sus padres la vendieron por una bolsa de arroz blanco.

EL ESPEJO MAGICO

(*Celestino*, p. 57)

Do not ask her whence she comes. Her story is of little account. In
their poverty, her parents sold her for a bag of white rice.

THE MAGIC MIRROR

(*Singing*, p. 47)

■ ■ ■ ■ ■

Fuiste a robar comida; pero tu abuela te vio y te dio un golpe con la
escoba.

MI TIA CELIA

(*Celestino*, p. 81)

You went to STEAL some food, but your grandmother SAW YOU and
gave you A WHACK WITH THE BROOM.

MY AUNT CELIA

(*Singing*, p. 71)

■ ■ ■ ■ ■

Todo le viene a la memoria ahora. Sin poderlo evitar, suspira y llora.

CANCION DE ROLANDO

(*Celestino*, p. 107)

It all comes back to his memory now. Unable to stop himself, he
sighs and weeps.

SONG OF ROLAND

(*Singing*, p. 97)

El palacio de las blanquísimas mofetas

In *El palacio de las blanquísimas mofetas* the use of subversive
documentation takes on a far greater role in the novel's narrative struc-

ture. As in *Celestino antes del alba* literary references appear alongside, and are given equal status to, the family's comments. In *El palacio de las blanquísimas mofetas* these references are at times anonymous, at times identified, and at other times simply labeled "Ellos" (Them). In addition, *El palacio de las blanquísimas mofetas* introduces fragments from newspaper accounts, beauty magazines, bulletins of guerrilla activity, advertisements, and film announcements.[2] It is difficult for the reader to validate their authenticity. Besides the fact that they cannot easily be corroborated, their juxtaposition in the text alongside the subjective words of different characters undermines any attempt at establishing documentary confidence. Still, the validity of the documents is really not important, since their job is not to factually document or to persuade the reader of their authenticity, but rather to represent the relativity of all documentation, as well as to undermine the linearity of the narrative discourse by creating a true collage structure. In actuality, the "documents" used in the novel go beyond the time of the novel's action (1958, the last year of Batista's dictatorship) to include two other eras: 1935 (the turbulent aftermath of Gerardo Machado's dictatorship) and 1968 (the inauguration of Fidel Castro's socialist regime). Thus, three decades (the 1930s, 1950s, and 1960s), each with its own set of problems for the island's sociopolitical and economic health, are blurred to reveal the inadequacies of the Cuban political system. Such poetic and political liberties could not be utilized, for example, by Miguel Barnet in his documentary novels, texts that respect chronology and are restricted to presenting orthodox Marxist thought and official Cuban revolutionary models.

Particularly interesting is the original manuscript of *El palacio de las blanquísimas mofetas* housed at the Princeton University library. The manuscript is a true collage. It contains a number of advertisements that were literally cut out and pasted directly onto the typed pages. In *El desamparado humor de Reinaldo Arenas* Roberto Valero informs us that Arenas had originally wanted to include photographs in the novel, but in the end the publisher did not include them: "Por ejemplo, cuando Fortunato desea escaparse de la casa con su maleta y diecisiete pesos, el autor hubiera insertado un anuncio local donde se veía a un hombre con su maleta tomando algún ómnibus de una línea holguinera" (p. 109) (For example, when Fortunato wishes to run away from home with his suitcase and seventeen dollars, the author would have inserted a local advertisement in which one could see a man with his suitcase getting on a bus on the Holguín line).

In the "fifth agony" there appear twelve *versiones* (versions) of the most significant event within the novel: Fortunato's rise in revolt and ultimate death. The idea that there can be an official version is denied by the contradictions of the different accounts of this event. However, the conflicting information surrounding Fortunato's decision to leave home in no way obscures the basic reasons for his departure: the extreme poverty, rigidity, and provincialism of his hometown, Holguín.

The twelve versions of Fortunato's departure to join the rebel army is reminiscent of Guillermo Cabrera Infante's use of multiple versions of a singular event in *Tres tristes tigres,* "La muerte de Trotsky referida por varios escritores cubanos, años después—o antes" ("The Death of Trotsky as Described by Various Cuban Writers, Several Years After the Event—or Before"). While the technique is used in Cabrera Infante's novel to exploit parodic possiblities, in *El palacio de las blanquísimas mofetas* it is more linked with the notion of multiple points of view of any given event. The seventh version is of particular significance; while the other versions are narrated by different family members, version seven is narrated by the third-person heterodiegetic narrator, traditionally the reliable omniscient narrator, who attempts from the very first sentence to emphasize the veracity of this version by contradicting everyone else's:

> ¡Mentira! ¡Mentira! Todo eso es mentira. Lo cierto es que cuando la situación llegó al extremo de que ya no había una vianda para ponerla en la mesa, Fortunato se fue a pasar una temporada a casa de su tía Emérita, la odiada, . . . (*El palacio,* p. 216)[3]

> It's a lie! It's a lie! It's all a lie! What *really* happened is that when they finally saw that they were between a rock and a hard place, when things got so bad that there wasn't so much as a sweet potato to put on the table, Fortunato left to go live a while in his aunt Emerita's house—the Obnoxious One's . . . (*The Palace,* p. 263)

Regardless of the initial seriousness and certitude of the narrator's words, his "testimony" crumbles under the weight of a game of uncontrolled verbal absurdities that closes the seventh version. Note below how the English translator gave up on translating many of these absurdities:

> Lo cierto es (justo es decirlo), que así fueron las cosas. Ay: lo cierto. Garr; lo cierto.
> Juiii: lo cierto.
> ¡Epa!: lo cierto.

Grapác: lo cierto.

Guirindán: lo cierto.

Cojones: lo cierto.

Vea: lo cierto.

Analice: lo cierto.

Medite: sobre lo cierto.

La certeza de lo cierto. La incertidumbre de lo cierto, la franqueza de lo cierto, la corteza de lo cierto, la tristeza de lo cierto, la impureza de lo cierto, la naturaleza de lo cierto. El desconcierto de lo cierto que aunque cierto se convierte en punto muerto y en nada remeda el entuerto. ¿No es cierto?

Ah: lo cierto . . . (*El palacio*, p. 217)

What really happened (as it's only fair to admit) is that that was what really happened. Oh, really! *Grrr,* really.

Grapáack!—really.

Ga-ga-*boom—really.*

The unhappiness of what really happened, which did happen like it happened, and so happens to be beyond haphazard telling, has left a telling bruise on all. Is that not true? Oh, the truth . . . (*The Palace,* pp. 264–65)

Otra vez el mar

Perhaps the most striking example of subversive documentation in *Otra vez el mar* is the service control sheet on José Rodríguez Pío, mechanic operator (*Otra vez,* pp. 294–97; *Farewell,* pp. 266–68). This parodic service control sheet ridicules the abundance of bureaucratic documentation so prevalent in revolutionary Cuba. For example:

(1) A long list of exemplary attitudes toward revolutionary state organizations and duties reaches absurd proportions. Mr. Pío's perfect record of service, his attitude, and his commitment to the Revolution is exemplified by his quarterly blood donations, regulation haircuts and dress, "normal" sleeping habits, lack of "special vices," and attendance at "national festivals, funerals, emergency meetings, and sporting events."

(2) The long list of attitudes and general information concerning Mr. Pío is completed by three secret references labeled: FESE, CACZTP, and RRTXZW. The use of the letter *W,* not used in any Spanish word, and *X,* rarely used (not to mention the absurd length of "CACZTP" and "RRTXZW") reveal a parodic discrediting of covert government organizations.

(3) Mr. Pío's mundane job description is derided by the stipulation that in case of "foreseen" death he may suggest who, in his judgment, would best replace him.

(4) The final "Causas del suicidio: Desconocidas" (Reasons for Suicide— Unknown) ridicules the state's inability to see beyond correct social and political attitudes to how individuals should conduct themselves. The strong tongue-and-cheek sarcasm evident in Mr. Pío's service control sheet undermines so-called official records that appear to be so important to the revolutionary bureaucracy.

El color del verano

Although the story of *El color del verano* takes place in the summer of 1999, the entire novel is but a carnivalesque document of what it was like to be young and homosexual in Cuba during the 1960s and 1970s. This is made evident in the prologue (pp. 246–50), which I have already studied in chapter 2. When Arenas (Gabriel/Reinaldo/the Tétrica Mofeta) writes: "*El color del verano* es un mundo que si no lo escribo se perderá fragmentado en la memoria de los que lo conocieron" (p. 249) (If I don't write about it, *El color del verano* is a world that will be lost and fragmented in the memory of those who knew and lived it), the concern for preserving in fiction this particular era in Cuban history is underscored.

In his autobiography, *Antes que anochezca,* Arenas informs the reader how he invented tongue twisters while living in Cuba as literary weapons against those individuals who betrayed him in one way or another (*Antes que anochezca,* p. 261). (Among others, Arenas mentions Miguel Barnet, Nicolás Guillén, and Roberto Fernández Retamar.) Taken as a whole, the tongue twisters lampoon the diabolical and back-stabbing literary scene in revolutionary Havana as well as that of the international literary establishment. According to Arenas the tongue twisters became quite famous in Havana in 1977. Roberto Valero confirms this in *El desamparado humor de Reinaldo Arenas* when he writes (p. 327), "La mayoría de los trabalenguas circularon ampliamente en La Habana. Los escritores los conocían de memoria. Se logró una especie de samizdat oral y satírico" (The majority of the tongue twisters circulated extensively throughout Havana. Writers knew them by heart, and a kind of oral and satirical samizdat was achieved). Valero's description of the tongue twisters as oral and satirical samizdats (from the Russian *samo* or self + *izdat* (*elstvo*) or publishing house)4 underscores their nature as subversive countertexts to the publications of the revolutionary regime that were officially sanctioned and freely distributed on the island. In *El color del verano* thirty of these tongue twisters are interspersed throughout the pages of the text. Printed for the first time in this novel, these "oral" documents are finally free to express what was once prohibited and censored in Cuba. Through their publication the tongue twisters become powerful literary "documents" of Arenas's turbulent years in Havana after falling into disfavor with the Castro regime. For the most part, each tongue twister is a scathing attack directed at a given writer for his or her literary ego, sexual inclinations, or hypocrisy in supporting the Castro regime.[5] In typical fashion, Arenas does not spare himself in these attacks; in one of the tongue twisters, he deprecates himself for his own conceit and sexual exploits:

> Ara, are, IRA, oro, uri . . .
> Con un aro y dos cadenas ara Arenas entre las hienas, horadando los eriales en aras de más aromas y orando a Ares por más oro porque todo su tesoro (incluyendo los aretes que usaba en sus areítos) los heredó un buga moro luego de hacerle maromas en el área de un urinario de Roma. Más no es Ares sino Hera quien con ira oye sus lloros. Y Arenas, arañando lomas, con su aro y sus cadenas, en el infierno carena teniendo por toda era (¡ella que era la que era!) un gran orinal de harina oriado con sus orinas.
>
> (*El color del verano,* p. 107)

> Ara, are, IRA, oro, uri . . .
> With a hoop and two chains Arenas ploughs among the hyenas, tunneling into uncultivated lands for the sake of more aromas and praying to Ares for more gold, because he lost all his treasures (including the earrings that he used for his dances) to a Moorish bugger after fooling around with him in a urinal in Rome. It isn't Ares but rather Hera who with ire hears his sobs. And Arenas, scraping hills, with his hoop and chains, careens into hell, having for all time (she who was who she was!) a great chamberpot of flour laced with his urine.

In *El color del verano* the inclusion of four letters written to and from the alter-egos (Reinaldo/Gabriel/the Tétrica Mofeta) is another example of subversive literary documentation that, while it ignores any pretense to the reproduction of precise facts and figures, poignantly captures through its poetic liberties the emotional weight, the trials and tribulations of living first under a revolution and then in exile. The first three letters (*El color*, pp. 84, 166, 288) are marked by a tone of despair, sadness, and disillusionment in having to live in exile (Paris, New York, and Miami). Although the individual enjoys free expression in these cities, Reinaldo/ Gabriel/the Tétrica Mofeta feels alienated and out of place. For example, the gray coldness of Paris is contrasted to the tropical climate of Cuba; the dirty beaches of Long Island, New York, are quite different from the warm and blue waters of the Caribbean; and despite its tropical climate Miami is presented as a plastic imitation, a mere shadow of Cuba. The three letters written from exile also document the horrors of AIDS. In the fourth letter (p. 344) the Tétrica Mofeta, who finds himself in Cuba, writes to Reinaldo, Gabriel, and to the Tétrica Mofeta, who are living in exile. In this final letter the Tétrica Mofeta sympathizes with the sorrows and afflictions of his alter-egos, but feels that their pain cannot compare to the horrors of living under a tyrannical system in which citizens must cooperate with the laws and whims of a dictator. In addition, living with AIDS under a system that persecutes homosexuals, and that furthermore cannot provide needed medical attention, is far more horrifying. But instead of concentrating on the negative, the Tétrica Mofeta goes on to talk about his (their) writings, all of which make up "una sola obra totali-zadora [cuyo] espíritu burlón y desesperado [sea tal vez] el de nuestro país" (*El color*, pp. 344–45) (a single complete work [whose] mocking and desperate spirit [is perhaps] that of our own country). In *El color del verano*, just as in all of the novels of the *pentagonía*, the precision of historical facts and figures is sacrificed for the vital and dynamic "docu-mentation" that only fiction can provide. The four letters of *El color del verano* poetically and intuitively capture the complex feelings of fragmen-tation, dissatisfaction, and confusion which the protagonist (Reinaldo/ Gabriel/the Tétrica Mofeta) experiences living both in and outside Cuba.

El asalto

In the futuristic world of *El asalto*, conventional language has been abolished and replaced by the party's official dialogues. "El Primer Diálogo Universal Autorizado a ser sostenido (en los momentos regla-mentarios) entre un hombre y mujer" (pp. 102–4) ("FIRST UNIVERSAL AUTHORIZED DIALOGUE to be spoken [at the appropriate time, place, and date] by a man and a woman"; Hurley trans.) is an example of the state's incessant repression of and control over its citizens. This dialogue, essen-tially a document of an Orwellian society that watchfully plans out, revises, and adjusts every intimate moment of a person's life, is reproduced in the text and commences in the following way:

HOMBRE: Viva el Reprimerísimo.
MUJER: Viva, viva, viva, viva.
HOMBRE: Con nuestro tesón más producción.
MUJER: Producción, producción, producción.
HOMBRE: Más conciencia y decencia.
MUJER: Decencia, decencia. (pp. 102–3)

MAN: Long live our glorious Represident!
WOMAN: Hurray, hurray, hurray, hurray.
MAN: With dedication, more production.
WOMAN: Production, production, production.
MAN: More efficiency, increased decency.
WOMAN: Decency, decency. (Hurley trans.)

This scripted dialogue, and the other one that appears in the text, "Diálogo Autorizado entre un niño y otro niño" (pp. 96–97) ("Authorized Dialogue between one child and another"), prohibits the expression of individual desire or need. In the world of *El asalto* the use of the first-person pronoun, fundamental to the documentary novel for being the voice of the witness who demands to be recognized, has been eliminated, censored from all discourse. Anyone heard using it is immediately identified as "un agente del enemigo, . . . individualista con ideas propias sobre la temperatura y sobre su persona, que comete además la arrogancia bárbara de confesarlo públicamente" (p. 62) ("an agent of the enemy, . . . an individualist with ideas regarding temperature and his own egoistic personhood, and who furthermore commits the barbarous and arrogant error of confessing that fact publicly"; Hurley trans.). These scripted dialogues ironically serve as (fictitious) "documents" that warn of how far, if allowed, totalitarian governments would go in controlling its citizens.

Contradictory Statements and Passages in the Pentagonía

In the documentary novel, to document implies that one is stating "facts," asserting unequivocal truths. The novels of the *pentagonía* reveal the relativity of documentation, that so-called facts are assembled, made up, fabricated by whoever wishes to use them to argue for or against any given idea. The pervasive use of flagrantly contradictory utterances and passages in the novels of the pentalogy is a narrative strategy that challenges the documentary novel's assertion that it can indeed record historical "truths" and "facts" through language. The contradictory utterances found in the pentalogy are utterances and phrases that purposely provoke ambiguity, thus undermining the deployment of any privileged discourse. What Sylvia Molloy states in her study *Las letras de Borges* concerning Borges's texts can equally apply to Arenas's writing. (Molloy's study is not a catalogue of themes, but rather an attempt to better understand what we might call the stylistic tics present in Borges's work.) It is Molloy's contention that the Borgesian text "inquieta al lector" (p. 10) (unsettles the reader) for it is not fixed or stable, but rather perpetuates an endless "vaivén" (coming and going), "un no fijar" (p. 11) (a lack of determinability). Arenas, like Borges, denies all that is stable and fixed through a derisive attitude that blurs genres, constantly fragments meaning, welcomes contradictions, and delights in the use of oxymoronic combinations, all with the end of critically questioning the validity of final interpretations. Below I have cited a few of the many examples of contradictory statements and passages that can be found in the five works of the *pentagonía*:

—¡Qué frío tan grande!
—¡Me aso de calor! (*Celestino*, p. 50)

"So cold!"
"I'm roasting." (*Singing*, p. 40)

▪ ▪ ▪ ▪

¿Apago la luz?
—Sí, pero enciéndela primero. (*Celestino*, pp. 87–88)

"Should I turn out the light?"
"Uh-huh, but turn it on first" (*Singing*, p. 74)

▪ ▪ ▪ ▪

Nada, nada se puede esperar. Todo, todo se puede esperar. (*El palacio*, p. 13)

Nothing. You can't expect a thing. Everything. You can expect just about everything. (*The Palace*, p. 6)

▪ ▪ ▪ ▪

Es un comemierda, es un buen muchacho, es una basura, es una gran persona, es un inútil, es un genio, no sirve. Ah, es de los buenos. (*El palacio*, p. 268)

He's a halfwit, he's a good boy, he's a worthless no-good, he's a wonderful person, he's hopeless, he's a genius, he's not worth five centavos. Ay, he's such a nice boy. (*The Palace*, p. 326)

In *Otra vez el mar* a lengthy introductory passage presents a seesawing of affirmations and contradictions around the image of the sea:

El mar. Azul. Al principio no. Al principio es más bien amarillo. Cenizo, diría . . . . Aunque tampoco es cenizo. Blanco, quizás. Blanco no quiere decir transparente. Blanco. Pero luego, casi también al principio, se vuelve gris. Gris, por un rato. Y después, oscuro. . . . Pero no hay olas. . . . Solamente el agua, tocando la tierra. Sin golpearla. Llega, blanca, no transparente, la toca, torpemente, y se aleja. No es la tierra: es la arena. . . . El agua sube, pero no se ve bajar. La arena la absorbe. Por debajo vuelve al mar. . . . Y, más allá, ya no es gris, sino pardusco. Muy oscuro. Casi negro. Hasta que al fin, efectivamente, es negro. Pero ya es muy alto. Se une con el cielo. Los dos, por separados, no se pueden distinguir. Así que entonces, mirando fijamente, nunca es azul . . . . (*Otra vez*, p. 9)

The ocean . . . . Blue . . . . Not at first. At first it's sort of sallow. Ashen, you might say . . . . Although it's not ashen either. White, perhaps. But not white meaning transparent. White. And then— though, still, almost at first—it turns gray. Gray for a while. And then dark. . . . Perhaps they're waves. No—just mirages of water, and sun. If they were waves they would reach the shore. That is, the *sand*. . . . The water rises, but you can't see it go down. The sand absorbs it. Underneath it goes back to the ocean. . . . And farther out, it's no longer gray, but dun-colored. Very dark. Almost black. Until finally, it really is black. But by then it's very high. It joins the sky. You can't make out where the two, as separate things, begin or end. So really, to be precise, it's never blue . . . . (*Farewell*, p. 3)

The above passage begins by stating that the sea *is* blue, then proceeds to describe the sea using various other colors (some diametrically opposed, such as black and white), only to reach the conclusion that the sea is *not* blue. These contradictions demonstrate a refusal to establish a stable and finalized meaning. Moreover, the statement "Los dos, por separados, no se pueden distinguir" ("You can't make out where the two, as separate things, begin or end") foreshadows the discovery at the end of the novel that Héctor and his wife are one and the same person.

In *El color del verano* the character Tedevoro, who first appeared in canto 6 of *Otra vez el mar*, carries around Havana a volume of Lenin's complete works. He tries to protect himself by drawing attention to his political correctness and deflecting attention from his identity as a homosexual. Throughout the novel the book's volume number constantly changes, a comic ruse that calls attention to the flighty nature of Tedevoro's political commitment. At one point the narrator's voice is challenged by another unidentified voice that breaks in saying: "¡Bueno! ¡Pero en qué quedamos! ¿Es el tomo 25, 26, 27, o 29? Decídete, querida, pues no haces más que saltar de tomo en tomo!" (p. 307) (Well! What is it finally? Is it volume 25, 26, 27 or 29? Make up your mind, sweetheart! All you do is jump from one volume to another).

The idea that dictatorships exploit their workers by only seeing them in terms of their service and productivity to the state is evident in the ironic, contradictory neologisms found throughout *El asalto*. If citation indeed confers authority, irony—a rhetorical technique often utilized by Arenas— destroys it. In the novel, "el Reprimerísimo Reprimero" (the President), who prohibits the expression of negativity in his society as an impediment to productivity, proclaims as law that only positive and encouraging language can be used by the people. Hence, all negative terms and ideas, all decadent and counterproductive language, all words that suggest weakness or noncompliance, are abolished. Thus, for example, citizens continue to work during "la nonoche" or "the not-night" (*El asalto,* p. 9) and spend less time resting as a result of the "noreposo" or "not-rest" (p. 24) and the "nodescanso" or "not-sleep" (p. 29).

A final narrative strategy used in *El asalto* to decenter meaning is the use of polysyndeton, as in the following example in which the repetition of the conjunction *o* (or) does not allow meaning to be anchored in the text: "La corneta, la lata *o* cuero *o* silbato *o* pito, *o* váyase usted a la porra retumba, *o* suena, *o* clama *o* llama, *o* váyase usted a la mierda" (emphasis added, *El asalto,* p. 45) ("the cornet, *or* tin can, *or* horn, *or* whistle, *or* conch shell, *or* whatever the hell it is—what do I care, anyway—echoes, *or* sounds, *or* cries out, *or* calls, *or* shit, you get the picture"; Hurley trans.).

SEVEN

Mistrust of Literary Forms

In the documentary novel the witness, anxious to give testimony, is forced to compromise the intimacy of his or her oral discourse as a result of the realization that a written text can reach a far larger audience. According to Nubya Casas:

> Prevalece en [la novela-testimonio] el conflicto que sufre el informante al tener que usar la forma escrita, que estima extemporánea, para poder alcanzar la difusión más amplia que pretende para su testimonio. Por lo tanto, se verá precisado a escoger entre una divulgación más inmediata: la voz—que tocará sólo a unos cuantos oyentes—, o una difusión más distante: la escrita—que llegue a un mayor número de lectores—pero siempre teniendo que hacer lo que considera como una concesión. Opta por lo segundo, aunque dejando en claro la aprensión anti-literaria que experimenta. Por eso, además, requerirá que se le juzgue como *testimonialista*, y no como literato, declarándolo explícitamente en la introducción, o dentro del propio testimonio. ("Novela-testimonio: historia y literatura," pp. 40–41)

Prevalent in the documentary novel is the conflict the witness suffers from having to use the written form, which he or she deems expedient, in order for the testimony to reach the largest possible audience. Hence, the witness will have to choose between a more immediate form of communication: the spoken form—which will only reach a few listeners—, and a far wider diffusion through the written form—that will reach a greater number of readers. Having always to make a concession, the witness will opt for the second choice, although making his or her apprehension clear for having to use a literary form. For this reason, the witness will ask to be judged as a *documentary witness* and not as a writer, a declaration he or she will explicitly make in the introduction, or within the actual testimony.

The creators—that is, the witness(es) and the compiler—of the documentary novel, having chosen a written discourse, fear that the literary form will adulterate, perhaps even falsify, the authenticity of the testimony. Hence, the importance of utility over aesthetics is underscored; the aesthetic use of narrative techniques—although not rejected—must in no way jeopardize the testimony. So it is that in the introduction to *Biografía de un cimarrón*, for example (p. 18), Barnet clearly highlights the documentary objective of his book over any literary intentions: "Sabemos que poner a hablar a un informante es, en cierta medida, hacer literatura. Pero no intentamos nosotros crear un documento literario, una novela"[1] (We know that to allow an informer to speak is, in a certain way, to create literature. However, we are not trying to create a literary document, a novel).

Celestino antes del alba (Cantando en el pozo), El palacio de las blanquísimas mofetas, El color del verano, and El asalto

Unlike the witness of the documentary novel, the child-narrator/Celestino, Fortunato, and Gabriel/Reinaldo/the Tétrica Mofeta find writing to be a refuge from the hate that surrounds them. For them, the written form is not rejected as a corruption of oral speech but rather embraced as a source of vitality and freedom. These characters are identified by their search for self-expression through the written form.

Through his incessant writing on tree trunks and branches in the countryside, the child-narrator/Celestino of *Celestino antes del alba* attempts to express his desires. This rebellious act, although the writing is still unintelligible, underscores an insatiable need to articulate intimate feelings and emotions through the written form, despite obstacles and intimidation.

Fortunato experiences the same urgency for expression as a means to survive the continual state of oppression he faces from his family as well as from the conservatism of his hometown. Like the child-narrator/Celestino, Fortunato starts to invent imaginary refuges that take him away from his asphyxiating situation. The young man steals paper from his grandfather's small vegetable and fruit shop and begins secretly to write, a labor of passion that he faithfully carries out under the most oppressive conditions:

> Mientras sudo, toso y espanto a los mosquitos, escribo. Mientras toso y toso, mientras sudo y sudo y palmeteo en el aire, escribo. No sé cómo me he hecho de una máquina de escribir y ya le he acabado al viejo todas las resmas de papel de la venduta. El viejo no dice nada porque no habla. Pero está que trina. Y abuela me quiere matar de la rabia que le da ver que el viejo tenga que despacharle la mercancía en la mano a la gente. Mientras la vieja me pelea yo escribo y escribo. Y no duermo. Y no como. Hasta que al fin se me quitan los deseos de escribir y tiro todas las resmas de papel en la fosa del baño. (*El palacio*, p. 16)

> While I sweat, cough, and shoo away the mosquitoes, I write. While I cough and cough and cough, while I sweat and sweat and fan the air, I write. I don't know how I managed to get my hands on a type-writing machine, but I've run the old man out of all the paper he had in the shop. The old man doesn't say anything, because he won't talk, but he's about to pop. And Grandma wants to kill me, she's so furious when she sees that the old man has to send goods home with the people carrying them in their bare hands. While the old woman scolds and fights with me, I write and write and write. And I don't sleep. Or eat. Until finally I get over the urge and I throw all the paper down the hole in the outhouse. (*The Palace*, p. 10)

Both the child-narrator/Celestino and Fortunato dream and idealize imaginative worlds and engage at the same time in the writing process. However, this writing is still of presignification, that is, what is written is a form of pre-writing, unintelligible and hidden from the other subjects in the novels as well as from the reader. The child-narrator/Celestino's literary efforts, as well as Fortunato's, are constantly criticized and re-ferred to as futile by the other characters. Yet the reader, even though he or she also is not given a key to decipher these writings, does perceive and recognize the writer's need, obsessive at times, for expression. This need, whose first and foremost purpose is but a pure expression of freedom through the word, appears in both novels as an aesthetic search for beauty. The following quotes illustrate how both the child-narrator/Celestino and Fortunato temporarily escape their respective repressive and hostile environments by projecting themselves into their imaginative worlds:

Si tú no existieras yo tendría que inventarte. Y te invento. Y dejo ya de sentirme solo. (*Celestino*, p. 210)

If you didn't exist, I'd have to invent you. So I invent you. And instantly that makes me not feel so lonesome. (*Singing*, p. 201)

▮▮▮▮▮

Y para sobrevivir tuvo que irse construyendo otros refugios, tuvo que darse a la tarea de reinventar, de cubrir de prestigios, de mistificar algún hueco, algún sitio predilecto por la frescura, por la sombra, tuvo que inventarse un amigo, nuevos territorios. (*El palacio*, p. 40)

And in order to survive he had to construct other refuges, he had to set himself and then meet the challenge of reinventing, of touching with mystery, of setting the halo of enchantment upon some hole, some place made dear to him by its coolness, by its shade, [he had to invent himself a friend, new territories]. (*The Palace*, p. 39)²

It is this creative process, the search in itself, that both novels underscore, for it is during these moments of writing that both the child-narrator/ Celestino and Fortunato are actualized. As Maurice Blanchot states in his essay "Literature and the Right to Death": "The writer only finds himself, only realizes himself through his work; before his work exists, not only does he not know who he is, but he is nothing. He only exists as a function of the work" (*The Gaze of Orpheus*, p. 24).

Blanchot's observation of how the writer achieves meaning and authenticity through the written form is apparent as Gabriel/Reinaldo/the Tétrica Mofeta struggles to write and rewrite his novel, *El color del verano*. At one point we read:

[Gabriel padecía] una vida doble, o triple, y [trabajaba] sin cesar en la sexta versión de su novela que ahora, mientras esperaba el tren, releía y aumentaba con goce furtivo. Tocar aquellas páginas era tocar una autenticidad que el mundo le negaba. (p. 118)

[Gabriel suffered from] a double or triple life, and he [worked] incessantly on the sixth version of his novel that now, while he waited for the train, he reread and modified with furtive pleasure. To touch those pages was to touch an authenticity that the world denied him.

In a beautiful passage entitled "En la biblioteca" (In the Library) (*El color*, p. 234), we see the excitement and bliss that the protagonist feels in the library when he is free to be transformed through the written word: ". . . una sensación de plenitud envolvía a la Tétrica Mofeta, a Gabriel y a Reinaldo fundiéndolos en un solo ser. Así, radiante, aquel ser tomaba el libro y volviendo a la mesa comenzaba la lectura" (. . . a sensation of plenitude would come over the Tétrica Mofeta, over Gabriel, and over Reinaldo fusing them into one single being. In this manner that radiant being would take the book, return to the table, and would begin reading). Through the written word (written or read, for writing and reading are reciprocal acts), Gabriel, Reinaldo, and the Tétrica Mofeta are harmoniously fused, shining radiantly as if spiritually transfixed.

The nameless narrator of *El asalto* is the only protagonist in the quintet that does not write, for in this futuristic world the individual, perceived only as a work dog that fuels the materialistic production of the state, has forgotten how to communicate, how to use language critically: "Sabes que muchos ya han olvidado el lenguaje hablado. En el último escrutinio de la lengua, se descubrió que la mayoría no maneja más que treinta o veinte palabras durante toda su vida. Los diálogos oficiales resolverán el problema" (p. 118) ("You know that many people have already forgotten the spoken language. In the last census, it was discovered that most people use no more than thirty or twenty words their whole life long. The official dialogues solve that problem"; Hurley trans.).

The world of *El asalto* represents a warning of how the individual, subordinated to the incessant demands, orders, utilitarian seriousness, and uncontested value system of a totalitarian regime, loses the ability to use language as an instrument for the articulation of his or her own profound disquietude. While all language is indeed ideologically motivated, the language of political propaganda, whether spoken or written, is perhaps the most sinister, for it intentionally hides behind the mask of legitimacy and finality.

Otra vez el mar

The adult Héctor of *Otra vez el mar* confronts the world with the same need for expression as the child-narrator/Celestino, Fortunato, and Gabriel/Reinaldo/the Tétrica Mofeta. However, Héctor's cantos are no longer scribbled on the leaves and trunks of trees like Celestino's, nor are they secretly written on stolen reams of paper like Fortunato's, nor do they fall victim to endless rewritings like those of Gabriel/Reinaldo/the Tétrica Mofeta. Héctor's cantos are simply invented, thought out, sung to himself while the reader is finally given the opportunity to hear—or rather, overhear—the poet's words. Héctor is a frustrated writer who has never published because of political censorship in Cuba. Consequently, his cantos are those impressions and ideas that he has thought of writing, that he wishes and intends to express.

Héctor is the poet-creator, the searcher for beauty, who, like the child-narrator/Celestino, Fortunato, and Gabriel/Reinaldo/the Tétrica Mofeta finds himself persecuted as a result of the conventions of a system unable to accept any expression of difference. His personal moments of inquietude and unhappiness are the consequence of living under a regime unwilling to accept any textual or sexual expressions not contributing to the established order of the revolutionary hegemony. Yet Héctor's frustrations run even deeper. Although *Otra vez el mar* is Arenas's most political novel, the text does not utilize politics as the only reason for the subject's estrangement. In *Otra vez el mar* Héctor's personal dilemma goes beyond the political, and even beyond his sexual frustrations. Although these two factors aggravate his abhorrence, they are reduced to a second plane by the recognition of the inherent contradictions of humanity, signs of which Héctor sees all around him. Héctor confronts the human condition, which denies individuals the fulfillment of desires and destroys all possibilities of permanent plenitude and satisfaction, through an urgent need to articulate, to cry out: "escucha ahora mi grito de hijo desesperado" (*Otra vez,* p. 199) ("hear now the cry of this desperate son," *Farewell,* p. 173).

In his cantos, Héctor struggles against the paltriness of human existence. Like the child-narrator/Celestino, Fortunato, and Gabriel/Reinaldo/the Tétrica Mofeta, his triumph, his redemption, is not so much in what he says but rather in his demanding need to *want to say*. Still, Héctor is quite conscious of the fragility of this endeavor. The writer in the face of his writings constantly questions their usefulness, their purpose. Thus, for example, in the second canto we hear:

La

litera

tura

es la consecuencia de una hipocresía legendaria. Si el hombre tuviese el coraje de decir la verdad en el instante en que la siente y frente al que se la inspira o provoca (al hablar, por ejemplo; al mirar, por ejemplo; al humillarse, por ejemplo) pues es en ese preciso instante que siente cuando padece o se inspira; si tuviese el coraje de expresar

la belleza o el terror cotidiano en una conversación; si tuviese el coraje de decir lo que es, lo que siente, lo que odia, lo que desea, sin
tener que escudarse en un acertijo de palabras guardadas para más
tarde; si tuviese la valentía de expresar sus desgracias como expresa
la necesidad de tomarse un refresco, no hubiese tenido que refu-
giarse, ampararse, justificarse, tras la confesión secreta, desgarradora
y falsa que es siempre un libro. (*Otra vez,* pp. 230–31)

Liter

ature

is the consequence of a traditional and well-established hypocrisy. If
man had the courage to speak the truth at the moment he feels it,
face to face with that person who inspires or provokes it—when he
talks, for example; when he looks at you, for example; when he hu-
miliates himself, for example (for it is then, at that very moment,
that one feels how much one suffers or is inspired); if man had the
courage to express day-to-day beauty or terror in his conversation;
if man had the courage to say what is, what he feels, what he hates,
what he desires, without having to shield himself with a riddle of
words saved for later; if he had the bravery to express his unhappiness in the same way he expresses the desire for a soft drink, he
wouldn't have to take refuge, seek shelter, justify himself, behind
the secret, heart-breaking, and false confession which a book always is. (*Farewell,* pp. 203–4)

This anxiety, however, is not limited exclusively to the written word, but
to all discourse (both oral and written) as can be seen when Héctor
immediately adds: "Se ha perdido—¿Existió alguna vez?—la sinceridad de
decir de voz a voz" (*Otra vez,* p. 231) ("The sincerity of one voice speaking
to another has been lost. Did it once exist?" *Farewell,* p. 204). This
interrogative insertion—"Did it once exist?"—reveals the writer's doubts
and ambiguity.[3] Therefore, this is not a deconstructive battle in which the
supremacy of the oral or written word is debated. What is underscored is
that language cannot be dominated as a transparent medium. Words, both
spoken and written, upon naming are merely echoes, not rigid object-
imitations of reality. Hence, since reality is inapprehensible, the illusion of
art as an accurate representation of the world is destroyed. *Otra vez el
mar,* like all of Arenas's texts, dismantles the traditional concept of the
literary work as a logocentric denotative agent of a singular exterior truth.
Instead, Arenas's texts rebelliously ramble and open themselves to contra-

dictory and ambiguous digressions that unfold an infinite number of possible "truths."

Héctor's skepticism of language as an effective instrument of expression—his obsession with the emptiness of speech—constantly resurfaces throughout the second part of *Otra vez el mar*. We read for example:

> Jamás podré relatar esos estados de quietud. Jamás podría relacionar pacíficamente esa belleza sin traicionarme. Jamás podré enumerar los diferentes colores del crepúsculo sin que en mis palabras no encuentre latiendo el desequilibrio de una angustia que llega quién sabe de dónde . . . (*Otra vez*, p. 235)[4]

> I will never be able to communicate those states of quietness. I will never be able to put down that beauty, peacefully, without betraying myself. I will never be able to list the colors of the sunset without my words having throbbing in them the imbalance of an anguish that comes, well, from who knows where? (*Farewell*, p. 208)

Still, as much as Héctor recognizes that his search for an adequate expression is illusory, he is forever forced back into language, for it provides his only solace. Héctor is ready to struggle with the word, to acknowledge its artifice, to enter language's unsettling game of seduction. In a moment of doubt he questions himself: "¿Es que no puedes vivir sin la palabra?" (*Otra vez*, p. 224) ("Can you not live without the word?" *Farewell*, p. 197). The answer is no, he cannot. As much as it divides and misrepresents him, the word is his vehicle of expression. And thus, he demands of himself, "Compone tu dolor antes de que sea aún más tarde. Di, señala, grita, canta tu padecer" (*Otra vez*, p. 387) ("Compose your pain before it gets any later. Say, point, cry, sing your suffering," *Farewell*, p. 377). Héctor must articulate, sing, cry out, call attention to his suffering; he must express himself. In the tones of Héctor's anguished cantos—whispered or imagined—he triumphs over his destiny. In the end, what lies at the center of *Otra vez el mar* is more than a denunciation of an authoritarian system. Far more urgent is an aesthetic search for an adequate expression, for an infuriating salvation, for a simple rhyme or reason.

In part 2 of *Otra vez el mar*, the poet-Héctor's literary activities are incorporated into the cantos. These compositions include tales, poems, anecdotes, political testimonies, allegories, and other fragments that the poet-Héctor privately composes for himself and to which the reader—unlike in *Celestino antes del alba* and *El palacio de las blanquísimas mofetas*—

is finally given access. One of these compositions, entitled "Monstruo" (Monster), and placed at the end of the fourth canto, articulates the poet-Héctor's, and the writer Reinaldo Arenas's, recognition of the writer's precarious relationship with language. Before its appearance in the text, Héctor splits himself in order to question the possibility of composing a clear and truthful expression, an immutable composition. The writer initiates a process of fictionalization, recounted by a heterodiegetic narrator, that will be allegorized in the subsequent tale:

> Supone él que aún puede expresar lo que se le antoja o pugna, que aún puede transmitir su venganza, su desesperación, su verdad, que alguien recogerá sus palabras, . . . que a pesar de todo (o por lo mismo) aún es. Y compone. (*Otra vez*, pp. 322–23)

> He imagines that he can still express what he yearns for or struggles against, that he can still convey his vengefulness, his desperation, his truth, that someone will pick up his words, . . . that in spite of everything (or because of it), he still is. And he composes. (*Farewell*, p. 294)

The possibility of composition—that is, of faithfully reproducing or transmitting Héctor's personal truth through words—is proposed. However, a close examination of the above passage reveals that at the same time that this proposition is being made, ambiguity, self-doubt, and controversy threaten to obscure the clarity of expression that Héctor hopes he will achieve. The heterodiegetic narrator first maintains that Héctor "imagines" that he "can" express what he capriciously desires to express ("what he yearns for") or "struggles against." The suggestion is made that the creative process is not a straightforward enterprise, but rather the result of an incessant tension between what the writer wants to say and what he must struggle to say. In addition, the verb *transmitir* (to convey) supposes the existence of an enunciator (writer) and an "enunciatee" (the reader) in a dynamic relationship that does not place the responsibility solely on the writer's desire for expression, but instead on both the writer and the reader in their actualization of the text. Further, this passage proposes that Héctor wishes to express "his" truth, not "a" truth or "the" truth, and that someone (an enunciatee, a reader) will receive it. This means that the work only comes into existence when it becomes the intimacy shared by the person who writes it and the person who reads it. Moreover, the heterodiegetic narrator informs us that Héctor "imagines" that in spite of everything ("or because of it") he still "is." The statement in parenthesis contradicts the writer's presumption that he exists, controlling the work, conveying precisely what he wishes, regardless of everything. The awareness that the writer, as Blanchot has stated, only exists as a result of the work, that he or she has no identity apart from the work, undermines the authority of traditional authorship. Finally, the use of the verb *componer* (to compose)—that is, to form, to construct, to connect from various sources a new order—presents writing as a composition of torn unity, always in struggle, never reconciled, an object constructed from conflicting discourses.

Regardless of the challenges that stand in the way of his desire for a clear and truthful expression, Héctor pushes forward in his attempt to articulate, to give presence to his ideas. The tale of "Monstruo" thus begins in the following way:

> En aquella ciudad también había un monstruo.
>
> Era una combinación de arterias que supuraban, de tráqueas que oscilaban como émbolos furiosos, de pelos encabritados y bastos, de cavernas ululantes y de inmensas garfas que comunicaban directamente con las orejas siniestras—De manera que todo el mundo elogiaba en voz alta la belleza del monstruo. (*Otra vez*, p. 323)

> In that city there was a monster, too.
>
> It was a complex of suppurating arteries, tracheas pumping like furious pistons, coarse hair streaming over its head, warbling caverns, and huge claws communicating directly with its sinister ears. All the world raised its voice in praise of the monster's beauty. (*Farewell*, p. 294)

The beauty of the monster so impressed the inhabitants of the city that it inspired innumerable odes; for example, one was dedicated to the delicate perfume the monster's anus exhaled. Sonnets were also written, inspired by the beauty of its mouth, a mouth divided into several compartments that saved the vomit the monster disgorged in its moments of greatest orgy. The city was so in love with the monster that when he shat, a line formed to inhale ("from afar") the great monstrous reek. Without a doubt everyone in the city loved the monster:

> Pero un día ocurrió algo extraño.
>
> Alguien comenzó a hablar contra el monstruo. Todos naturalmente, pensaron que se trataba de un loco, y esperaban (pedían) de

un momento a otro su exterminio. El que hablaba pronunciaba un discurso ofensivo que comenzaba más o menos de esta forma: "En aquella ciudad también había un monstruo. Era una combinación de arterias que supuraban, de tráqueas que oscilaban como émbolos furiosos . . ." Y seguía arremetiendo, solitario y violento heroico . . . Algunas mujeres, desde lejos, se detuvieron a escuchar. Los hombres, siempre más civilizados, se refugiaron tras las puertas. Pero él seguía vociferando contra el monstruo: "sus ojos siempre rojizos y repletos de legañas" . . . En fin como nadie lo asesinaba todos comenzaron a escucharlo; luego, a respetarlo. Por último, lo admiraban y parafraseaban sus discursos contra el monstruo.

Ya cuando su poder era tal que había logrado abolir al monstruo y ocupar su lugar, todos pudimos comprobar—y no cesaba de hablar contra el monstruo—que se trataba del monstruo. (*Otra vez*, pp. 323–24)

But one day a strange thing occurred.

Someone began to speak out against the monster. Everyone, of course, thought this was a question of a madman declaiming, and they expected (prayed) that he would quickly be exterminated. The man who was speaking delivered an insulting speech that began more or less like this: "In that city there was a monster, too. It was a complex of suppurating arteries, tracheas pumping like furious pistons. . . ." And he went on, attacking—solitary, violent, and heroic. A few women, keeping their distance, stopped to listen. Men, always more civilized, peeked out from behind doors. But he went on shouting horrible things about the monster: "Its eyes, always bloodshot and rheumy . . ." Finally, since no one murdered him, everyone began listening to him; then, respecting him. Then they even came to admire him, and they paraphrased his tirades against the monster.

At last when his power was such that he had managed to abolish the monster and take his place, we could all see for ourselves—and he never stopped speaking against the monster—that it was all a question of a monster. (*Farewell*, pp. 295–96)

Before the composition, Héctor's desire was to express and transmit his personal "truth" through words. This desire, however, is totally undermined by the irony of the very tale that he composes.[5] On the most basic level, "Monstruo" is a criticism of all types of hegemonic discourses and those who blindly follow them. Yet, more importantly, this tale unmasks, in a self-conscious manner, the ideology inherent in all discourse. That is, the ideological power of the word inevitably consumes whoever consents to be blinded by the illusion of pure objectivity or neutrality.

In "Monstruo" the precise words that start the tale are exactly those that the heroic man within the story uses to dethrone the monster, revealing his "true ugliness." At the same time, it is this very man—who has dared attack the monster from a position of so-called truth—who in the end is also revealed as the monster. The suggestion that a similar process will endlessly be repeated exposes the monstrosity of the narration itself. Still, let us not forget that it is the poet-Héctor who composes this allegorical tale that attacks all who place themselves in a discourse of power. Yet, Héctor himself is not above falling into the trap of seduction as the man within the story. The writer of "Monstruo" is guilty of the same logocentric desire to present his "truth"—here, the desire to present the "truth" about the arbitrariness of "truth." This vertiginous deconstructive game reveals that despite the writer's attempts to escape from the ideological power of the word, he or she is destined to fail. Héctor, who before the composition had wanted to suppose the possibility of expression free of subjectivity, likewise fails. But in fact, and here the distinction must be carefully made, the writer Héctor recognizes and anticipates this inherent failure and actually inscribes it into the anecdotal level of the narration. That is, the awareness that all processes of articulation represent falsehood and betrayal—that words do not evoke, but rather murder the reality they attempt to name—is not ignored but intentionally woven into the very fabric of the text. For this reason, "Monstruo" can be called a self-conscious or metafictional composition about the very process of writing.[6]

Critical studies have made it common knowledge that the literary form is always ideological, even when written by those who claim their writing has no message. The writer of "Monstruo" (or rather the writers, Héctor and Reinaldo Arenas) reveal the fundamental ideological intention of their tale instead of hiding, like the documentary novelist, behind a supposed neutrality of truth. It is precisely here that the very honesty of this writing can be found, in revealing and holding up its condition of artifice for the reader to see. In "Literature and the Right to Death," Maurice Blanchot proposes that the language that most communicates or articulates is that which reveals its condition of artifice:

What is striking is that in literature, deceit and mystification are not only inevitable but constitute the writer's honesty, whatever hope and truth are in him. Nowadays people often talk about the sickness of words, [yet] this sickness is also the words' health. [Words] may be torn apart by equivocation, but this equivocation is a good thing—without it there would be no dialogue. They may be falsified by misunderstanding—but this misunderstanding is the possibility of our understanding. They may be imbued with emptiness—but this emptiness is their very meaning. Naturally, a writer can always make it his ideal to call a cat a cat. But what he cannot manage to do is then believe that he is on the way to health and sincerity. (p. 30)

In Spanish American literature, thanks to Borges's own reflections on these very ideas, Blanchot's words are easy to assimilate. The inevitable failure and futility of any perfervid quest for truth or objectivity through the written form is a constant of the Borgesian text. Yet, despite this failure, the creative impulse, the desire for expression, is always present. Similarly, in Arenas's texts, in spite of the risk and inevitable failure of the word, the need for self-expression asserts itself on the writer. Arenas's texts display no attempt to produce an objective monolithic system of language, but rather to inscribe the writer's own particular social and historical experiences into the text in an aesthetic game of reflections, deformations, and transformations.

EIGHT

Reinterpreting and Rewriting Recorded History

> Nunca me he considerado un ser ni de izquierda ni de derecha,
> ni quiero que se me catalogue bajo ninguna etiqueta oportunista
> y política; yo digo mi verdad, lo mismo que un judío que haya
> sufrido el racismo o un ruso que haya estado en un gulag, o
> cualquier ser humano que haya tenido ojos para ver las cosas
> tal como son; grito, luego existo (I have never considered my-
> self to be from the left or from the right; nor do I want to be
> catalogued under any opportunistic or political label; I tell my
> truth, the same as a Jew who has suffered racism or a Russian
> who has been in a gulag; or any human being who has had eyes
> to see things as they are; I cry out, therefore I exist).
>
> Reinaldo Arenas, *Antes que anochezca*

In "La novela testimonio: socio-literatura," Miguel Barnet
found it necessary to point out that the overriding objective of the writer-
promoter of the documentary novel is not merely aesthetic, but rather more
functional, more practical. The writer-promoter should serve as a link in the
chain of his or her country's traditions by contributing to the articulation
of the collective memory, the *we* and not the *I*: ". . . la historia de las gentes
sin historia . . . ha encontrado sus portavoces en estos excavadores de la conciencia colectiva" ("La novela testimonio: socio-literatura," p. 143) (. . . the
story of people without a history . . . has found its expression in these
excavators of the collective consciousness). According to Barnet, this desire
to reveal, recover, excavate the so-called truth of the past of the collective
consciousness from the distortion of conventional accounts is the documentary novel's most important feature. He is never clear, however, on how *el*

artista gestor (the writer-promoter) should go about revealing, recovering, or excavating the "true" face of lost or distorted historical accounts. One assumes that truth is determined by scrutinizing the past against the framework of the official revolutionary ideology of class struggle and historical materialism. Still, regardless of how the revelation is achieved, it appears that a critical attitude toward any history recorded by a group in power is germane to the documentary novel format.

In the documentary novel the direct voice of the witness, with its claim on referential transparency, attempts to gain the confidence of the reader in the face of so-called objective evidence and facts. In *Biografía de un cimarrón*, for instance, the recurrent use of the archaic predicate statement "yo vide" (*yo vi* 'I saw') demonstrates this desire constantly to verify Esteban Montejo's testimony. *Biografía de un cimarrón*, like Barnet's *Canción de Rachel, Gallego*, and *La vida real*, seeks to refamiliarize the reader with lost or distorted historical events. Esteban Montejo revises (rewrites) what was the accepted history. He elucidates on the scarcely improved conditions after abolition and presents the black man's active participation in the struggle for Cuban independence. Similarly, *Canción de Rachel* reveals the corruption of the Cuban republican era, *Gallego* uncovers the exploitation of the immigrant struggle, and *La vida real* presents the prerevolutionary misery and inequality that forced thousands of Cubans to emigrate to the United States. These novels, like other Cuban documentary novels, revise (rewrite) Cuban history, always from the vantage point of the revolutionary government. These are texts with an ideological function: to reveal the deplorable situations that justified the Cuban Revolution. It is telling that none of Barnet's documentary novels go beyond 1959, the year in which the Cuban Revolution triumphed. To date, Barnet has not written a documentary novel that attempts a critical analysis of the history that has been recorded over the three-plus decades of the Castro regime.

The novels of Reinaldo Arenas's *pentagonía* can be read as texts that call into question the official revolutionary historiography's selection and arrangement of "facts" by revealing the ideological intention behind all narratives, both historical and fictional. These novels, rather than support the concept of an official history of the collective consciousness, prefer to examine the enigma of individual human existence. The novels of the pentalogy explore the individual's spirit of creativity, a spirit that rebels against all hierarchical systems of power that attempt to simplify the human experience or reduce its vitality to historical facts or figures.

El mundo alucinante

Although *El mundo alucinante*, a novel based on the fictionalization of a historical figure, is not one of the novels studied in this book,
its irreverent attitude toward the historian's claim to "facts" provides the
clearest expression of Arenas's attitude toward the incorporation of history into literature. Because of its explicit criticism of the lack of liberty
that often accompanies the institutionalization of a revolution (a criticism
that naturally implicated the Cuban revolutionary experience), this novel
has been read by many as a direct attack against the Castro regime. *El
mundo alucinante* is a creative juxtaposition of historical and literary discourses in which history is twice subordinated to fiction—first through
the memoirs of Fray Servando Teresa de Mier, and again through Arenas's
refabrication of those memoirs. The historical Fray Servando Teresa de
Mier (1763–1827) of the Mexican struggle for independence is recreated by
Arenas's investigations and thorough reading of what was written about
this extraordinary individual's adventurous life: "Comencé a tratar de
localizarte por todos los sitios. Revolví bibliotecas infernales, . . . fui a
embajadas, a casas de cultura, a museos . . ." (*El mundo,* p. 19); "I have
been everywhere trying to find you. I've turned libraries upside down, . . .
I've been to embassies, cultural mission houses, and museums . . ." (*The
Ill-fated Peregrinations,* p. xxi).

In *El mundo alucinante* Friar Servando Teresa de Mier shares the position of being a rebellious writer like the child-narrator/Celestino, Fortunato, Héctor, and Gabriel/Reinaldo/the Tétrica Mofeta. This is evident in his rewriting of what had been the generally accepted account of
the appearance of the Virgin of Guadalupe to the humble peasant Juan
Diego. Indeed, it is the friar's subversive sermon that the Virgin did not
appear to the Indian peasant but to the Apostle Saint Thomas—who in
fact was Quetzalcoatl, the feathered-serpent deity—that sets into motion
his whirlwind of adventures. Like the protagonists of the *pentagonía,* the
friar is an insolent spirit who refuses to adapt to the criteria established by
those in power.

In the introductory essay to the 1982 edition of *El mundo alucinante,*
Arenas stated: "siempre he desconfiado de lo 'histórico', de ese dato
'minucioso y preciso'" (p. 15); "I have always distrusted the 'historical,'
those 'minutiae,' the 'precise date' or 'fact'" (*The Ill-fated Peregrinations,*
p. xvi). This distrust for historical facts and figures is most cleverly shown
in the text by the use of different points of view (first, second, and third)

to narrate the same past episodes. This shifting focalization underscores the relative nature behind any attempt to reconstruct past events as static "facts."

By comparing a portion of the introduction to Miguel Barnet's *Canción de Rachel* to the epigraph Arenas wrote for *El mundo alucinante* we can uncover some telling differences regarding each writer's vision of history. In Barnet we read, "*Canción de Rachel* habla de ella, de su vida, tal y como ella me la contó y tal como yo luego se la conté a ella" (*Canción de Rachel* is about Rachel, her life, just as she told it to me and just as I later told it back to her). In the epigraph to *El mundo alucinante* it is stated: "Esta es la vida de Fray Servando Teresa de Mier, tal como fue, tal como pudo haber sido, tal como a mí me hubiese gustado que hubiera sido. Más que una novela histórica o biográfica pretende ser, simplemente, una novela" ("This is the story of Friar Servando Teresa de Mier y Noriega— just as it was, just as it might have been; just as I wish it had been. Neither a historical nor a biographical novel strictly speaking, but more than those, this tale aspires to be, quite simply, a novel"; Hurley trans., *The Ill-fated Peregrinations of Fray Servando*, p. vii).

First, one cannot help but notice the (accidental?) similarity in vocabulary (*tal [y] como* 'just as') and tone in these two statements. Yet, when examined more closely, each statement reveals a very different and distinct narrative approach. Barnet's words display how the power and authority of the narrator-investigator's voice has evolved since his first novel. The narrative pact initiated by *Biografía de un cimarrón,* which anchored the novel in the original story of the narrator-informant, appears to be devalued in *Canción de Rachel* as it now accommodates and acknowledges the narrator-investigator's participation in the story ("just as I told it back to her"). In *Canción de Rachel* Barnet (the narrator-investigator) finds in fiction a way of allowing the "other" to speak. But as we have seen, this fictionalization in *Canción de Rachel* in no way implies a rejection of the documentary (sociohistorical) foundation of the text. Rather, Barnet commences a process of (re)negotiation between history and fiction, one that acknowledges the existence of fiction but in no way tries to establish it as the stronger discourse of the enunciation. What is permitted in *Canción de Rachel* is a modest fictionalization that will exercise itself over less important segments of the text—for example, the fictionalization of the protagonist's name or the use of other voices marked off in italics that ridicule Rachel's vision of the world. Still, the excavation of the "truth" of the collective past remains the documentary novel's most important feature.

In Arenas's epigraph to *El mundo alucinante* there is no negotiation between history and fiction, since fiction is not set against history ("facts"). The writer's fictional creation ("this tale aspires to be, quite simply, a novel") is clearly more important than any desire for a faithful historical recreation of a collective consciousness. According to P. H. Nowell-Smith, oppositions like fact versus fiction, fact versus opinion, and fact versus interpretation are only necessary for the historian wishing to deploy a discourse of "truth." For Nowell-Smith: "Facts exist nowhere and no-when. And this is not because they are timeless entities not located in space, but because they are not entities at all."[1] Unlike the documentary novelist who must always struggle with the dichotomies of "fact versus fiction," "fact versus opinion," and "fact versus interpretation," Arenas places more trust in the power of pure fiction as a vital (symbolic) expression of the complexities of human existence. While the documentary novel aspires to communicate a truth-value grounded in representation, iconic rather than symbolic, Arenas's novels refuse any such identification with so-called verifiable historical information. In contrast, Arenas's texts defamiliarize and undermine any claim to historic objectivism through various structural and rhetorical techniques (for example, "subversive documentation," irony, parody, discursive contradictions, among others) that impede the reader from ever identifying directly with any single discourse of authority.

The Pentagonía

Arenas's declaration that the *pentagonía* can be read as both a secret history of Cuba and a writer's autobiography underscores the polysemous and intentionally paradoxical nature of these texts that are part history, part autobiography, and part lyrical cry against the malevolent social forces that impede the individual's search for happiness. Despite, or perhaps as a result of, their fictitious, magical, and lyrical qualities, these novels succeed in presenting a vital and critical commentary on twentieth-century Cuban politics, economy, and society, and on a more universal level, on mankind's propensity for discrimination, bigotry, and intolerance. In the end, the novels of the *pentagonía* speak not only to the Cuban community in and outside of Cuba, but to all individuals who cherish and respect the individual's right to free expression.

Celestino antes del alba, El palacio de las blanquísimas mofetas, Otra vez el mar, El color del verano, and *El asalto* never give a simple historical explanation for a character's existential dilemmas, nor do they try to rewrite history from a singular point of view. In the pentalogy, historical circumstances are treated with the greatest economy; when they appear, they reveal the existential situation of a character, not a specific sociopolitical or historical moment. Nonetheless, the historical dimension of existence is not ignored: each novel is embedded in a specific sociohistorical context (the prerevolutionary years, last years of the Batista regime, revolutionary years, an imagined future totalitarian society). There is a fundamental difference between the novels of the pentalogy and documentary novels in regard to the question of historiography in general. While Arenas's pentalogy examines the historical dimensions of individual human existence, documentary novels are novelized historiography that describe, illustrate, and depict a specific historical situation; that is, they write the history of a society, not of human beings.

In the novels of the pentalogy, contrary to the notion that history can be re-interpreted through documentary accuracy, the reader often discovers a magical and poetic time-space where dreams, hallucinations, memory, and imagination crisscross in a nonsequential time. Unlike Esteban Montejos's reliable "yo vide" (I saw), the allegations of Arenas's protean main character, as we have noted, are many times contradictory and doubtful. Yet, despite the unreliability of his voice, the strong and vital testimony that he presents concerning his hopes, dreams, despair, and the destitute conditions of life under a (pre-revolutionary, revolutionary, and future revolutionary) totalitarian regime is not betrayed or any less convincing or authentic for these flights of fantasy. The reader senses the need of the protagonist to redress through his imagination the harshness of his immediate surroundings. Hence, as the protagonist blurs the boundaries and limits of empirical reality, the reader intuits the monstrous and crude conditions of a hostile and impoverished life in which fantasy and imagination provide the only escape. In the pentalogy the aesthetic discourse is never sacrificed for the accuracy of a historical discourse that hopes for referential transparency. The concern in these novels is not to rewrite history but to subordinate history to fiction and thus question individual experience.[2]

The documentary novelist wishes the reader to believe that past events contain meaning in and of themselves. However, there is no "meaning" that belongs to the past in and of itself for "meaning" is assigned to past "facts" in the present. The legitimization of events in Barnet's *Biografía de un cimarrón*, *Canción de Rachel*, *Gallego*, and *La vida real*, for example, occurred (were given meaning) the moment Barnet chose to investigate, assemble information, and finally write these narratives. While the documentary novel predominantly uses the past tense to create an illusion that what is being "recorded" did "in fact" occur, the novels of the pentalogy are composed, with minor exceptions, in the present tense. Arenas's novels are not a rewriting, or a recording, or an excavating of past life, but a vital artistic expression that articulates human experience in the full immediacy of action. For this reason, the *diégèse* of these novels is predominantly composed in the present tense. Arenas allows his readers to view his novels in their present singularity, at the level of the *énoncé*. Moreover, since it is contemporary with the reading act, the present tense emphasizes each text's condition of artifice. Discourse is seen as a surface, as a network of exchanges in a signifying field, and not as signs that correspond to exterior historical "facts."

The novels of the *pentagonía* dismantle historiographical discourse through fictionalization; they deny and reject any pretense to an official history of the Cuban Revolution. Arenas does not build his texts on historical facts or figures but constantly undermines and discredits any claim to veracity or exclusivity. In a 1970 review entitled "Con los ojos abiertos," Arenas wrote:

> Los escritores que se apoyan en fechas, cifras, crónicas (lo que también se le llama historia), olvidando que en todo tiempo quien miente y ama, quien destruye, traiciona, recuerda y crea es el hombre, nos han dejado una literatura polvorienta, a veces bostezable, a veces elegante, pero siempre un producto de gabinete. (p. 10)

> Writers who base their work on dates, numbers, chronicles (what is also called history), forgetting that throughout time man lies and loves, destroys, betrays, remembers and creates, have left us a dusty literature, at times boring, at times elegant, but always a product of a laboratory.

Celestino antes del alba, El palacio de las blanquísimas mofetas, Otra vez el mar, El color del verano, and *El asalto* display no attempt to produce an objective monolithic system of language; rather their intention is to inscribe the writer's particular social and historical experiences into the text. Dissonance, subversion, and ambiguity are inscribed into Arenas's novels, texts that do not presume to be anything but what they are, pure fiction.

As we have seen, the Cuban documentary novel is a curious construct, an overlapping of fact and fiction designed to "give voice to the voice-less." Yet, in actuality, the witnesses who are chosen or recreated provide information about their personal experiences only to highlight the importance of the revolutionary historical reality shaping their lives. Hence, the tendency of documentary novels is more to explore the areas of history than of fiction, with the purpose of granting veracity to the witnesses' discourse by means of referential descriptions and verifiable references. But modern criticism has shown that no writing, including history, is free of ideological intention. While the Cuban documentary novel attempts to hide its ideology behind a monolithic text of historical facts and figures, the novels of the pentalogy display no attempt to present themselves as a historical "truth." Ironically, however, this does not weaken their validity. Arenas's deliriously humorous and simultaneously poignant accounts lyrically inscribe the emotional, imaginative, and hallucinatory experiences of characters—linguistic creations that represent individuals who have been ignored and silenced by the revolutionary regime—into a creative text that indeed presents vital "testimonies" of human existence.

APPENDIX

Conversation with Reinaldo Arenas

The following conversation took place in New York City in December 1987. The conversation, conducted entirely in Spanish, was taped and later transcribed and included in my doctoral dissertation. In 1989 I sent Arenas the transcript, which he updated, edited, and authorized for publication. It appeared in Spanish in 1990 in *Conversación con Reinaldo Arenas* (Madrid: Editorial Betania). The following translation is mine.

F.S. While you lived in Cuba, before falling out of favor with the Revolution, you wrote articles, reviews, and even stories for *La Gaceta de Cuba* and *Unión*. Until what year did you write for these two periodicals?

R.A. I think that the last articles I wrote for these journals were in 1969. I don't believe that in 1970 I published many articles.

F.S. Well, in 1970 the essay "El reino de la imagen" (The Reign of the Image) was published in *La Gaceta de Cuba*.

R.A. Of course, my homage to José Lezama Lima. This article was written around the time Lezama turned sixty. I believe this was practically one of the last things that I published. After this came the famous Congress on Education and Culture in 1971 and subsequently everything changed. In fact, there are many things missing, which were censored, from the Lezama article. I wrote the article in 1969, but it wasn't published until 1970. I wrote this homage to Lezama after having read *Paradiso* and Lezama's complete poems. Now I have a book in which the complete article appears.

F.S. You're referring to *Necesidad de libertad*, aren't you?

R.A. Yes. In Cuba they cut out some parts in which I talked about the poet's task, which above all is to write the work. I also said that no one bothered to think about poets, and when they did it was only to attack them. In short, there was a series of details that they thought alluded too directly to the revolutionary regime. They took out parts in which I stated that in no era had the writer been an instrument of the state, or something to that effect, and that the writer would always have to be a sort of freelance sniper who had to survive by his or her own resources. All this was taken out of the original. Yes, I believe that this was one of my last pieces of work that was published in Cuba. I collaborated with *La Gaceta de Cuba,* more or less, from 1968 until 1970. Perhaps in 1967 I published something.

F.S. And in *Unión?*

R.A. The first piece of work I published appeared in *Unión,* before the publication of *Celestino antes del alba.* Around 1965 I published three short stories.

F.S. You also published other stories in *Unión,* and even some parts of *El palacio de las blanquísimas mofetas.* Also the essay "Celestino y yo."

R.A. "Celestino y yo" appeared in *Unión* in 1967, but I had previously published some very short stories, "La punta del arco iris" (The Tip of the Rainbow), "Soledad" (Solitude), and "La puesta del sol" (Sunset), in 1965. All three stories deal more or less with rural themes. I have never published these stories again. In fact, I don't consider them to be very good.

F.S. Why not?

R.A. Well, before publishing *Celestino antes del alba*—which is the first and only book I published in Cuba, a book in which, more or less, I start to do something that I consider not to be so bad—I had already written about two books of poetry, which fortunately were lost before they were ever published, and a book of stories with childhood themes in which the protagonist was always a child. Those stories ["La punta del arco iris," "Soledad," and "La puesta del sol"] and another story that I really liked, entitled "Los zapatos vacíos" (The Empty Shoes), which was also lost, appeared in this book. I believe that this book of stories was my first step in later writing *Celestino antes del alba.*

F.S. Then these stories were in fact the genesis of *Celestino antes del alba?*

R.A. At that time I was still close to my childhood. It was 1963, I was more or less twenty years old and my experiences were precisely those experiences from the countryside that upon abandoning it, when I left the countryside for Havana, I felt nostalgic for. In short, having left all that behind, that very countryside became something rather magical that made me, I would say, reconstruct it through my imagination. Those were the first things I wrote, those stories with rural and childhood themes that are also somewhat autobiographical. In fact, those stories helped me get a job at the National Library. I had been working in a rather wretched place called the National Institute of Agrarian Reform. One day there was a contest for storytellers in the National Library and I took along that very story that was lost, "Los zapatos vacíos." I narrated it and they liked it very much, although they didn't know who the author was since they had only called for storytellers and not authors. From that I got a job at the National Library. That was an important experience in my life.

F.S. How many years did you work at the National Library?

R.A. I worked at the National Library from 1963 until 1968. It was an important experience because at that time it was fundamental for me to be able to have access to a number of texts that were practically unattainable in Cuba. For example, where was I going to buy a copy of Joyce's *Ulysses*? Or where was I going to read Proust, or Yeats, or almost any other great writer? In the library there also were a number of individuals that at that time helped me, people like Eliseo Diego, Cintio Vitier, and the director of the library, María Teresa Freyre de Andrade, a very well read and educated person. Through these individuals I met José Lezama Lima, who frequented the library. In the library I discovered a cultural and creative atmosphere. At that time almost everyone— including Cintio Vitier and Eliseo Diego, who are now almost officials of the regime—were people who were out of favor with the Revolution, and precisely for being out of favor they worked in the library. The library was no place for people with political ambitions. Eliseo Diego, for example, worked in the children's literature department. They were all, I would say, up to a certain point, outcasts. And I . . . well, grew up in that atmosphere of exclusion and isolation (which I think is healthy for writers), reading and writing among them. Sometimes we would get together at their houses or in the library and create a literary, almost underground, atmosphere. Later things changed. The director, María Teresa Freyre de Andrade, a revolutionary, was dismissed, and people like Eliseo Diego and Cintio Vitier, who had been antirevolutionaries, changed completely and became spokesmen for the regime. In 1968, when the situation got very difficult at the library, I went to work at the Institute for Cuban Books. I only worked there for one year and later went to work at the UNEAC (Unión Nacional de Escritores y Artistas de Cuba or National Union of Writers and Artists of Cuba). That is why in 1969, and even in 1968 and 1970 there appear things that I wrote in the journals *Unión* and *La Gaceta de Cuba,* both periodicals published by UNEAC.

F.S. How did you manage to get your manuscripts out of Cuba?

R.A. Well, almost as if by magic. From 1967, the same year I published *Celestino antes del alba,* I started to send my manuscripts out of Cuba. At that time writers who weren't altogether in favor of the regime still came to Cuba. I remember that in 1967 Cuba celebrated an important event, the May Salon, in which many important works were exhibited. Well-known painters and writers came to Cuba and many had the opportunity to read *Celestino antes del alba.* The French surrealist group, who were the most interested in the novel, helped me smuggle out *El mundo alucinante* with the help of the painter Jorge Camacho. I also smuggled out other stories I had that formed part of the collection *Con los ojos cerrados.* In 1968 a French editorial house translated *El mundo alucinante*; thus it appeared first in French rather than Spanish. Of course after this my situation became more difficult in Cuba, since I had published a book outside the island, in France no less, without having first consulted the Cuban government. That was enough to cause me problems. Never again was I able to publish in Cuba. Yes, a few articles, but nothing else. However, since I already had certain connections, whenever a tourist would visit Cuba, for example a professor, I would give him or her my manuscripts. *El palacio de las blanquísimas mofetas* was smuggled out disguised as a botany book.

F.S. Isn't it correct that when you arrived in the United States in 1980 you had to publish new editions of your work as a result of the many pirated editions that had appeared?

R.A. In fact I never received a penny for any edition. They were all "pirated" editions. Moreover, while I was in Cuba many times I wasn't even notified of these publications. Of all the editions of *El mundo alucinante* that were published I only knew about one, and that was because the editor (Emanuel Carballo) was more or less a friend of Fidel Castro. It's rather incredible considering that at the same time he was a friend of the Castro regime he was publishing and selling my books. He had many ties with Casa de las Américas. Once I sent him a letter complaining about my situation in Cuba, and he turned the letter over to Casa de las Américas, to Haydée Santamaría, who finally ended her life by shooting herself. . . . But in reality, I wasn't aware of the published editions of my work. For example, a book like *Con los ojos cerrados*, which was published in Uruguay in 1972, I only saw for the first time when I arrived here in the United States in 1980.

F.S. Why did you change the title of *Celestino antes del alba* to *Cantando en el pozo* when you published the new edition?

R.A. I personally never wanted to change the title of *Celestino antes del alba* to *Cantando en el pozo*. I prefer the original title. The problem was that the editorial house thought that they couldn't publish the book with the title *Celestino antes del alba* because of copyright issues. Once *Celestino antes del alba* was published in Cuba, the government owned the rights. Since the book belongs to what is called the national art heritage, there existed the theoretical possibility that the Cuban government could bring a lawsuit against the editorial house because the book had been originally published in Cuba. Since the editorial house thought that it couldn't be published with the original title there was no other recourse but to find a new title. Among the number of titles that were possible I felt that *Cantando en el pozo* at least had a certain relationship to the novel. That is, it was the least harmful. Curiously when the book, which presently is being translated, finally appears in English the editorial house has preferred the new title *Cantando en el pozo*. It's going to be called *Singing from the Well*.

F.S. When you wrote *Celestino antes del alba* did you already have the plan for the *pentagonía*?

R.A. When I wrote *Celestino antes del alba*, no. I wrote *Celestino antes del alba* in the National Library where I worked. I was scheduled to start work at one in the afternoon. Since I didn't own a typewriter, I would go earlier to use the one at the library. When I wrote *El palacio de las blanquísimas mofetas* I realized that it was a continuation of *Celestino antes del alba*, and in fact around that same time I already had the idea for *Otra vez el mar*. I conceived of *Otra vez el mar* in 1966; the first version is from 1969.

F.S. Yet it wasn't published until 1982. That is, sixteen years pass from the time you first conceive of the novel until its actual publication.

R.A. The tragedy surrounding that novel is so great that I still don't feel there exists a Spanish edition that is worthwhile. I would like to publish a new edition in Spanish. Also, one can hardly find a copy of that edition anymore. Argos Vergara is an editorial house that is practically out of business. I plan to publish a new edition, but the editorial world is as fantastic and absurd a world as that of Fray Servando. No one ever knows what can happen. The Argos Vergara edition is incomplete.

F.S. In *El palacio de las blanquísimas mofetas* Celestino is reincarnated as the adolescent Fortunato. In *Otra vez el mar* he reincarnates as the adult Héctor. Will this "reincarnation" of the protagonist occur in the last two novels of the quintet, *El color del verano* and *El asalto*?

R.A. *El asalto* is the only novel in which the protagonist doesn't die. The story of *El asalto* is the culmination of the *pentagonía*. The story takes place in a future time, in a completely tyrannical and automated society where even language is impoverished. The *pentagonía* commences with the apolitical world of *Celestino antes del alba,* a completely primitive era. Later *El palacio de las blanquísimas mofetas* continues with the Batista era, which coincides with the protagonist's adolescence. The third novel, *Otra vez el mar,* unfolds during the time of Fidel Castro and coincides with the protagonist's early adult years. The fourth novel, *El color del verano,* is a bit of the world of the picaresque or "underground" in Cuba from 1970 to 1999 (the novel ends with the century). It deals with the maturity of the protagonist, who is mixed up with a whole world of picaresque characters who survive and read clandestinely and live in the most rebellious but at the same time dark and dismal fashion. The novel ends with the mass exodus off the island. In the fifth novel, *El asalto,* the protagonist, who always dies, doesn't die. He's a character who after having lived under a dictatorship for so long has degraded and debased himself and goes along with a regime that he hates. But his hate is not the result of wanting to destroy the regime, but rather of wanting to destroy his mother. He believes that he resembles his mother more and more each day and that the moment will arrive when he will turn into his very own mother. His face will be like hers. As a result, he decides that the only way to eliminate that resemblance is by killing her, but to kill her he must go across the island looking for her, and in order to do this, he first has to obtain a special permission from the government, which no longer allows its citizens to move around freely. He then becomes a member of the "Bureau of Counterwhispering." Because the people are forced to say what the government tells them to say, they sometimes rebel by whispering other words, something that is prohibited. As a Counterwhisper the protagonist can freely go across the country looking for his mother; however, he never finds her. One day when "the Represident," the absolute dictator, is about to speak, the protagonist, who as an agent finds himself protecting the platform where the dictator is about to speak, suddenly realizes that the dictator is his mother in disguise. He advances toward her in order to kill her, but as he advances he begins to get an erection. His member grows to excessive proportions as he advances toward his mother, who is "the Represident." The mother, recognizing her son, fears for her life. Then the battle between them commences.

F.S. This scene reminds me of that fantastically amusing episode in part one of *Otra vez el mar* in which the warriors of the Trojan War battle each other with their erect members.

R.A. Exactly. At the end of *El asalto* the protagonist penetrates his mother with his erect member. The mother cries out and explodes. What remains are some nuts and bolts, oil and mechanical gears. That is why the novel is called *El asalto* [The Assault], because the protagonist overtakes his mother's power and control. In the end, the people who had been enslaved start to whisper louder and louder as they advance forward. There is a final moment when the protagonist retreats to the sea while the people destroy everything and finally take control.

F.S. This theme of the castrating mother appears in many of your texts. For example, it appears in the allegorical empire of the second canto in *Otra vez el mar* and in the story "La Vieja Rosa," among others. In many of your texts mothers tyrannize or oppress their sons, they want to destroy them.

R.A. It's a dual relationship. There's this type of relationship in all my novels. It's not completely a tyrannical relationship. The mother is destructive, but at the same time she is affectionate. She can destroy but also love. It's a relationship of power and control that she has with her son. She dominates him, but also cares for him; she destroys him, but also loves him. To a certain extent I see in this the tradition of the Cuban mother, a tradition that is the result of our Spanish heritage. The son loves his mother but also realizes that he must get away from her. I believe that Cuban mothers have had a negative and positive influence on our writers. For example, Lezama Lima publishes *Paradiso* after his mother's death. Perhaps he wouldn't have dared to publish that novel beforehand, which, among other things, pays homage to his mother. We don't dare reveal our true selves to our mothers, much less if we're homosexual. Mothers see that as absolutely taboo, completely immoral and prohibited; at least the majority of mothers see it that way. That love/hate, rejection and rapprochement of the mother is a contradictory relationship, but very real. In *El asalto* at the same time the protagonist destroys his mother he does it by possessing her. Therefore, there isn't total hate, but rather obsession and passion.

F.S. The character of the wife in *Otra vez el mar* at times hates her son. She also isn't the typical Cuban mother.

R.A. Perhaps that's why she doesn't exist. She's Héctor's invention. In *Otra vez el mar* there is an entire gallery of mothers. There is the wife's mother, who is an important figure in her life. She is a mother that doesn't see beyond practical things, someone very typical in Cuba. For example, she says, "But dear you have a beautiful kitchen, I'm never going to have a kitchen like this." She represents the type of person that wants to solve everything in a practical way. In the novel there's also the adolescent's mother, who is the dedicated mother. She's the mother who lives for her son—"my son, my son, my son"—and is incapable of imagining that he would do anything that she didn't approve of. There is also Héctor's vision of his mother. That mother he evokes from far away. And there's also the mechanical mother, the dictator mother who's a precursor of the last novel. And finally there's the omnipresent mother represented by the moon.

F.S. Could you talk a little bit about the different sequences of time that appear in *Otra vez el mar?*

R.A. Before I started to write *Otra vez el mar* I had made a series of maps concerning the time sequences in the novel. They were spherical maps because in this novel, obviously, time is represented as circular. First, there are the six or seven hours that represent the time from when the couple leave the beach and arrive at the tunnel leading into Havana. Then there are the six days that the couple spends at the beach.

F.S. Here there's a parodic allusion to the story of the six days of creation in the Bible, isn't there?

R.A. Yes, when each day is described there's a passage from the Bible. It's the first thing that she describes each morning. In addition to the six days, there's the time that describes their life together in Havana. Also there's a regression to a childhood time. In her case it was difficult for me to create the changes in time since all of part one is narrated in the present tense. She is in the present but at the same time the present is like a past that never ends. The past is the present. Once a person remembers, he or she is living in the present.

F.S. And from there the epigraph of part one, "Memory is a present which never stops going past."

R.A. Of course.

F.S. Your desire to rewrite, which Alicia Borinsky has studied in her article "Re-escribir y escribir: Arenas, Menard, Borges, Cervantes, Fray Servando," is not limited exclusively to *El mundo alucinante,* but is also present, for example, in *La Loma del Angel.*

R.A. I see rewriting as a way of interpreting reality, this reality that for me is multiple like in *El mundo alucinante* or *Otra vez el mar.* I find in rewriting a manifestation of the different realities that exist in the world. One reads a text and that same text provokes a series of ideas that perhaps are not in the text, and for that reason one decides to rewrite that text in order to explore those ideas. I'm basically interested in two things in the narrative world. One is the exploration of my personal life, my experiences, my sufferings, my own tragedies. The other is the historical world. To take that history to a completely fictitious plane. To interpret history perhaps like the people who suffered it experienced it. In this plane of rewriting history through fiction or parody I would place *El central, El mundo alucinante,* and *La Loma del Angel.*

F.S. How is this manifested in *El central?*

R.A. In *El central* there are three eras of slavery represented: that of the Indians, later that of the blacks, and lastly that of the present time. They are historical eras that even include historical figures like Fray Bartolomé de las Casas. But in *Otra vez el mar* there are also moments of rewriting. For example, the rewriting of the Trojan War. There are also characters that are absolutely real and appear as if revived by Héctor. In the sixth canto, for example, Héctor transforms himself into different characters. At one moment he's a black slave who is serving his masters. At other times he's a character in a camp cutting down sugar cane while also serving as a cook. There is also a passage in which he's a medieval monk in a castle.

F.S. And the character of Tedevoro from *Otra vez el mar,* is he a rewriting of Adolfina from *El palacio de las blanquísimas mofetas?*

R.A. Yes, he's like Adolfina, who never finds what she's searching for. The sixth canto, in which Tedevoro appears, is like the intersection of another time and of another rhetoric in the novel. The narration at the beginning of the sixth canto, everything that is written in prose up until the moment of Tedevoro's death, is the same as that of the world of the fourth novel of the *pentagonía.* That tone of the first part of the sixth canto is the same as that of *El color del verano.*

F.S. And why do you appear as "la Tétrica Mofeta" (the Gloomy Skunk) in the Tedevoro story?

R.A. That was the pseudonym I gave myself in that world. All that is explained in *El color del verano*.

F.S. And Donald Duck, Popeye, Mighty Mouse, and the others that appear?

R.A. Well, that's also the world of childhood that I mythicize somewhat because we were raised watching all those cartoons or buying comic books. Tedevoro is a character who has idealized that world so much that in the end he becomes like those cartoon characters, simply a piece of paper. He is nothing, he gets folded and folded like a piece of cardboard.

F.S. The Tedevoro story ends with the words "Go on? Not go on? That is the question." This moment marks a transition in the novel. From this moment on there is a sort of frenzy, fury, or hysterical desire on Héctor's part to be able to express himself.

R.A. This is the transition toward Héctor's death. During those intervals of time that occur in the novel, for example, the time of the wife's narration in the car in which she returns to the beach, to the past, and looks toward the future, Héctor is composing his poems, "Quick, quick, sing before it's too late." As the car approaches Havana the possibility of singing that imaginary poem begins to disappear. If he arrives he will turn himself over to the slavery of the city, to conventionalism, to defeat: "Don't arrive, don't ever get here, because arriving is turning yourself over to them." In the end he decides to commit suicide before entering Havana.

F.S. Is Héctor then like one of the characters of *Pedro Páramo* who speaks from his grave?

R.A. No. In my novel the text is what remains after death. It is a text that Héctor thinks of, creates when he is alive. The cantos survive the death of the character. The actual text is written in the void of death.

F.S. You told me before that you first conceived of *Otra vez el mar* in 1966, precisely during the "Boom" in Latin American letters. What effect, if any, did the "Boom" have on a novel like *Otra vez el mar* in which the structure is so singular?

R.A. One of the things that I always attempted to do was to make each novel an experiment, something completely new. In the *pentagonía* each novel had to have its own tone, rhythm, language, a special structure for each narrative world. Perhaps now in the late 1980s I have other ideas.

F.S. In what way are your ideas different now?

R.A. I believe that language and sorrow change according to the circumstances we find ourselves in. I'm no longer that character who wrote *Otra vez el mar*. Now I live in another context; one that is perhaps more ironic, more desolate, more tragic, more cosmopolitan or whatever you want to call it.

F.S. I understand, but I also feel that that subversive spirit present in your earlier work is still present in *Otra vez el mar* and in your other novels. That transgressive mode of writing that wages war on the concept of the novel as a closed and linear genre continues to appear in your work.

R.A. Absolutely. I believe that from a linguistic and structural point of view a novel has to be an innovative text, contradictory and conflictive, that incessantly provides multiple interpretations. However, the contradictions and concerns that I now pose or raise are more numerous. Now I don't only question time and structure in the novel, but I also question my role as author. In my latest novels the author not only disappears but is also violently attacked and insulted by the characters. Metaphorically speaking, a novel like *El portero*—which I just completed—is not written by Reinaldo Arenas but by a million anonymous individuals. There's a moment in the novel when a group of editors, who aren't writers, explain why they didn't ask Guillermo Cabrera Infante, Severo Sarduy, or even Reinaldo Arenas to write the novel. According to the editors, these writers would have written things that simply didn't interest them. My novel *Viaje a La Habana*—presently in the process of being published in Spain—is supposedly written by various individuals who are enemies among themselves and who fill up the text with endless footnotes. In one of these footnotes it is reported that Reinaldo Arenas "was an insignificant writer who died of AIDS in 1987." It's possible that this is true and that what you're seeing before your eyes is a ghost. Anyway, my texts, in their apparent simplicity, are now much more complex and disguised. The author is no longer the master of life or of the characters; neither is the author the master of his or her fate or of anything. In reality, the author no longer exists.

F.S. Something similar to what you have just said occurs at the end of *Otra vez el mar* when a "*chorus of characters* (emerging from the page)" starts to question the author.

R.A. You're right. However, now I feel differently about the world and I express it differently. Naturally that doesn't mean I want, in any way, to write a traditional linear novel. It just means that each novel is an experimental world unto itself and that once it's complete you can't repeat it formally. You have to find other avenues, and the experiences of living in exile have brought me other narrative worlds. Living in exile has brought me the world of nostalgia, it has offered me a series of things that I never would have experienced in Cuba. Perhaps my fortune has been the historical, social, and personal calamities I have suffered, which have given diversity to my creative experience.

F.S. There appears to be a doubling game of mirrors, of opposites, in *Otra vez el mar*. For example, Héctor/the adolescent; the nameless wife/ Héctor; the nameless wife who hates being a mother/the adolescent's mother who dedicates herself totally to her son's every need. Also, the sea, a fundamental character, is presented as both a symbol of freedom and slavery. What do you think?

R.A. All my novels pose a constant and contradictory duality, which is characteristic of every human being. I candidly presented this idea in my prologue to *El mundo alucinante* in which I wrote: "I will never tire of discovering that the tree of six o'clock in the morning is not the tree of noon, nor that tree whose soughing brings us consolation at evening. And that breeze that springs up at night, can it possibly be the same breeze as at morning? And that ocean water the swimmer cuts through at sunset as though it were meringue, are those the choppy waters of midday? As time flows, permeates, so obviously and fully, into a tree or a beach or a landscape, can we, the earth's most sensitive creatures, remain insensitive to its signs? I think not—we are cruel and tender, greedy and generous, impassioned and meditative, laconic and rowdy, terrible and sublime, like the ocean . . ." (Hurley trans., p. xviii). The sea is the summary and the mirror of all the characters in the novel.

F.S. Could you talk a little about the possible ways of reading *Otra vez el mar*, because I think there are more than one.

R.A. My idea was to publish a canto and then a chapter, a chapter and then a canto and so forth. The editor, however, told me it was a crazy idea and that no one would understand anything. Another idea, even more crazy, was to publish both parts side by side. That is, to read the novel in a parallel fashion, to read both parts at the same time in order to see how the two characters, who in fact are traveling in the same car, develop along the same time. There was that remote possibility that was also rejected. And in the end we agreed on the idea of publishing the wife's part first followed by Héctor's cantos, which is not altogether such a bad idea.

F.S. I also think that one can read the first or second part by itself, for its own aesthetic value, although obviously the reading would be incomplete.

R.A. The first part is a complete but partial novel. There is a problem with many readers, they don't want to read the second part. I have many friends who called and said to me how is it possible that after the first part you wrote *"that other part?"* I believe that the second part is simply the complement of the first, or vice versa. Moreover, if you read carefully you discover that *she* leaves gaps in the text that only *he* can fill. The first part is like the map of the second. The first part is the "novel" in the most conventional sense of the word; the second part is the explosion.

F.S. I found a letter in the Reinaldo Arenas manuscript collection at the Princeton University library from Enrico Mario Santí in which he states the following concerning *Otra vez el mar*: "There are parts that remind me of Dostoevsky; other parts remind me of a neighborhood carnival while others of the most risqué passages of the Bible; in many cases it is a disturbing reading experience because it is something completely new, the novel as a blender that mixes everything together. . . ."

R.A. Of course, that has always been one of my ideas concerning the novel. Pío Baroja—although I don't think that he ever put it into practice—used to say that the novel was like a sack into which the author could throw everything. I believe that this is one of the most marvelous things about the novel, that the author can experiment in every sense of the word. For example, in *El portero* I present the idea that the novel is written by a million individuals (Cuban exiles) who are writing a biography about one of their own. To achieve this I utilize a tone that is more or less that of the essay. At other times the animals in the story speak and each animal tells its own story. For this I utilize a parodic tone. All of this could not be done in a poem. The novel is precisely that genre that can participate in all the others without losing its identity, its essence.

F.S. In *Otra vez el mar* there exists a tension between what we might call an aesthetics of freedom or art for art's sake and an aesthetics of *engagement* (quite the other extreme). However, I believe that in the end neither extreme wins out; rather the reading is actualized somewhere in the middle where these two tendencies battle each other out.

R.A. For me the novel is an open text for the reader who must answer for him- or herself all those questions. It's the reader who must give the final verdict, not the author. If the author gives this verdict the book becomes uninteresting. What I'm interested in is that once the reader finishes the book he or she begins the other reading; that other reading that the reader who is concerned with interpreting and to a certain extent (re)writing that text will do.

F.S. In the English translation of *Otra vez el mar, Farewell to the Sea,* there appear a number of short stories in the sixth canto—for example, "Negroes," "The Table," "Monster II"—that are not in the original novel. Why were these stories included in the English version?

R.A. The idea behind the stories is that they are the things that Héctor writes or plans to write and wishes to publish. Héctor is a writer who has never been able to publish in Cuba. These are the stories that he is thinking about writing or has already written. They appear in canto six as a transition. In this, the last canto, there is a sexual, creative, and sentimental explosion. In fact, these stories were in the original Spanish manuscript but did not appear in the 1982 Argos Vergara edition.

F.S. Also, one of the very last sentences in the English version is different from the Spanish edition. The line reads: "To the last second equanimity and rhythm—fantasy." The word *equanimity* doesn't appear in the Spanish edition.

R.A. In the original manuscript the word *ecuanimidad* does indeed appear, but in the final published edition there were many things left out; also there were many errata. What should have appeared is exactly what appears in the English translation: "To the last second equanimity and rhythm—fantasy." Both equanimity and rhythm. Rhythm, because it refers to Héctor's creation, to his poem, a rhythmic poem; equanimity because without it there's nothing, not even madness, that can be told or narrated. Up to the end, up to the last second, Héctor cannot lose his sense of rhythm or equanimity, without which he would lose his sense of creation. Fantasy persists up until the moment when both equanimity and rhythm, and with it poetry, die. "*Héctor, Héctor,* I say, rushing forward. Imprisoned, unleashed, furious, and crashing, like the ocean." In the Spanish edition [Barcelona: Argos Vergara] it says "estallado" (shattered) instead of "estallando" (crashing). This type of error is abominable. I have jotted down all these mistakes in the Spanish edition so that if I publish a new edition I can make the corrections. So in fact, the English edition is more faithful to the original manuscript than the Spanish edition. [No new edition has been published.—F.S.]

F.S. I think that the English translation of *Otra vez el mar* is very good. The only thing I didn't care for was the title, *Farewell to the Sea.*

R.A. The title was chosen simply to make it more marketable. I think it could have been translated differently, perhaps something like *Once*

More the Sea or *Again the Sea*. Sometimes there's just nothing you can do.

F.S. What was the revolutionary government's reaction to your writing in Cuba?

R.A. The revolutionary government never has approved of this type of writing, not back then and not now. Like all orthodox systems the revolutionary government is more interested in promoting literature that has a message, a literature that is as little experimental as possible. And what I have always been interested in, in all my books, is the power of experimentation, in language as well as in structure. That is why I told you that I'm interested in pursuing a different experiment in each novel. There's no sense for me to narrate now using a tone like Balzac's. When he originally did it he was experimenting, but if I adopted it today I would only be copying it. I believe that a writer must always renew him- or herself. In Cuba, my way of writing was never going to interest the government. The revolutionary government is not interested in any type of experimental, avant-garde, or irreverent writing.

F.S. What type of writing was the government then interested in when you found yourself writing in Cuba?

R.A. In the 1960s, writers like Lisandro Otero, Edmundo Desnoes—those types of dreadful realistic novels.

F.S. And Miguel Barnet's novels?

R.A. Naturally, that type of thing also interests the state because they aren't in fact novels, they're testimonies that are written in the form of books. But they're testimonies from the masses that give a historical perspective, up to a point a dialectic, Marxist perspective. Barnet's novels are like pages taken out of the Marxist-Leninist manual. That is, first we have the runaway black slave who becomes free, then comes the republican era with its nominal power, and we are introduced to the singer from *Canción de Rachel*. Finally in *Gallego* we have the Revolution and everything is now paradise. As if in real life there were such a paradisiacal political scale, that everything is negative until in the end all is marvelous with the Revolution. I think that the mistake is believing in a positive happy ending. Human beings carry both a negative and positive load. Social systems, however, whatever they are, generally tend to degrade human beings. They ask human beings to renounce their freedom, and hence their vitality. In a democratic system this is less obvious, but nonetheless it still exists. All societies are hypocritical.

F.S. What interested you when you wrote *Arturo, la estrella más brillante*?

R.A. What interested me the most in that novel was the creative rhythm. The idea that as the protagonist perishes he creates in order to survive and transcend his immediate reality.

F.S. And when you wrote *Necesidad de libertad*?

R.A. That is a collection of essays. Obviously I don't consider it to be a book that falls within a tradition of fiction. However, I did want to maintain in that book that same tone that appears in almost everything I've done. That is, a contradictory tone with diverse perspectives or points of view. The book is made up of essays, but at the same time there are also personal letters, documents, some very serious and others very ironic.

F.S. I've always seen humor as an important element in all your work.

R.A. A sense of humor is fundamental, it's one of the gifts we have. If we lose our smile we don't have anything. I believe that humor is one of our most autochthonous traits, that sense of humor, of irony, of joking that Cubans have. With humor you evoke reality in a more disrespectful manner and therefore you can come closer to it without the distancing effect that is typical of all seriousness. All rhetoric implies certain useless formalities that humor interrupts and challenges as it gives us a more human reality.

F.S. When you finish writing a novel, does it always turn out as you planned?

R.A. It's impossible to believe that a novel, or any other literary work, can turn out to be what the author originally conceived it to be. In the first place, it's impossible to conceive of a novel in its totality. The author has a series of notes, ideas, maps, things jotted down, in short, an entire series of things that are done before writing. But as the characters come to life they free themselves from the author. The author is an instrument of the characters who directs them, because if not it would be total chaos. The author has all those characters trapped in his or her head until they begin to clamor, to cry out for help. And only the author can give them help, through words. The author is like a medium, an interpreter between this world and that mysterious world of characters who cry out. Writing is not a profession, but rather a type of illumination that an author can have and also lose. When an author finishes a novel he or she is not sure of being able to write another. An author who writes novels in a professional way produces things like Julio Cortázar wrote in his last years, that is, stylistic exercises, which is what is in fashion today in Spanish literature. This is horrible. That magical thing that is a book, something that is simply mysterious and innovative is lost when the work of the writer becomes simply professional. That mysterious creative visitation that comes to the author is completely separate from the ability that a person has to draft and write a paragraph. Nevertheless, that ability is also vital: it's necessary for the author to know how to write, to know the grammatical rules and all the other rules of the game. But more than that, there is a mysterious game, that is what it is, a laborious game of breathing vitality into those characters that goes beyond our own narrative talent. And that's where the mystery of creation lies. It is something that can't be manifested under a dictatorship. Dictatorships don't accept mystery, everything has to be explicit and clear. As if life itself were explicit and clear. Life is an endless mystery, mystery and terror. That's what we are, a desperate flash sheltered by poetry and tenderness.

F.S. Who are the authors that you read?

R.A. Just now when I was in Miami I read Proust again. At first I thought that I wasn't going to be able to read him again, but when I started I liked him more. I believe that Proust renewed literature in a way that we must be eternally grateful to him for. There are moments in which he even makes fun of the characters, of the novel itself, and of his readers.

F.S. Borges also does that.

R.A. Borges is one of my favorite authors. His death marked for me the end of a particular way of viewing literature, which is very important. For example, it's not important that five thousand kilograms of potatoes were produced in Cuba or that a number of children were taught how to read and write. That is not the job of literature. Similarly, it's not important that Sartre or Solzhenitsyn have been published in Cuba. And to use that as an example of a merit is actually a serious problem. Literature is a mystery that can't participate in petty political causes. That isn't what's important. What's important is that literature requires an act of inspiration. Literature is something mysterious that can't be labeled or categorized as useful or not useful, literature goes beyond the political machinery. When the political machinery uses literature—and that is what every totalitarian system does, it uses literature for its own purposes—it's very dangerous; literature then stops being literature and becomes propaganda. Borges's greatness existed in the fact that he placed his faith in the act of creation itself, a faith that went beyond the circumstances in which he lived. This faith is indispensable for the writer because behind this faith or innocence lies the real creator, alone and naked, clothed only by his or her words and surrounded by the world he or she is going to put down on paper. That faith is the only thing that makes us exist as writers. The rest are just individuals who produce books in order to make money or to obtain a special post within a given regime. Borges's example can be compared to Lezama Lima, whose creative ingenuousness also placed faith in words. In Borges each poem is a masterpiece in itself that was written not to be on good terms with Augusto Pinochet or Fidel Castro, but to be on good terms with literature. The same is true of Lezama Lima, who lived for words and for literature. However, that enchantment or bewitching fascination with words and literature is slowly being lost. In most conferences that I attend people are more interested in hearing papers in favor or against Fidel Castro.

F.S. What are some of your projects for the future?

R.A. I still have things that I wrote in Cuba and that I still haven't put in order, which now I would like to work on. Also I've just completed a book of stories. I would like to finish the *pentagonía,* which is what I'm most interested in doing. In addition, I've always been interested in poetry. I have already published *El central* and *Voluntad de vivir manifestándose.* I also have a poetic trilogy: *Leprosorio,* which includes *El central, Morir en junio y con la lengua afuera,* and *Leprosorio,* which soon will be published.

F.S. I've always thought that the distinction between poetry and prose in your work is very difficult to discern. It all seems very poetic to me.

R.A. I believe that a writer should have a knowledge of poetry and from there get all the rest. Poetry is the source of everything. I read poetry. That is why I've always admired Borges, who is a great poet. Borges never abandoned poetry. Even when he wrote his last books of prose he always wrote poetry. One should never forget poetry or underestimate its power. Neither should one limit poetry to a genre, rather it should be a literary necessity. When a text requires a more poetic tone a writer should use one; if it isn't required then he or she should not use it. But a writer should always keep poetry in mind; if not, the text becomes journalistic, very arid. One of my aspirations is that after I'm dead some reader will remember me for the rhythm of some of my sentences. I'm obviously very optimistic. I can't help it.

NOTES

Introduction

1. In addition to the English translations mentioned in the bibliography, Grove Press has purchased the rights to contract for and publish *Viaje a La Habana* and the poetic trilogy *El central, Morir en junio y con la lengua afuera*, and *Leprosorio*. Viking Press has under contract the fourth and fifth novels of the pentalogy (*El color del verano* and *El asalto*). The English translation of *El asalto* has been completed by Andrew Hurley and is scheduled to appear in 1994. Hurley is currently working on the translation of *El color del verano*, which is expected to be released in 1995.

2. Although Arenas's texts have enjoyed popularity in the Spanish-speaking world, only five books dedicated exclusively to the study of his work have been published to date. These are: *Reinaldo Arenas: narrativa de transgresión* (1986) by Perla Rozencvaig; *La textualidad de Reinaldo Arenas* (1987) by Eduardo C. Béjar; *Reinaldo Arenas: alucinaciones, fantasía y realidad* (1990), a collection of articles selected and edited by Julio Hernández-Miyares and Perla Rozencvaig; *El desamparado humor de Reinaldo Arenas* (1991) by Roberto Valero; and *La escritura de la memoria* (1992), a series of short essays and interviews edited by Ottmar Ette.

3. Poe's precepts governing the short story are to be found in his famous essay "Twice-Told Tales." Even though his predilection was for the short narrative, Poe twice ventured to write a full-length novel, *The Narrative of A. Gordon Pym* (1837–38) and *The Journal of Julius Rodman* (1840). Borges, on the other hand, never attempted the writing of a novel: "Desvarío laborioso y empobrecedor el de componer vastos libros; el de explayar en quinientas páginas una idea cuya perfecta exposición oral cabe en pocos minutos. Mejor procedimiento es simular que esos libros ya existen y ofrecer un resumen, un comentario" (The composition of vast books is a laborious and impoverishing extravagance. To go on for five hundred pages developing an idea whose perfect oral exposition is possible in a few minutes! A better procedure is to pretend that the books already exist, and then to offer a résumé, a commentary), prologue to *Ficciones*.

4. *El color del verano* and *El asalto* were finally published in December of 1991

(Miami, Ediciones Universal). I am including in the number of published novels: *La Vieja Rosa* (written in 1966 and published in Caracas in 1980), *Arturo, la estrella más brillante* (Barcelona, 1984), and *Viaje a La Habana* (Miami, 1990).

The English translations of *La Vieja Rosa* and *Arturo, la estrella más brillante* appeared together for the first time in 1989 in *Old Rosa: A Novel in Two Stories*. In the past, both *La Vieja Rosa* and *Arturo, la estrella más brillante* have been identified, on different occasions, as either long stories or novellas. Arenas's correspondence for the years 1980–83, housed at the Princeton University library, contains a number of exchanges between the writer and the prominent film director Néstor Almendros. In one letter Arenas writes to Almendros in regard to *Arturo, la estrella más brillante,* a text he refers to as "un cuento" (a story). In his reply Almendros corrects Arenas by calling the work "una narración larga" (a long narration) with a political thrust. I consider the debate over whether *La Vieja Rosa* and *Arturo, la estrella más brillante* are stories, short novels, or novellas unproductive, especially considering the writer's designation of both texts as two instances, two narrative moments, that together constitute a novel—that elastic, inherently open, ill-defined, and inexhaustible genre that critics have spent centuries unsuccessfully trying to pin down.

Arenas subtitled *Viaje a La Habana,* "Novela en tres viajes" (A Novel in Three Trips). Published a few months before the author's death, this work is a collection of three stories ("Que trine Eva," "Mona," and "Viaje a La Habana"), each with its own plot, characters, and action. Still, all three stories are connected by a central theme: the search for a homosexual identity that produces a personal liberation.

5. *Celestino antes del alba* (1967) and *Cantando en el pozo* (1982) are the same novel, but with different titles. When *Celestino antes del alba* was reissued in 1982, it was published under the new title *Cantando en el pozo* because of copyright issues. (See my interview with the author, in the appendix preceding these notes.) Throughout this book I will refer to Arenas's first novel by its original title, *Celestino antes del alba*. All quotes, however, will be from the authorized 1982 edition, *Cantando en el pozo*. Although the citations will be listed as *Celestino antes del alba*, the pages correspond to the 1982 authorized edition of *Cantando en el pozo*.

6. In the preliminary notes to the revised and definitive edition of *Celestino antes del alba*, entitled *Cantando en el pozo* (1982), Arenas stated for the first time that it, together with *El palacio de las blanquísimas mofetas* and *Otra vez el mar,* formed part of a *pentagonía* (pentagony) that would be completed by *El color del verano* and *El asalto*.

A number of published articles have studied *Celestino antes del alba, El palacio de las blanquísimas mofetas,* and *Otra vez el mar* as individual works. None of the five Spanish-language studies of Arenas's work cited above in note 2 has attempted to examine or explore the distinctively intradependent structure of the writer's pentalogy. In *El desamparado humor de Reinaldo Arenas,* Roberto Valero studies what he calls the *tetragonía,* the four novels *Celestino antes del alba, El palacio de las blanquísimas mofetas, Otra vez el mar,* and *El asalto* (the novel that Valero helped Arenas organize and complete shortly before his death). However, Valero does not study *El color del verano.*

7. Reinaldo Arenas. See the interview that appears in the appendix of *La Vieja Rosa* (Caracas: Editorial Arte, 1980), pp. 109–10.

8. In an interview with Franz-Olivier Giesbert of the *Nouvel Observateur* (September 19–25, 1981), later translated into English in *Encounter* (January 1982), Arenas recounts the vicissitudes he experienced (re)writing and publishing *Otra vez el mar.* In my conversation with Arenas, he explained that he conceived of *Otra vez el mar* in 1966 and completed the first version in 1969 (see p. 141).

9. Severo Sarduy, "Carta privada a Reinaldo Arenas," p. 4.

10. In Andrew Hurley's unpublished translation of *El asalto,* he renders the Spanish "el Reprimerísimo Reprimero" (literally, "The Very Repressive, Very First One") as the "Represident." Unless otherwise specified, I will cite from Hurley's unpublished translation throughout.

11. Reinaldo Arenas, *Antes que anochezca,* pp. 12–13. Like many of Arenas's works, the autobiography first appeared in French, as *Avant la nuit,* trans. Liliane Hasson (Paris: Julliard, 1992).

12. Over the years Arenas repeatedly stated his intention to complete the *pentagonía.* Yet, after the publication of *Otra vez el mar* he published four other novels: *Arturo, la estrella más brillante* (1984), *La Loma del Angel* (1987), *El portero* (1989), and *Viaje a La Habana* (1990). The preliminary manuscripts of *El color del verano* and *El asalto* have been available for some time at the Princeton University library. Arenas made the final versions of *El color del verano* and *El asalto* available to me in the summer of 1990, shortly before his death. Since that time I have been researching and organizing my ideas for this book.

1. The Emergence of the Cuban Documentary Novel

1. Alberto Baeza Flores, "La cultura cubana en la encrucijada de su decenio conflictivo 1959–1969," in Carlos A. Montaner's *Diez años de Revolución cubana,* as quoted in Seymour Menton's *Prose Fiction of the Cuban Revolution,* p. 125.

2. The original 1975 English edition of *Prose Fiction of the Cuban Revolution* was translated into Spanish as *La narrativa de la Revolución cubana* in 1978 by Marisela Fernández (Madrid: Playor, S.A.). In 1982, a second Spanish-language edition was published under the same title (México: Plaza y Janés, S.A.) with an appendix that extended the survey to 1981. For purposes of my study, *Prose Fiction of the Cuban Revolution* provides the most extensive compendium of Cuban revolutionary literature up to 1981, one year after Arenas left Cuba. I will quote from both the original English edition of 1975 and the Mexican edition of 1982. Two other works that record the literary production of the Revolution, but in more modest terms, are: Lourdes Casal, "The Cuban Novel, 1959–1969: An Annotated Bibli-

ography," and Ernesto Méndez y Soto, *Panorama de la novela cubana de la Revolución (1959–1970)*.

3. Despite the fact that José Rodríguez Feo coined the term *exorcismo* in reference to the Cuban short story, many critics have made use of the term to study the Cuban novelistic production of the first half of the 1960s.

4. In 1964 the Revolution was still tolerant over polemics concerning artistic freedom, as is evident by the publication of Seymour Menton's article "La novela de la revolución cubana" in *Casa de las Américas*. The article, however, was accompanied by an editorial note that stated: "Aunque se trate de un enfoque superficial y académico, que además repite los viejos argumentos en contra de la Revolución cubana, consideramos que su reproducción en Cuba—y especialmente en este número dedicado al nuevo movimiento literario nacional—es ya una respuesta" (p. 150) (Although it has a superficial and academic focus, which furthermore repeats the old arguments against the Cuban Revolution, we consider that its publication in Cuba—and especially in this issue dedicated to the new national literary movement—is a response in itself).

5. In 1975 Emir Rodríquez Monegal suggested that without the Cuban Revolution (a "boom" with a small *b*), Latin America's literary "Boom" (with a capital *B*) might never have occurred. See "La nueva novela vista desde Cuba," p. 649.

In his own personal account of the "Boom" (*Historia personal del "Boom"*), José Donoso identifies the two most important factors that, in his estimation, contributed to its success: the Cuban Revolution, which served to create a dialogue among Latin American intellectuals; and the founding of the literary journal *Mundo Nuevo* under Emir Rodríguez Monegal, which helped rapidly to disseminate the new literature. Although Reinaldo Arenas never published in *Mundo Nuevo*, Rodríguez Monegal wrote in his book-length study, *El Boom de la novela latinoamericana*: "Esa corriente central [del Boom] de la novela del lenguaje encuentra su expresión más experimental en la obra de tres narradores cubanos (Guillermo Cabrera Infante, Severo Sarduy, Reynaldo [*sic*] Arenas) y un cuarto, argentino (Manuel Puig). Que Cuba tenga tal preeminencia en la actual narrativa hispanoamericana puede explicarse no sólo por el *boom* creado desde la isla por la política cultural del Gobierno, . . . sino también [por] la obra de Lezama Lima, [quien] . . . situó la búsqueda de una expresión americana al nivel más experimental del mito y del lenguaje" (p. 94) (That central current of the Boom, with its preoccupation with language in the novel, finds its most experimental expression in the work of three Cuban narrators (Guillermo Cabrera Infante, Severo Sarduy, Reinaldo Arenas) and a fourth, an Argentine (Manuel Puig). That Cuba should have such dominance in contemporary Spanish American fiction can be explained not only by the boom created on the island by the cultural policies of the government, . . . but also by the work of Lezama Lima, whose search for an American expression can be found at the most experimental level of myth and language).

6. *Paradiso* did in fact encounter numerous obstacles and governmental censor-

ship before it was finally published in a limited edition of four thousand copies. In his article "La novela de Lezama Lima," Armando Alvarez Bravo discusses at length the censorship of *Paradiso* in Cuba and the subsequent decision by the Castro regime finally to lift the ban on the novel's distribution.

In *Historia personal del "Boom"* (pp. 51–52), José Donoso recalls the enormous international prestige and wide circulation that Julio Cortázar's *Rayuela* received, thanks to its cult following in universities in the United States. However, Donoso goes on to state how in certain sectors of Spain, the popularity of *Rayuela* was not unanimous; an irreconcilable debate arose over whether it was in fact *Rayuela* or José Lezama Lima's *Paradiso* that was the superior work. Regardless of which is the better novel, if indeed such a judgment can be made, the popularity of Lezama's *Paradiso* is singularly important in that it provided an alternative to the engagement that the Cuban Revolution was asking from its writers.

7. As stated in the introduction, *El mundo alucinante* first appeared in Paris in 1968 as *Le monde hallucinant* and one year later was published in Spanish in México. The stories of *Con los ojos cerrados*, although published in Uruguay in 1972, were all written in Cuba between 1967 and 1969. Three of the stories—"Con los ojos cerrados," "A la sombra de la mata de almendras," and "El hijo y la madre"—were published in Cuba in *Unión* and *La Gaceta de Cuba*. See the bibliography, *Stories, Essays, Reviews, and Other Literary Fragments Published in Cuba*, for their dates of publication.

8. I have judged appropriate the use of the term *documentary novel* for the Spanish *novela testimonio*. Other writers have likewise translated the term as "documentary novel." See, among others, Paul Bundy and Enrico Mario Santí, "The Documentary Novel," *Cuban Studies/Estudios Cubanos* 11, no. 1 (January 1981: 19–32); Roberto González Echevarría, "*Biografía de un cimarrón* and the Novel of the Cuban Revolution," in *The Voice of the Masters*; and David William Foster, "Latin American Documentary Narrative," *PMLA* 99, no. 1 (January 1984): 41–55.

9. In "The Politics of Memory and Miguel Barnet's *The Autobiography of a Runaway Slave*," William Luis states that for a number of years Miguel Barnet was associated with a group of poets known as "El Puente" (The Bridge), who fell out of grace because many of its members were accused of being antisocial and homosexual by the regime. During this period Barnet's work was not published in Cuba. William Luis hypothesizes: "Perhaps Barnet seized upon the story of Montejo as an opportunity to resume a public literary life. . . . He may have stressed the independent and revolutionary aspects of Montejo's life as a way of overcoming bureaucratic censorship. Whatever the causes, the results were clear. After the publication of *The Autobiography of a Runaway Slave*, Barnet was not only reintegrated into the literary establishment, but he became an important writer. . . . His subject matter was appropriate, one which the literary and political establishments were committed to support" (p. 485).

10. This essay originally appeared in *Unión* 6, no. 4 (December 1969) and was

later included as the appendix to the 1969 edition of *Canción de Rachel*. It is from this appendix that I will quote. In 1981 Paul Bundy and Enrico Mario Santí translated parts of Barnet's essay into English as "The Documentary Novel." I have consulted this essay for my own translations.

11. Although Heberto Padilla's case reached its most dramatic phase in 1971, with the poet's meeting and subsequent confession before the Cuban Writers' Union, his problems with the regime can be traced back as early as 1968. In that year Padilla wrote and published a favorable review of Guillermo Cabrera Infante's novel *Tres tristes tigres* for the weekly review *El caimán barbudo* (The Bearded Alligator). At the time, the exiled Cuban's novel was considered by those in power to be frivolous and empty of political and social commitment. Thus, Padilla's review was interpreted as a counterrevolutionary act. In 1968 Padilla also received the Casa de las Américas prize for his book of poems *Fuera del juego*. Although the Writers' Union and the police pressured the jury to disqualify the book for its deviation from correct revolutionary opinion, Padilla was still awarded the prize. However, from that moment on Padilla became a marginal person in Cuba whose individual and literary activities were closely monitored.

This political case, whose objective was to make Padilla an example of the ideological deviation that the revolutionary system was struggling to eradicate, is now generally considered to have been nothing more than a setup by top government officials intent upon dominating all aspects of Cuban culture. Indeed, Padilla's case turned out to be an embarrassment for the Revolution, an episode that shattered the hopes of many who had expected much more than browbeating, censorship, and paranoia from a Revolution they had supported. The Padilla affair permanently upset the intellectual Left all over Latin America and Europe.

In 1989 the editorial house Plaza y Janés published Padilla's long-expected autobiography, *La mala memoria*. The English translation, *Self-Portrait of the Other*, appeared in 1990 (Farrar, Straus and Giroux). That a Cuban poet's memoir would be translated and published in less than a year by a top North American publishing house attests to the fascination that still surrounds this highly controversial figure. *Self-Portrait of the Other* provides for the reader a personal analysis of the precarious relationship between power and artistic freedom that has plagued the Cuban Revolution since its beginning in 1959. The Padilla incident is also extensively chronicled by Lourdes Casal in *El caso Padilla: Literatura y Revolución en Cuba*.

12. Quoted by Menton as it appeared in *Granma Weekly Review*, October 27, 1968. *Prose Fiction of the Cuban Revolution*, p. 112.

13. Juan Marinello, "Sobre nuestra crítica literaria," *Vida Universitaria* 21, no. 219 (May–June 1970), as quoted by Menton in *Prose Fiction of the Cuban Revolution*, p. 113.

14. For the full text of Padilla's confession before the UNEAC, see "Heberto Padilla: intervención en la Unión de Escritores y Artistas de Cuba," *Casa de las Américas* nos. 65–66 (March–June 1971), pp. 191–203.

15. Oscar Lewis, Ruth M. Lewis, and Susan M. Rigdan, *Living the Revolution: An Oral History of Contemporary Cuba, Four Men Four Women*, p. xi.

16. In 1965 Miguel Barnet, praising Lewis's work, wrote: "*Los hijos de Sánchez* es un libro para el gran público. Lo mismo podemos decir de su *Antropología de la pobreza*. Ambos están considerados por la ciencia y la literatura. . . . Quisieran muchos reaccionarios quemar el libro de Lewis en la plaza pública. Les ofende la verdad así tan descarnada. No quieren admitir que, como la familia Sánchez, existen otras más marginales aún" ("Los hijos de Sánchez," p. 104) (*The Children of Sánchez* is a book for the general public. We can say the same of *Anthropology of Poverty*. Both are respected by science and literature. . . . Many reactionaries would love to burn Lewis's book in the public square. They are offended by the bare truth. They do not want to admit that, like the Sánchez family, there exist other families even more marginalized). For more positive remarks concerning Oscar Lewis's *Los hijos de Sánchez* see issue no. 43 of *Casa de las Américas* (1967), p. 122.

17. In an article translated for the *Partisan Review*, "Twenty-Six Rue de Bièvre," the Spanish novelist Juan Goytisolo gives a personal account of how the Padilla affair tore apart the Hispanic literary community.

18. In *Cuba: The Shaping of Revolutionary Consciousness* (1990), Tzvi Medin observes: "The antidogmatism that had been promoted as an alternative to Soviet orthodoxy began to bear rather undesirable fruit on the domestic level, and in that year, 1968, began the precipitate closure of the obtuse and oscillating angle of divergence permitted within the elastic Marxism-Leninism of 1962–1968. This phenomenon found explicit official expression, definitive to this day, in the First Congress of Education and Culture held in April 1971 . . . [which] saw the definitive imposition of a cultural control that closed the angle of divergence almost completely, leaving an opening only for variations of form; and here, too, in certain channels of expression, *a documentary realism predominated*" (pp. 22–23, emphasis added).

19. In 1972 the Cuban Ministry of Internal Affairs (MININT) established an annual prize to promote Cuban detective fiction that would identify justice with the new socialist governing structure. This is how the MININT defined its literary competition: "El concurso está dirigido al desarrollo de este género en nuestro país, por lo que las obras que se presenten serán de temática policial y tendrán un carácter didáctico, sirviendo asimismo como estímulo a la prevención y vigilancia de todas las actividades antisociales y contra el poder del pueblo" ("Concurso Aniversario de la Revolución 1982," *Moncada*, Oct. 1981, p. 16) (The contest's goal is to develop this genre in our country. Therefore, the works presented should have law-enforcement themes and be of a didactic nature, serving in this way as stimulus for the prevention and monitoring of all antisocial activities that go against the will of the people).

The Cuban detective genre reflects the values of the Revolution and of the *hombre nuevo* or "new man" (a term coined by Che Guevara) which it hopes to create. Some examples of antisocial behavior include: ideological divergence, disloyalty to the regime, and all forms of "extravagance," such as homosexuality or social aberrations. Correct revolutionary conduct requires uniformity and ideological solidarity.

20. The flourishing of documentary texts in revolutionary Cuba is recounted in Alejandro García Alvarez's essay "El testimonio: su divulgación en Cuba revolucionaria" (The Documentary: Its Dissemination in Revolutionary Cuba). The author notes: "La publicación de testimonios por parte de las editoriales cubanas puede ser calificada de abundante. . . . Si se toman en consideración exclusivamente aquellos trabajos de mayor extensión publicados individualmente, el número de obras de este tipo publicadas en los últimos veinte años se aproxima al centenar. Esto implica un promedio de cinco obras anuales que desde luego, no refleja exactamente el ritmo editorial verdadero. Dicho ritmo sólo comenzó a acelerarse entre 1968–1970, para incrementarse significativamente durante la década del setenta y alcanzar su intensidad mayor durante el último quinquenio. En este progresivo auge han jugado un estimulante papel los concursos convocados por la Unión de Escritores y Artistas de Cuba, Casa de las Américas y Ministerio de las Fuerzas Armadas, por sólo mencionar algunos de los más importantes, cuyos premios incluyen la publicación de las obras seleccionadas" (pp. 110–11) (The publication of documentary texts by Cuban editorial houses can be classified as abundant. . . . If one takes into consideration only those longer works that have been published separately in the last twenty years, the number approaches one hundred. This suggests an average of five books per year, a number that does not precisely reflect the actual editorial rate. Documentary texts began to increase during 1968–1970, significantly proliferating during the 1970s and reaching their period of maximum production during the last five years. In this steadily increased production, a decisive role has been played by the literary competitions sponsored by the National Union of Writers and Artists of Cuba, Casa de las Américas, and the Armed Forces Ministry, to mention only a few of the more important, whose prizes include the publication of the winning entries).

21. While Nubya C. Casas ("Novela-testimonio: historia y literatura") proposes that the documentary genre can be traced back to Father Bartolomé de las Casas's transcription of Columbus's diary of discovery, other critics have seen it as a more recent development. (Among others, see the work of John Hollowell, Mas'ud Zavarzadeh, and Barbara Foley.) For purposes of this study there is no need to enter into such a theoretical debate. What is important is that after the 1959 Revolution the genre was in fact actively disseminated in Cuba. The documentary novel in the United States (for example, Truman Capote's *In Cold Blood* and Norman Mailer's *The Executioner's Song*) is totally different from its Cuban counterpart. The North American version is not connected in any way to an official state policy, nor does it contain a political message, as it does in Cuba. I do not

believe that any North American reader is politically stirred as a result of reading either Capote or Mailer. Rather, it is more a case in which the reader is allowed to indulge his or her curiosity regarding the workings of the criminal mind.

22. Che Guevara's testimonial text was one of the first to document the insurrectional struggle. In 1972 Roberto Fernández Retamar described it as "una nueva literatura, caracterizada por su despreocupación de toda moda literaria, y su apego escueto, y por lo mismo conmovedor al hecho real" ("Apuntes sobre revolución y literatura en Cuba," p. 39) (a new literature, characterized by its freedom from all literary conventions and by its solitary, but at the same time moving account of the true facts).

23. John Beverley, "The Margin at the Center: On *Testimonio* (Testimonial Narrative)," p. 14.

24. Miguel Barnet, "El creador y su obra," p. 10.

25. Raúl González de Cascorro, "El género testimonial en Cuba," *Unión*, no. 4 (1978), p. 78.

26. *Casa de las Américas* 11, no. 62 (Sept.–Oct. 1970), p. 226.

27. Lourdes Casal, "La novela en Cuba 1959–1967: una introducción," p. 208. For further discussion on this issue also see Pamela María Smorkaloff's *Literatura y edición de libros*, pp. 265–77.

28. *Granma*, July 30, 1971, p. 4.

29. The January 16, 1975, issue of *Granma* states: "de acuerdo a las nuevas bases los 16 premios [corresponderán] a las tres categorías de ficción (cuento, novela, poesía y teatro), investigación (ensayo y testimonio) y literatura para niños" (p. 3) (in accordance with the new guidelines the 16 prizes [will correspond] to the three categories of fiction (short story, novel, poetry and theater), investigation (essays and documentaries) and children's literature).

30. *Granma*, February 8, 1975, p. 3.

31. *Granma*, January 24, 1975, p. 5.

32. "The Margin at the Center: On *Testimonio* (Testimonial Narrative)," pp. 12–13. John Beverley provides a useful introduction to *testimonio* writing. He dedicates a few pages of his article to establishing a distinction between *testimonio* and "documentary fiction" (pp. 25–26). More than achieving this goal, however, Beverley's argument only illustrates the difficulties in trying to pin down this genre.

33. Nubya C. Casas, "Novela-testimonio: historia y literatura," p. 22.

34. "Las . . . novelas testimoniales de Miguel Barnet tienen como sujeto literario personajes marcados por la otredad" (The literary subjects of Miguel Barnet's documentary novels are marked by their otherness). See Elzbieta Sklodowska, "La visión de la gente sin historia en las novelas testimoniales de Miguel Barnet," p. 60. Ms. Sklodowska has synthesized important parts of her dissertation in the essay "Aproximaciones a la forma testimonial: la novelística de Miguel Barnet."

35. Miguel Barnet, "Testimonio y comunicación: una vía hacia la identidad," p. 142. This very idea of giving voice to the voiceless was introduced by Oscar

Lewis in his anthropological work. In the introduction to *The Children of Sánchez,* Lewis states: "With the aid of the tape recorder, unskilled, uneducated, and even illiterate persons can talk about themselves and relate their observations and experiences . . ." (p. xii). It is interesting to note that Barnet, who had previously hailed Lewis's work, reverses his position after *Project Cuba* is shut down in 1970: "Oscar Lewis que ha escrito un libro como *La vida,* que es un ladrillo que nadie lee. . . . [E]s tremendamente aburrido" (Oscar Lewis who has written a book like *La Vida: A Puerto Rican Family in the Culture of Poverty,* a doorstop that no one reads. . . . [I]t is terribly boring). See Barnet's interview with Emilio Bejel, *Hispamérica* 10, no. 29 (1981): p. 50. Indeed, it appears that the title of Barnet's *La vida real* (The Real Life) is intended as a parodic allusion to Oscar Lewis's work.

36. For a detailed and well-documented study of the controversies surrounding this very issue, see William Luis's essay "The Politics of Memory and Miguel Barnet's *The Autobiography of a Runaway Slave.*"

37. When I asked Arenas about Barnet's novels in 1987, he responded: "Claro. Ese tipo de cosa también interesa mucho al estado porque no son en realidad novelas, son testimonios que se llegan a escribir en forma de libro. Pero son testimonios de la masa que dan una visión histórica, hasta cierto punto dialéctica, marxista. Las novelas de Barnet son como páginas desprendidas del manual del marxismo-leninismo. O sea, aquí tenemos el cimarrón, que es el negro esclavo, ahora viene el proceso en que el cimarrón se independiza y viene la República mediatizada y entonces la corista de *Canción de Rachel.* Finalmente llega la Revolución con *Gallego* y entonces ya es el paraíso. Como si la vida tuviese esa escala política paradisíaca, que todo lo demás es negativo y al final todo es maravilloso con la Revolución" (Naturally, that type of thing also interests the state because they aren't in fact novels, they're testimonies that are written in the form of books. But they're testimonies from the masses that give a historical perspective, up to a point a dialectic, Marxist perspective. Barnet's novels are like pages taken out of the Marxist-Leninist manual. That is, first we have the runaway black slave who becomes free, then comes the republican era with its nominal power, and we are introduced to the singer from *Canción de Rachel.* Finally in *Gallego* we have the Revolution and everything is now paradise. As if in real life there were such a paradisiacal political scale, that everything is negative until in the end all is marvelous with the Revolution) (see appendix, p. 151). This statement makes it quite clear that Arenas was not only aware of Barnet's work but also of the strong support it received by the revolutionary regime.

2. The Pentagonía: Giving Voice to the Voiceless

1. David Viñas's *Los hombres de a caballo,* for example, relates the activities of an Argentine army unit sent to Peru to stop a guerrilla revolt. Viñas's portrayal of corruption and brutality in the Argentine army, supported and influenced by the

imperialistic United States, is anything but subtle. "El chulo regresa" (The Return of the Pimp), a short story from the collection *Gente de playa Girón* by Raúl González de Cascorro, one of Cuba's most outspoken supporters of the documentary novel, was published in the January–February issue of *Casa de las Américas* (2, no. 10, 1962) and is indicative of the type of literature that was actively supported by the Revolution. In this story a pimp, with no redeeming values whatsoever, returns to fight as a soldier in one of the battalions of the Bay of Pigs invasion. The story ends with the protagonist violently drowning a fellow black soldier whom he describes as "a repulsive monster." Eventually the pimp also drowns after his boat is destroyed by the Cuban Air Force. Finally, the stories of *Cualquiercosario* by Jorge Onetti all use a common, functional language to reject bourgeois values and support the social world of the proletariat.

2. *Literatura y edición de libros*, p. 146. In her book Smorkaloff provides a study of the post-revolutionary Cuban literary enterprise. She attempts to review the new social functions of the writer, reader, and the literary publishing industry that began with the triumph of the 1959 Revolution. For this purpose she investigates the extraliterary factors (for example, publishing infrastructure, mechanical aspects of production, literary workshops, and competitions that were created to foster further writing) that were and still are responsible for the increased production of (state-supported) literature on the island.

3. For a summarized account of the author's fall from grace with the Cuban revolutionary government, see Enrico Mario Santí, "Entrevista con Reinaldo Arenas." This interview was conducted shortly after Arenas left Cuba in 1980. For a more detailed account of Arenas's problems in Cuba, see the author's autobiography, *Antes que anochezca*.

4. In the interview that appears in the appendix of this book (p. 141), Arenas states that he had preferred the original title *Celestino antes del alba* for the 1982 edition. However, since the original had been published in Cuba there was the theoretical possibility of copyright infringement.

5. Whether Arenas's use of the words *testigo* (witness) and *testimonio* (testimony) specifically refers to the generic structure of the documentary novel or to the broader question of moral witness is not important. It has been shown how the cultural policy makers of the Revolution actively promoted a documentary-testimonial realism to assist in the deployment of a new revolutionary consciousness. Arenas was indeed aware of this and was also quite aware, as I demonstrated earlier, of Miguel Barnet's work and the strong support it received by the revolutionary regime. Hence, my thesis that Arenas drew material from, and built off, the Cuban documentary novel tradition in order to articulate his own particular concerns should not be controversial.

6. At the First National Congress on Education and Culture in 1971 it was stated that in Cuba "the cultural media cannot serve as a medium for the proliferation of false intellectuals who try to convert snobbishness, extravagance, homosexuality,

and other social aberrations into expressions of revolutionary art, and who are far removed from the masses and from the spirit of our Revolution" (Tzvi Medin, *Cuba: The Shaping of Revolutionary Consciousness*, p. 23).

7. Monica Morley and Enrico Mario Santí, "Reinaldo Arenas y su mundo alucinante: una entrevista," p. 118.

8. In fact, it was the manuscript of *Otra vez el mar* that was confiscated and destroyed twice by the Cuban security police while Arenas was in Cuba. The author recounts his protracted struggles to rewrite and hide the manuscript of this novel in his autobiography, *Antes que anochezca*.

9. In 1980, the same year he escaped from Cuba during the Mariel exodus, Arenas granted the *Nouvel Observateur* an interview (later translated into English in *Encounter*, January 1982) in which he spoke out against the hostility of the Cuban revolutionary regime toward subversive individuals, uncommitted writers, and homosexuals. In this interview, Arenas maintained that while he lived in Cuba, the expression of any form of difference or opposition was considered counterrevolutionary, for it went against the archetype of the disciplined revolutionary.

As early as 1965 forced labor camps under the name of UMAP (an acronym for Unidades Militares de Ayuda a la Producción or Military Units for Aid to Production) were constructed in the province of Camagüey for the purpose of correcting so-called antisocial and deviant behaviors that, according to the government, threatened the creation of a true revolutionary consciousness. This period of repression has been documented by Néstor Almendros and Orlando Jiménez-Leal in their 1984 film *Conducta impropia* (Improper Conduct). *Conducta impropia* is made up of individual testimonies that document the atrocities committed by the Cuban revolutionary government against homosexuals. In the film Arenas himself recounts his experiences with homosexual discrimination while living in Cuba. During the height of the homosexual purges, Arenas states that any individual who was identified as homosexual or "extravagant" was carted off to a UMAP camp for not adapting to the revolutionary model. Allen Young's account of homophobia in Cuba (*Gays under the Cuban Revolution*, 1981) supports Arenas's accusations of the regime's intolerance toward any manifestation of "extravagant" behavior. Allen Young writes: "The people carted off to UMAP camps included youths who showed 'too much' concern with their personal appearance (long hair, colorful clothing, etc.); they were said to be victims of *la enfermedad* (the disease) or of 'cultural imperialism' "(p. 22).

10. In 1968 Arenas delivered a supportive paper on García Márquez's *Cien años de soledad* at the University of Havana entitled "*Cien años de soledad* en la ciudad de los espejismos." The paper was later published in Peter Earle's collection of essays titled *Gabriel García Márquez*, pp. 51–58. Over the years García Márquez has been an active and highly visible political supporter of Fidel Castro. Since his arrival in the United States in 1980, Arenas was extremely critical of García Márquez for his support of Castro and made his views repeatedly known in articles

hostile to the Colombian Nobel laureate. See, for example, "Gabriel García Márquez, ¿esbirro o es burro?" (pp. 66–69) and "Gabriel García Márquez, C. de M." (p. 245) in *Necesidad de libertad*.

11. Arenas appears to have done his math correctly when he makes Esteban Montejo "un anciano de más de 130 años" (an old man of more than 130 years). In *Biografía de un cimarrón*, published in 1966, Montejo is presented as being 104 years old. Thus, if Montejo lived to 1999, the story time of *El color del verano*, he would indeed be around 133 years old.

12. In Cuban slang a person who hides behind a mask or does not reveal his or her true self is accused of having a *barniz* (literally, "varnish." An English equivalent might be "veneer"). Throughout *Antes que anochezca* Arenas refers to Barnet as *Miguel Barniz*. The editorial house that published the autobiography (Barcelona: Tusquets Editores) decided to use the name *Miguel Barniz* in order to avoid legal problems with Barnet, who is depicted in a very negative light in the autobiography.

3. The First-Person Narrative Voice

1. For a more detailed explanation of *mimesis of process* and how Linda Hutcheon distinguishes it from *mimesis of product* see chapter 2, "Process and Product: The Implications of Metafiction for the Theory of the Novel as a Mimetic Genre," of *Narcissistic Narrative: The Metafictional Paradox*.

2. Utilizing Gérard Genette's terminology (as presented in *Narrative Discourse: An Essay in Method* and *Narrative Discourse Revisited*), the child-narrator/Celestino, Fortunato, Héctor, Gabriel/Reinaldo/the Tétrica Mofeta, and the nameless narrator of *El asalto* would be considered *homodiegetic narrators,* that is, narrators who are also characters in the situations and events recounted (*diégèse*).

3. With Descartes's famous maxim "cogito ergo sum"—the belief that a conscious, willing, thinking self, soul, or mind exists—modern philosophy was born as a system identifying the locus of "truth" within human self-consciousness. The basic principles of Cartesian rationalism have persisted into the present. Standing at the threshold of the twentieth century, Nietzsche was the first philosopher to shatter the privileged oneness and unity of the subject by insisting on the forces of difference and plurality at work in all consciousness. In *The Will to Power* he states: "The assumption of one single subject is perhaps unnecessary; perhaps it is just as permissible to assume a multiplicity of subjects, whose interaction and struggle is the basis of our thought and our consciousness in general? A kind of aristocracy of 'cells' in which dominion resides? To be sure, an aristocracy of equals, used to ruling jointly and understanding how to command? *My hypothesis*: The subject as multiplicity" (p. 270).

4. Eliseo Diego, "Sobre *Celestino antes del alba*," p. 163. I am also reminded of Paul de Man's declaration concerning Borges's work: "The creation of beauty

thus begins as an act of duplicity. The writer engenders another self that is his mirror-like reversal. In this anti-self, the virtues and the vices of the original are curiously distorted and reversed," Paul de Man, "A Modern Master," p. 8.

5. In "The Margin at the Center: On *Testimonio* (Testimonial Narrative)" John Beverley states: "One should note [in *testimonios*] the insistence on and affirmation of the individual subject evident in titles like *I, Rigoberta Menchú* (even more strongly in Spanish: *Me llamo Rigoberta Menchú y así me nació la conciencia*)" (p. 17).

In 1982, in an interview with José Batalló, Barnet stated that the individual whose story is recreated in *Canción de Rachel* was the actress Amalia Sorg. According to Barnet, the collage of voices that make up *Canción de Rachel* do not need to have a fixed reality outside of the text to establish authenticity; the proper name "Rachel" acts as a nominal unit for a collection of characteristics that establishes an equivalent relationship between the narrative sign and the sum. See José Batalló's interview with Miguel Barnet, "Encuentros con Miguel Barnet," pp. 51–60.

6. The use of the double in *Celestino antes del alba* is not limited to the child-narrator/Celestino pair. This pair further proliferates in the choruses of voices present in the text. Toward the end of the novel the narrative "I" of the child-narrator becomes lost in a dramatic scene in which a theatrical carnival of family members' voices are united to a chorus of elves, goblins, witches, and dead cousins. The use of the personal pronoun *nosotros* (we) by these choruses of voices is at times (con)fused with the personal pronoun *yo* (I) of the child-narrator. In her book *Reinaldo Arenas: narrativa de transgresión* Perla Rozencvaig states: "El coro de duendes también se confabula con el protagonista. . . . [Al] final de la historia [Celestino] reencarna en un duende, mientras el narrador se queda contando las nubes en cuyas caprichosas formas busca nuevos estímulos su imaginación. Si Liebgeher aumentó el número de *doppelgänger* a cinco, Arenas lo sobrepasó, haciendo imposible precisar cuántos son en total los dobles del personaje" (p. 59) (The chorus of elves also confabulates with the protagonist. . . . At the end of the story [Celestino] is reincarnated as an elf, while the narrator counts clouds, seeking further stimulus for his imagination in their capricious forms. If Liebgeher increased the number of doppelgänger to five, Arenas went beyond, making it virtually impossible to say how many doubles the character has).

7. According to Bakhtin, although the menippea takes its name from Menippus of Gadara (third century B.C.), it was Marcus Terentius Varro who introduced the term by calling his satires "saturae menippeae." Mikhail Bakhtin, *Problems of Dostoevsky's Poetics*, pp. 112–13.

8. Humor is an aspect of Arenas's work that colors his language and is an integral part of his narrative style. In the pentalogy laughter is much more than derision or mockery, it is utilized by the characters as a positive strategy for survival. In *El desamparado humor de Reinaldo Arenas* Roberto Valero observes: "Es curioso destacar, ya que nuestras aproximaciones están en función de la obra

de Reinaldo Arenas, que las dictaduras, cualquiera que éstas sean (nazismo, sta-linismo, franquismo, castrismo . . .) imponen su férrea censura prácticamente en todos los campos del pensamiento, pero sobre todo, en cualquier manifestación humorística" (p. 37) (It is curious to point out, and our assumptions are made in light of Reinaldo Arenas's work, that dictatorships, whatever they may be [Na-zism, Stalinism, Francoism, Castroism . . .] impose an ironfisted censorship on virtually all fields of thought, and especially on any humorous manifestation).

9. See Ernesto Méndez y Soto, *Panorama de la novela cubana de la Revolución (1959–1970)*; George R. McMurray, *Spanish American Writing Since 1941*; Kessel Schwartz, *A New History of Spanish American Fiction*, among others.

10. Present in the death of Carmelina is a foreshadowing synthesis of both Fortunato and Adolfina of *El palacio de las blanquísimas mofetas*; Fortunato is supposedly hanged by the Batista police and Adolfina sets herself afire. This meta-morphosis or permutation of the character (Carmelina into Fortunato and Adol-fina) further illustrates the pentalogy's dismantling of the notion of a concrete and stable subjectivity. In Arenas's novels characterization is not closed or finalized, but proceeds like a continuous permutation, what Julia Kristeva calls the "subject-in-process" (*The Kristeva Reader*, p. 15), from one novel to the next.

11. Within Cuban slang *pájaro* (bird) is a pejorative term used to refer to homo-sexuals. Throughout the novel Celestino is accused of being *loco* (crazy), *pervertido* (perverted), *maricón* (faggot) simply because he writes poetry. The poet Celes-tino, like the homosexual, is ostracized and becomes the victim of scorn simply because he is different. The representation of homosexuality, hinted at in this first novel, becomes more explicit in Arenas's future novels. See my article "*Celestino antes del alba*: escritura subversiva/sexualidad transgresiva" for a more detailed study of this theme.

12. Rita Guibert was the first to speak of Cabrera Infante's novel as a "gallery of voices." See "The Tongue-Twisted Tiger," p. 14.

13. Perla Rozencvaig, "Entrevista," *Hispamérica* (1981), pp. 47–48.

14. This deconstruction of gender is not a case of metamorphosis as it is, for example, in Virginia Woolf's *Orlando* (a character who incidently makes a brief appearance in Arenas's *El mundo alucinante*). Also, in Julio Cortázar's *Rayuela*, a novel where the use of the doppelgänger is central to the story, the double is limited to the same-sex combination La Maga–Talita and Oliveira-Traveler.

15. Jay Cantor's review (*New York Times Book Review*) of the English translation of *Otra vez el mar* (*Farewell to the Sea*) criticizes Arenas for not having granted the wife "a wider life, given her a name." This suggestion obviously reveals a lack of understanding of the role of the nameless wife within the novel.

16. Perla Rozencvaig, "Reinaldo Arenas's Last Interview," p. 79.

17. Perla Rozencvaig calls this a heterodiegetic narrator. See "Entrevista," *Hispa-mérica*, p. 47. In *Narrative Discourse* Gérard Genette states: "We will therefore distinguish here between two types of narrative: one with the narrator absent from

the story he tells, the other with the narrator present as a character in the story he tells. I call the first type, for obvious reasons, *heterodiegetic*, and the second type *homodiegetic*" (pp. 244–45).

18. Perla Rozencvaig, "Entrevista" (*Hispamérica*, 1981), p. 47.

19. In the first four novels of the pentalogy the presentation of the figure of the mother fluctuates between two diametrically opposed images: the loving, caring, affectionate and nurturing mother and the brutal, diabolical, chastising witch. In *Otra vez el mar* there is a foreshadowing of the last novel of the pentalogy in the allegory of the tyrannical Great Big Mama of *Canto segundo,* a type of tropical female Big Brother. This diabolical mother, malevolent, forever vigilant, described as cupping her imaginary testicles, attempts to procreate an ideal society of the future. The allegory is centered around her pursuit of a couple whose only crime is that they wish to escape to a place where dreaming is permitted. But their refusal to adhere to her orders drives Great Big Mama into a frenzy, for she is not accustomed to disobedience by her faithful subjects who, always submissive, have modeled themselves after the dog ("¡El perro! ¡El perro! SEAMOS COMO EL," *Otra vez,* p. 243; "The dog! The dog! LET US ALL BE LIKE HIM," *Farewell,* p. 215). Thus begins an interplanetary search for the fugitives: it ends in their deaths, but at the cost of an apocalyptic destruction of the universe. For Arenas's own comments on the presentation of the figure of the mother in his novels, see the conversation in the appendix, pp. 143–44.

4. "Real" Witnesses

1. Elzbieta Sklodowska, "La visión de la gente sin historia en las novelas testimoniales de Miguel Barnet," p. 21.

2. Adriana Méndez, "Conversación con Miguel Barnet," p. 42.

3. Ramón López, "El danzón de Rachel," p. 122.

4. Nedda G. de Anhalt, "Reinaldo Arenas: *aquel* mar, una vez más," pp. 153–54.

5. Miguel Barnet, "Celestino antes y después del alba," p. 21.

6. Reinaldo Arenas, "Magia y persecución en José Martí," p. 13.

7. In *Problems of Dostoevsky's Poetics* Bakhtin speaks of the "crisis dream" that leads to rebirth and renewal. The dream of the boy in Wilde's story is indeed a crisis dream. This type of dream, however, is not the kind that is present in *Celestino antes del alba,* where dreams are more in line with the tradition of the menippean satire in which dreams destroy the unity of a represented life. "The dream [is] . . . counterposed to ordinary life as *another* possible life. Such an opposition (from one or another viewpoint) appears for the first time in the menippea. The dream is introduced there precisely as the *possibility* of a completely different life, a life organized according to laws different from those governing ordinary life (sometimes directly as an 'inside-out-world')." Mikhail Bakhtin, *Problems of Dostoevsky's Poetics,* p. 147.

8. Emir Rodríguez Monegal informs us in *Jorge Luis Borges: A Literary Biography* (pp. 274–75) that this poem first appeared in *Sur* (December 1936, pp. 71–72) and was later included in the 1943 edition of *Poemas*.

9. In his essay "Sobre Oscar Wilde" (*Otras Inquisiciones*) Borges notes the peculiar difference between the nightmarish work of Chesterton, who in life led a joyous existence, and the unassailable innocence of the work of Wilde, who was the victim of imprisonment, bankruptcy, and scandal. It is precisely this element of innocence, an ability to maintain virtuous simplicity in the face of continual abuse, that appears as the most salient characteristic of the child-narrator/Celestino of *Celestino antes del alba*.

10. Arenas's texts, with their comic view of the world, clearly draw from the popular humor of Caribbean laughter. In Cuba this particular brand of laughter and joking has been termed *choteo*. The *choteo* is the prevalent use of derision and practical jokes, an attitude of not taking anything too seriously: "[E]l choteo ataca o esquiva por medio de la burla lo demasiado serio, si por tal se entiende lo que el choteador estima demasiado autorizado o ejemplar" (Jorge Mañach, *Indagación del choteo*, p. 17) (Through its mockery *choteo* attacks or avoids that which is too serious, meaning that which the *choteador* considers to be exceedingly respectable or that which is presented as exemplary).

11. Reinaldo Arenas, "La vida es riesgo o abstinencia," p. 56.

5. Chronology

1. Raúl González de Cascorro, "El género testimonial en Cuba," pp. 78–79.

2. From Perla Rozencvaig's 1981 interview (*Hispamérica*) with Arenas, p. 43.

3. In Miguel Barnet's interview with Arenas, "Celestino antes y después del alba," Arenas explains his transgression of time: "En esta novela he tratado de que el tiempo quede deformado, de tal manera que llegue a desaparecer. El tiempo no existe en esta obra. Me parece que sólo hay una manera eficaz de hacer que el tiempo desaparezca, y es eliminando la muerte. . . . Por eso en esta novela los personajes son inmortales; parece como si murieran, y luego surgen de nuevo, riéndose de toda acción temporal" (p. 21) (In this novel I have attempted to deform time in such a way that it seems to disappear. Time doesn't exist in this novel. I feel that there's only one way to make time disappear, and that's by eliminating death. . . . That's why all the characters are immortal in this novel; they seem to die only to reappear laughing at all temporal action.)

4. Concerning the symbol of the sea Robert Alter states: "When we encounter the symbolic presence of the sea—to cite a central example—in symbolist fictions like Conrad's *Nostromo,* Mann's *Death in Venice,* Joyce's *Ulysses,* Virginia Woolf's *To the Lighthouse,* and Agnon's *Betrothed,* the symbol, now in the foreground, becomes so potently semantic that discursive reason can no longer encompass it: the sea is at once the source of life and form and the image of dissolution, the

pulsating surge of Eros and the corrosive wash of indifferent death" (*Motives for Fiction,* p. 135).

At one point (p. 148) in the interview that appears in the appendix I suggest to Arenas that the image of the sea in *Otra vez el mar* appears as both freedom and incarceration. His reply: "En todas mis novelas se plantea una constante dualidad contradictoria que es característica de todo ser humano" (All my novels pose a constant and contradictory duality, which is characteristic of every human being). After this Arenas then proceeded to read the following passage from his essay "Fray Servando, víctima infatigable" ("Fray Servando, Tireless Victim"): "No me cansaré de descubrir que el árbol de las seis de la mañana no es éste de las doce del día, ni aquél, cuyo halo nos consuela al anochecer. Y ese aire que en la noche avanza, ¿puede ser el mismo de la mañana? Y esas aguas marinas que el nadador del atardecer surca cortándolas como un pastel, ¿son acaso las de las doce del día? Influyendo, de manera tan evidente, el tiempo en un árbol o en un paisaje, ¿permanecemos nosotros, las criaturas más sensibles, inmunes a tales señales? Creo todo lo contrario: somos crueles y tiernos, egoístas y generosos, apasionados y meditativos, lacónicos y estruendosos, terribles y sublimes, como el mar . . ." (*El mundo alucinante,* pp. 16–17); "I will never tire of discovering that the tree of six o'clock in the morning is not the tree of noon, nor that tree whose soughing brings us consolation at evening. And that breeze that springs up at night, can it possibly be the same breeze as at morning? And that ocean water the swimmer cuts through at sunset as though it were meringue, are those the choppy waters of midday? As time flows, permeates, so obviously and fully, into a tree or a beach or a landscape, can we, the earth's most sensitive creatures, remain insensitive to its signs? I think not—we are cruel and tender, greedy and generous, impassioned and meditative, laconic and rowdy, terrible and sublime, like the ocean . . ." (*The Ill-fated Peregrinations of Fray Servando,* p. xviii).

5. Bakhtin used the term *chronotope,* literally "time-space," to designate the intrinsic interconnectedness of time and space relationships as they are artistically represented in literature. Borrowed from mathematics, where it was introduced and adapted as part of Einstein's theory of relativity, the term designates the spatiotemporal organization characteristic of all literature. In *The Dialogic Imagination* (p. 84) Bakhtin argues that the word's special scientific meaning is not important for purposes of literary criticism; he merely borrows the term as a metaphor—but then adds parenthetically, "almost, but not entirely" as a metaphor. The link to Einstein's revolutionary theories should not be totally ignored. Beyond laying the foundation for modern physics, Einstein's work contained philosophical implications suggesting that our human understanding and relationship to reality will always be relative. These powerful questions proposed by Einstein at the beginning of the twentieth century dramatically challenged the homogeneous and rational laws of seventeenth-century Newtonian cosmology. Einstein's introduction of the relativity of individual perception into the objectified view of

Newton's universe completely refuted Newtonian concepts of absolute time and absolute space that had survived over two hundred years and acquired the status of scientific dogma. Einstein's theory of relativity disproved the classical conception of separateness of time and space by arguing that we cannot experience space in the abstract, independent of the matter that fills it, nor can we experience absolute time, since time experienced by separate observers differs according to their relative motion. Likewise, for Bakhtin the literary artistic chronotope is but the fusion of spatial and temporal coordinates that appears within each literary genre. In the glossary to *The Dialogic Imagination* there appears a brief definition of the term: "Literally, 'time-space.' A unit of analysis for studying texts according to the ratio and nature of the temporal and spatial categories represented. The distinctiveness of this concept as opposed to most other uses of time and space in literary analysis lies in the fact that neither category is privileged; they are utterly interdependent" (*The Dialogic Imagination*, p. 425).

6. According to Bakhtin, the carnival was not just a ritual in the European culture of the late Middle Ages and Renaissance, but rather a way of inverting and reinvigorating the official seriousness of culture and authority. However, according to Bakhtin, this festive carnivalesque humor, which had flourished since antiquity (the Roman Saturnalias) and climaxed during the sixteenth century, began to lose power in the seventeenth century. The deterioration of subversive humor was largely due to the stabilization of the new absolute monarchy, the aesthetics of classicism reflecting the seriousness of the new culture, and Cartesian rationalistic philosophy (*Rabelais and His World*, p. 101). A popular spirit of classicism and rationalism came to characterize the new official culture of the seventeenth century. The process was completed in the eighteenth century, when singularity became indisputable; Voltaire, for example, criticized Rabelais's work for being extravagant and nonsensical (*Rabelais and His World*, pp. 116–17).

7. Perla Rozencvaig, "Reinaldo Arenas's Last Interview," p. 80.

6. Documentation

1. The novel also contains seven footnotes (pp. 195–200)—left out of the English translation—that are rather erudite and far removed from the rural atmosphere of the novel. These are to be accommodated by each reader, who will find their applicability difficult to validate. In *El desamparado humor de Reinaldo Arenas* (p. 103), Roberto Valero reproduces an interview with Arenas in which he asked about these obscure footnotes:

Valero: "Pero esas citas tan eruditas al pie de la página. Por ejemplo aquí en la 143 dice: 'El ramo del poeta,' inspirado en un poema de Mao Wensi, poeta de la dinastía rebelde de los Chou (Tsin Chou). Nota: El Palacio de Cristal de la Luna. . . ."

Arenas: "Claro, pero es el mismo tono de lo que ha aparecido dentro de la novela. . . . La parte teatral es como el resumen de la novela. . . . [Es] la culminación del proceso de la novela. Cuando llega la parte dramática en que los personajes se mezclan las citas son personajes también, participan como cosa dramática."

(*Valero:* But these erudite footnotes. For example, here on page 143 it says: "The branch of the poet," inspired by a poem by Mao Wensi, a poet from the rebel dynasty of the Chous (Tsin Chou). Note: The Glass Palace of the Moon. . . ."

Arenas: Of course, but it's the same tone that has appeared up to that point in the novel. . . . [It's] the culmination of the novelistic process. The play mixes the characters and footnotes, the footnotes in themselves acting as characters, participating dramatically.)

From the above quote it is obvious that Arenas intended these footnotes to add to the chorus of voices already present in the novel.

2. *El palacio de las blanquísimas mofetas* incorporates banal newspaper articles and advertisements—for example, an advertisement for a local theater (p. 74), a funeral home (p. 182), Pond's cold cream (p. 227), a laxative (p. 247), and so forth—alongside reports of controversial revolutionary activity. The *boletines* (bulletins) serve as the official mouthpiece for the revolutionary struggle. The first reports concerning the insurrectional struggle begin far into the novel (*El palacio,* p. 177) with rapidly increasing testimony of military advances into the "fifth agony." These so-called official versions are juxtaposed with articles from four other periodicals: the newspaper "El Norte," the biweekly "La Justicia," the local "El Eco de Holguín," and the magazine "Cuadernos populares." These four periodicals serve as mouthpieces for the established government and concern themselves more with such events as the weather, the Pope's birthday, beauty hints, and so forth, than with the military advances of the Revolution. All these subtexts or intertexts parallel the cacophony of family voices already present within the novel.

3. The seventh version also introduces the story of *Otra vez el mar.* Here the reader is introduced to the figure of the young girl who falls in love with her cousin along with other elements that will make up the story of the nameless wife and Héctor in the subsequent novel of the pentalogy.

4. In the old Soviet Union a samizdat was a dissenting manuscript whose official publication was forbidden. It was reproduced by typewriting copies and carbons and then circulating them clandestinely.

5. The tongue twister dedicated to Virgilio Piñera (*El color,* p. 136) is an exception, for in it Arenas playfully pays homage to a famous Cuban writer whom he greatly admired:

"Bar, ber, bir, bor, bur, ver, vir . . . ¡Ah, Virgen!, el virgo de Virgilio birlado. ¿En qué barbacana, en qué barbacoa, en qué bergantín varado en Birmania, en qué burdo burdel de Burdeos, en qué barandal infernal en que un barbudo de Borneo en sin igual albur le dijo abur? ¡No!, ni bergantín ni bergante ni verga albergaron sin embargo tal virgo. Una mañana, en simple verbena abierta, un San Bernardo Burlado abordado por el bardo desesperado lo birló con su bermejo berbiquí a cambio de unas berenjenas" (*El color del verano*, p. 136) (Bar, ber, bir, bor, bur, ver, vir . . . Oh Virgin, Virgilio's virginity knocked down and tarnished! In what barbican, in what loft, in what isolated brig in Burma, in what seedy brothel in Bordeaux, on what infernal banister where a bearded man without equal from Borneo said to him goodbye? No! Neither brig nor scoundrel nor penis was able to lodge that Virgo. One morning, in an outdoor fair, an outwitted Saint Bernard approached by the desperate bard knocked him down with his red carpenter's brace just to get his eggplants).

7. Mistrust of Literary Forms

1. This well-defined assertion that places the documentary goal of the book over any aesthetic considerations in *Biografía de un cimarrón* lost its authority in Barnet's later novels. While *Biografía de un cimarrón* was unanimously applauded for its fidelity in representing its era—slavery and the War of Independence— many criticized *Canción de Rachel* for its frivolity. Still, other critics have defended the majority of Barnet's novels as documentary texts. In 1990 Angel Luis Fernández Guerra defended the term *documentary novel* for Barnet's *Biografía de un cimarrón, Canción de Rachel, Gallego*, and *La vida real* in an article published in *Casa de las Américas* entitled "Edipo y Cayo Graco (Para leer a Miguel Barnet)." Fernández Guerra does state, however, that Barnet's latest novel, *Oficio de ángel* (1989), is a post-documentary text "porque aquí sí el creador asume la personalidad del yo-narrador, del informante, y se convierte en objeto informativo de sí mismo" (p. 52) (because here the creator assumes the personality of the narrator, of the informer, and converts himself into an object of information).

2. What is translated in brackets only appears in the Spanish edition and has been left out of the English translation. The phrase obviously alludes to Celestino, the imaginary creation of the child-narrator of *Celestino antes del alba*.

3. Dashes as well as parentheses are generally used to introduce supplementary information that complements and explains stated ideas. In contrast, Arenas often utilizes dashes and parentheses as subversive tools (counter-statements) that undermine and challenge a cohesive flow of ideas, thus further opening and modifying the text. As a result of these transgressive interruptions the reader is forced to revise beliefs, accommodate new positions, and make more complex inferences concerning his customary codes and expectations.

4. This passage repeats in spirit the scene from Virginia Woolf's *Orlando* in which the young Orlando faces a similar frustration in attempting to describe the color green: "He was describing, as all young poets are forever describing, nature, and in order to match the shade of green precisely he looked (and here he showed more audacity than most) at the thing itself, which happened to be a laurel bush growing beneath the window. After that, of course, he could write no more. Green in nature is one thing, green in literature another. Nature and letters seem

to have a natural antipathy; bring them together and they tear each other to pieces" (pp. 16–17).

5. Hayden White has proposed that irony clearly reflects the sentiment that language does not reveal "reality" but rather obscures it. This ironic unmasking of the ambiguities of language as a precise tool of expression is at the heart of "Monstruo." Hayden White writes: "Irony thus represents a stage of consciousness in which the problematical nature of language itself has been recognized. It points to the potential foolishness of all linguistic characterizations of reality as much as to the absurdity of the beliefs it parodies" (*Metahistory: The Historical Imagination in Nineteenth Century Europe*, p. 57).

6. I use the terms *self-conscious* and *metafictional literature* to refer to a type of writing that refers to itself and to those elements or components by which it is constituted and communicated. For these concepts I have consulted Robert Alter, *Partial Magic: The Novel as a Self-Conscious Genre*, and Linda Hutcheon, *Narcissistic Narrative: The Metafictional Paradox*.

8. Reinterpreting and Rewriting Recorded History

1. P. H. Nowell-Smith, "Historical Facts," p. 323, as quoted in Didier Coste's *Narrative as Communication*, p. 21.

2. Although, to varying degrees, a political discourse is present in the novels of the pentalogy, these texts do not make politics the sole reason for the characters' frustrations. What John Alexander Coleman has stated in regard to *Otra vez el mar* is equally true of the other novels: ". . . this is not denunciatory fiction, though politics weighs heavily enough on . . . [the wife and Héctor's] ruminations." From a letter written by Coleman to Kathryn Court of Penguin Books concerning the English translation of *Otra vez el mar*. Found in Arenas's correspondence 1980–83, housed at the Princeton University library.

BIBLIOGRAPHY

Works by Reinaldo Arenas

Books

Where published English-language translations exist, their titles are given in brackets. See "English Translations" below.

Celestino antes del alba [*Singing from the Well*]. Havana: Ediciones Unión, 1967. Quotations in this volume are taken from the 1982 edition (see *Cantando en el pozo,* below).

Con los ojos cerrados. Montevideo: Editorial Arca, 1972.

La Vieja Rosa ["Old Rosa" in *Old Rose: A Novel in Two Stories*]. Caracas: Editorial Arte, 1980.

El central [*El Central: A Cuban Sugar Mill*]. Barcelona: Seix Barral, 1981.

Termina el desfile. Barcelona: Seix Barral, 1981.

Cantando en el pozo [*Singing from the Well*]. Barcelona: Editorial Argos Vergara, 1982.

El mundo alucinante [*Hallucinations/The Ill-fated Peregrinations of Fray Servando*]. Caracas: Monte Avila Editores, 1982.

El palacic de las blanquísimas mofetas [*The Palace of the White Skunks*]. Barcelona: Editorial Argos Vergara, 1982.

Otra vez el mar [*Farewell to the Sea*]. Barcelona: Editorial Argos Vergara, 1982.

Arturo, la estrella más brillante ["The Brightest Star" in *Old Rose: A Novel in Two Stories*]. Barcelona: Montesinos, 1984.

Lazarillo de Tormes (lecturas fáciles). New York: Regents Publishing Company, 1984.

Necesidad de libertad (*Mariel: testimonios de un intelectual disidente*). México: Kosmos-Editorial, 1986.

Persecución (*Cinco piezas de teatro experimental*). Miami: Ediciones Universal, 1986.

La Loma del Angel [*Graveyard of the Angels*]. Málaga: DADOR/ediciones, 1987.

El portero [*The Doorman*]. Málaga: DADOR/ediciones, 1989.

Voluntad de vivir manifestándose. Madrid: Editorial Betania, 1989.

Leprosorio (*Trilogía poética*). Madrid: Editorial Betania, 1990.

Un plebiscito a Fidel Castro (with Jorge Camacho). Madrid: Editorial Betania, 1990.

Viaje a La Habana. Miami: Ediciones Universal, 1990.

El asalto. Miami: Ediciones Universal, 1991.

El color del verano. Miami: Ediciones Universal, 1991.

Final de un cuento. Huelva: Diputación Provincial de Huelva, 1991.

Antes que anochezca (*Autobiografía*) [*Before Night Falls*]. Barcelona: Tusquets Editores, 1992.

Stories, Essays, Reviews, and Other Literary Fragments Published in Cuba

"La punta del arcoiris," "Soledad," and "La puerta del sol." *Unión* 4, no. 1 (1965): 113–19.

"Con los ojos cerrados." *Unión* 5, no. 4 (1966): 12–15.

"El encadenamiento del fraile." *La Gaceta de Cuba* 5, no. 53 (1966): 6.

"Celestino y yo." *Unión* 6, no. 3 (1967): 117–20.

"El hijo y la madre." *Unión* 6, no. 4 (1967): 222–26.

"Estancia en Pamplona." *Casa de las Américas* 7, no. 43 (1967): 87–90.

"Benítez entra en el juego." Review of *Tute de reyes. Unión* 7, no. 2 (1968): 146–52.

"Carta a la revista *Mundo Nuevo.*" *La Gaceta de Cuba* 6, no. 66 (1968): 16.

"Magia y persecución en José Martí." *La Gaceta de Cuba* 6, no. 66 (1968): 13–16.

"Bajo el signo de enero." Review of *Viento de enero. La Gaceta de Cuba* 7, no. 67 (1968): 20.

"Literatura y revolución (Encuesta): los autores." *Casa de las Américas* 9, nos. 51–52 (1968): 119, 164.

"A la sombra de la mata de almendras." *La Gaceta de Cuba* 7, no. 69 (1969): 5–7.

"Tres mujeres y el amor." Review of *Tres mujeres. La Gaceta de Cuba* 7, no. 71 (1969): 26–28.

"El páramo en llamas." In *Recopilación de textos sobre Juan Rulfo,* edited by Antonio Benítez Rojo, 60–63. Havana: Casa de las Américas, 1969.

"Con los ojos abiertos." Review of *Abrir y cerrar los ojos. La Gaceta de Cuba* 8, no. 81 (1970): 10–11.

"Mariana entre los hombres." Review of *Mariana. La Gaceta de Cuba* 8, no. 86 (1970): 28–29.

"Tres sobre la mosca." *La Gaceta de Cuba* 8, no. 87 (1970): 9.

"El reino de la imagen." *La Gaceta de Cuba* 8, no. 88 (1970): 23–26.

"Granados en la casa del sol." Review of *El viento en la casa sol. La Gaceta de Cuba* 8, no. 88 (1970): 30.

"El palacio de las blanquísimas mofetas." *Unión* 9, no. 4 (1970): 37–45.

"En la ciudad de los espejismos." In *Gabriel García Márquez*, edited Peter G. Earle, 151–58. Madrid: Taurus Ediciones, 1981.

Selected Interviews

With Miguel Barnet. "Celestino antes y después del alba." *La Gaceta de Cuba* 6, no. 60 (1967): 21.

With Enrico Mario Santí. "Entrevista con Reinaldo Arenas." *Vuelta* 47 (1980): 18–25.

With Jorge Olivares and Nivia Montenegro. "Conversación con Reinaldo Arenas." *Taller literario* 1, no. 2 (1980): 53–67.

With Franz Olivier-Giesbert. "Pourquoi j'ai fui Fidel Castro." *Le Nouvel Observateur* no. 880 (September 19–25, 1981): 64–68. Later reprinted as "Dangerous Manuscripts: A Conversation with Reinaldo Arenas." *Encounter* 58, no. 1 (January 1982): 60–67.

With Perla Rozencvaig. "Entrevista." *Hispamérica* 10, no. 28 (1981): 41–48.

With Rita M. Molinero. "Donde no hay furia y desgarro no hay literatura." *Quimera*, no. 17 (1982): 19–23.

With Mónica Morley and Enrico Mario Santí. "Reinaldo Arenas y su mundo alucinante: una entrevista." *Hispania* 66 (March 1983): 114–18.

With Nedda G. de Anhalt. "Reinaldo Arenas: *aquel* mar, una vez más." 1987 interview in *Rojo y naranja sobre rojo*. México: Editorial Vuelta, 1991: 133–67.

With Carlos Espinosa Domínguez. "La vida es riesgo o abstinencia." *Quimera*, no. 101 (1990): 54–61.

With Perla Rozencvaig. "Reinaldo Arenas's Last Interview." *Review: Latin American Literature and Arts* 44 (January–June 1991): 78–83.

English Translations

Hallucinations (translation of *El mundo alucinante*). Trans. Gordon Brotherson. New York: Harper and Row, 1971.

El Central: A Cuban Sugar Mill (translation of *El central*). Trans. Anthony Kerrigan. New York: Avon Books, 1984.

Farewell to the Sea (translation of *Otra vez el mar*). Trans. Andrew Hurley. New York: Viking Penguin, 1986.

Graveyard of the Angels (translation of *La Loma del Angel*). Trans. Alfred MacAdam. New York: Avon Books, 1987.

Singing from the Well (translation of *Celestino antes del alba/Cantando en el pozo*). Trans. Andrew Hurley. New York: Viking Penguin, 1987.

The Ill-fated Peregrinations of Fray Servando (new translation of *El mundo alucinante*). Trans. Andrew Hurley. New York: Avon Books, 1987.

Old Rose. A Novel in Two Stories (translation of *La Vieja Rosa* ["Old Rosa"] and *Arturo, la estrella más brillante* ["The Brightest Star"]). Trans. Andrew Hurley and Ann Tashi Slater. New York: Grove Press, 1989.

The Palace of the White Skunks (translation of *El palacio de las blanquísimas mofetas*). Trans. Andrew Hurley. New York: Viking Penguin, 1990.

The Doorman (translation of *El portero*). Trans. Dolores M. Koch. New York: Grove Press, 1991.

Before Night Falls (translation of *Antes que anochezca*). Trans. Dolores M. Koch. New York: Viking Penguin, 1993.

The Assault (translation of *El asalto*). Trans. Andrew Hurley. New York: Viking Penguin, in press.

The Color of Summer (translation of *El color del verano*). Trans. Andrew Hurley. New York: Viking Penguin, in press.

Works about Reinaldo Arenas

Books

Béjar, Eduardo C. *La textualidad de Reinaldo Arenas*. Madrid: Editorial Playor, 1987.

Ette, Ottmar, ed. *La escritura de la memoria*. Frankfurt: Vervuert, 1992.

Hernández-Miyares, Julio, and Perla Rozencvaig, eds. *Reinaldo Arenas: alucinaciones, fantasía y realidad*. Glenview, Ill.: Scott, Foresman and Company, 1990.

Rozencvaig, Perla. *Reinaldo Arenas: narrativa de transgresión*. México: Editorial Oasis, 1986.

Soto, Francisco. *Conversación con Reinaldo Arenas*. Madrid: Editorial Betania, 1990.

Valero, Roberto. *El desamparado humor de Reinaldo Arenas*. North Miami: Hallmark Press, 1991.

Selected Articles and Reviews

Beaupied, Aida. "De lo anecdótico a lo conceptual en *El mundo alucinante* de Reinaldo Arenas." *Revista de Estudios Hispánicos* 11 (1984): 133–42.

Borinski, Alicia. "Re-escribir y Escribir: Arenas, Menard, Borges, Cevantes, Fray Servando." *Revista Iberoamericana* 41, nos. 92–93 (1975): 605–16.

Bovi-Guerra, Pedro. "*El mundo alucinante*: ecos de *Orlando* y otros ecos." *Románica* 15 (1978–79): 97–107.

Bush, Andrew. "The Riddled Text: Borges and Arenas." *MLN* 103, no. 2 (1988): 374–97.

Cantor, Jay. "Fantasies of Escape and Love." Review of *Farewell to the Sea. The New York Times Book Review*, November 24, 1985, 31.

Diego, Eliseo. "Sobre *Celestino antes del alba*." *Casa de las Américas* 7, no. 45 (1967): 162–66.

Ellis, Edwin E. "Reinaldo Arenas and His Act of Fury. A Writer in Exile Documents Repression in *El central*." *New York Advocate* 398, July 10, 1984: 38–40.

Foster, David William. "Critical Monographs, Dissertations, and Critical Essays about Reinaldo Arenas." In *Cuban Literature: A Research Guide*, 89–91. New York: Garland Publishing, 1985.

————. Study of *Arturo, la estrella más brillante*. In *Gay and Lesbian Themes in Latin American Literature*, 66–72. Austin: University of Texas Press, 1991.

González, Eduardo G. "A razón de santo: últimos lances de Fray Servando." *Revista Iberoamericana* 41, nos. 92–93 (1975): 593–603.

González Mandria, Flora María. "Repetición y escritura en la obra de Reinaldo Arenas." In *Historia y ficción en la narrativa hispanoamericana*, edited by Roberto González Echevarría, 395–408. Caracas: Monte Avila Editores, 1984.

Gordon, Ambrose. "Rippling Ribaldry and Pouncing Puns: The Two Lives of Friar Servando." *Review: Latin American Literature and Arts*, no. 8 (Spring 1973): 40–44.

Jara, René. "Aspectos de la intertextualidad en *El mundo alucinante*." *Texto crítico* 5, no. 13 (1979): 219–35.

Jiménez Emán, Gabriel. "La transgresión imaginaria." *Quimera*, nos. 9–10 (1981): 70–74.

MacAdam, Alfred. "La vocación literaria en Arenas." *Linden Lane* 1, no. 4 (1982): 9–10.

Méndez Rodena, Adriana. "*El palacio de las blanquísimas mofetas*: ¿narración historiográfica o narración imaginaria?" *Revista de la Universidad de México* 39, no. 27 (1983): 14–21.

Olivares, Jorge. "Carnival and the Novel: Reinaldo Arenas' *El palacio de las blanquísimas mofetas*." *Hispanic Review* 53, no. 4 (1985): 467–76.

Ortega, Julio. "The Dazzling World of Friar Servando." *Review* 8 (Spring 1973): 45–48.

Oviedo, José Miguel. "Reinaldo Arenas, *Termina el desfile*." *Vuelta* 7, no. 74 (1983): 43–46.

Rivera, Carlos. "Tres escrituras: *Cobra*, *El mundo alucinante* y *Sobregondi retrocede*." *Románica* 12 (1975): 55–61.

Rodríguez Monegal, Emir. "The Labyrinthine World of Reinaldo Arenas." *Latin American Literary Review* 8, no. 16 (1980): 126–31.

————. "*Celestino antes del alba* de Reinaldo Arenas." *Vuelta* 5, no. 53 (1981): 33–34.

Rodríguez Ortiz, Oscar. "Reinaldo Arenas: la textualidad del yo." In *Sobre narradores y héroes*, 17–73. Caracas: Monte Avila Editores, 1980.

Sánchez-Grey Alba, Esther. "Un acercamiento a *Celestino antes del alba* de Reinaldo Arenas." *Círculo: Revista de Cultura* 10 (1982): 15–24.

Santí, Enrico Mario. "The Life and Times of Reinaldo Arenas." *Michigan Quarterly Review* 23, no. 2 (Spring 1984): 227–36.

Sarduy, Severo. "Carta privada a Reinaldo Arenas." *Unveiling Cuba*, no. 3 (New York, April 1983): 4.

Schwartz, Kessel. "Homosexuality and the Fiction of Reinaldo Arenas." *Journal of Evolutionary Psychology* (March 1984): 12–20.

Soto, Francisco. "*Otra vez el mar*: el escritor frente a la escritura." *Selected Proceedings of the Pennsylvania Foreign Language Conference* (1988–90): 352–58.

―――. "Reinaldo Arenas: gran patriota y escritor singular." *Diario las Américas,* January 21, 1990, 10–11A.

―――. "Conversación con Reinaldo Arenas." Madrid: Ediciones Betania, 1990.

―――. Review of *Old Rosa. The Americas Review* 18, no. 1 (Spring 1990): 114–15.

―――. Review of *El portero. Revista Iberoamericana* 56, nos. 152–53 (July–December 1990): 1399–1401.

―――. Review of *Voluntad de vivir manifestándose. Revista Iberoamericana* 56, nos. 152–53 (July–December 1990): 1401–3.

―――. "El mensaje de Reinaldo Arenas." *El Nuevo Herald,* January 3, 1991, 6-A.

―――. "El escritor Reinaldo Arenas" (article in response to two articles by Celedonio González published in *Diario las Américas* on January 16 and 23, 1991). *Diario las Américas,* March 17, 1991, 12-A.

―――. "*Celestino antes del alba*: escritura subversiva/sexualidad transgresiva." *Revista Iberoamericana* 57, no. 154 (January–March 1991): 345–54.

―――. "*El portero*: una alucinante fábula moderna." *INTI,* nos. 32–33 (Fall 1990–Spring 1991): 106–17.

―――. Review of *The Palace of the White Skunks. Review: Latin American Literature and Arts* 44 (January–June 1991): 90–91.

―――. Review of *Viaje a La Habana. Revista Iberoamericana* 57, nos. 155–56 (April–September 1991): 806–9.

―――. "Reinaldo Arenas's Literary Legacy." *Christopher Street Magazine* 156 (May 1991): 12–16.

―――. Review of *The Doorman. Review: Latin American Literature and Arts* 45 (July–December 1991): 109–10.

―――. "Reinaldo Arenas and the Cuban Documentary Novel: A Study of *Celestino antes del alba, El palacio de las blanquísimas mofetas,* and *Otra vez el mar*." *Utah Foreign Language Review* 1 (1991–92): 1–18.

―――. "*Celestino antes del alba, El palacio de las blanquísimas mofetas,* and *Otra vez el mar*: The Struggle for Self-Expression." *Hispania* 75, no. 1 (1992): 60–68.

―――. "La transfiguración del poder en 'La Vieja Rosa' y *Arturo, la estrella más brillante*." *Confluencia* 8, no. 1 (1992): 71–78.

Vesterman, William. "Going No Place with Arenas." *Review: Latin American Literature and Arts* 13 (Spring 1973): 49–51.

Volek, Emil. "La carnavalización y la alegoría en *El mundo alucinante* de Reinaldo Arenas." *Revista Iberoamericana* 51, nos. 130–31 (1985): 125–48.

Walter, Claudia Joan. "Reynaldo Arenas' *El mundo alucinante*: Aesthetic and Thematic Focal Points." *Kentucky Romance Quarterly* 19 (1972): 41–50.

Wood, Michael. Review of *Farewell to the Sea. The New York Review of Books,* March 27, 1986, 34–37.

Zaldívar, Gladys. "La metáfora de la historia en *El mundo alucinante*." In *Novelística cubana de los años 60,* 41–71. Miami: Editorial Universal, 1977.

Alter, Robert. *Partial Magic: The Novel as a Self-Conscious Genre.* Berkeley: University of California Press, 1975.

──────. *Motives for Fiction.* Cambridge, Mass.: Harvard University Press, 1984.

Alvarez Bravo, Armando. "La novela de Lezama Lima." In *Coloquio Internacional sobre la obra de José Lezama Lima,* 87–97. Madrid: Editorial Fundamentos, 1984.

Arenal, Humberto. *El sol a plomo.* Havana: Cruzada Latinoamericana de Difusión Cultural, 1959. Translated as *The Sun Beats Down: A Novella of the Cuban Revolution.* Trans. Joseph M. Bernstein. New York: Hill and Wang, 1959.

Bakhtin, Mikhail. "From the Prehistory of Novelistic Discourse." *The Dialogic Imagination.* Trans. Caryl Emerson and Michael Holquist. Austin: University of Texas Press, 1981.

──────. *Problems of Dostoevsky's Poetics.* Trans. Caryl Emerson. Minneapolis: University of Minnesota Press, 1981.

──────. *Rabelais and His World.* Trans. Helene Iswolsky. Bloomington: Indiana University Press, 1984.

──────. *Speech Genres and Other Essays.* Trans. Vern W. McGee. Austin: University of Texas Press, 1986.

Barnet, Miguel. "Los hijos de Sánchez." *Casa de las Américas* 5, no. 32 (September–October 1965): 100–104.

──────. *Biografía de un cimarrón.* Madrid: Ediciones Alfaguara, 1966. Translated as *The Autobiography of a Runaway Slave.* Trans. Jocasta Innes. London: The Bodley Head, 1968.

──────. "La novela testimonio: socio-literatura." In the appendix to *Canción de Rachel.* Barcelona: Editorial Estela, 1969. Translated as *Rachel's Song.* Trans. W. Nick Hill. Willimantic, Conn.: Curbstone Press, 1991.

──────. "El creador y su obra." *La Gaceta de Cuba* no. 85 (August–September 1970): 10.

──────. "Testimonio y comunicación: una vía hacia la identidad." *Unión,* no. 4 (1980): 131–43.

──────. *Gallego.* Madrid: Ediciones Alfaguara, 1981.

──────. *La vida real.* Madrid: Ediciones Alfaguara, 1984.

──────. *Oficio de ángel.* Madrid: Ediciones Alfaguara, 1989.

Batalló, José. "Encuentros con Miguel Barnet." *Camp de l'arpa. Revista de literatura,* no. 96 (1982): 51–60.

Becerra Ortega, José. *La novena estación.* Havana: El Siglo XX, 1959.

Bejel, Emilio. "Entrevista con Miguel Barnet." *Hispamérica* 10, no. 29 (1981): 41–52.

Benedetti, Mario. "Situación del escritor en América Latina." *Casa de las Américas* 7, no. 45 (1967): 31–36.

Benítez Rojo, Antonio. *Tute de reyes.* Havana: Casa de las Américas, 1967.

Beverley, John. "The Margin at the Center: On *Testimonio* (Testimonial Narrative)." *Modern Fiction Studies* 33, no. 1 (1989): 11–28.

Blanchot, Maurice. *The Gaze of Orpheus*. New York: Station Hill Press, 1981.

Bloom, Harold. *The Anxiety of Influence*. London: Oxford University Press, 1975.

Borges, Jorge Luis. *Obras completas*. Buenos Aires: Emecé Editores, 1974.

Bundy, Paul, and Enrico Mario Santí. "The Documentary Novel." *Cuban Studies* 11, no. 1 (1981): 19–32.

Cabrera Infante, Guillermo. *Tres tristes tigres*. Barcelona: Seix Barral, 1984. Translated as *Three Trapped Tigers*. Trans. Donald Garner and Suzanne Jill Levine. New York: Harper & Row, 1971.

Calderón González, Jorge. *Amparo: millo y azucenas*. Havana: Casa de las Américas, 1970.

Casal, Lourdes. "La novela en Cuba, 1959–1967: una introducción." *Exilio*, nos. 3–4 (Winter 1969–Spring 1970): 184–217.

———. "The Cuban Novel, 1959–1969: An Annotated Bibliography." *Abraxas* 1, no. 1 (Fall 1970): 77–92.

———. *El caso Padilla: Literatura y Revolución en Cuba*. Miami: Ediciones Universal, 1971.

Casas, Nubya C. "Novela-testimonio: historia y literatura." Ph.D. diss., New York University, 1981.

Casaus, Víctor. *Girón en la memoria*. Havana: Casa de las Américas, 1970.

Castro, Fidel. "Discurso de clausura." *Casa de las Américas*, nos. 65–66 (1971): 21–33.

———. "Palabras a los intelectuales." In *Fidel Castro. Obras escogidas*, vol. 1, 1953–62, 135–74. Madrid: Editorial Fundamentos, 1976.

Colón, Cristóbal. *Diario de Colón*. Madrid: C. Sanz, 1962.

Cortázar, Julio. *Rayuela*. México: Editorial Seix Barral, 1985. Translated as *Hopscotch*. Trans. Gregory Rabassa. New York: Pantheon Books, 1966.

Coste, Didier. *Narrative as Communication*. Minneapolis: University of Minnesota Press, 1989.

Culler, Jonathan. "Presupposition and Intertextuality." In *Pursuit of Signs—Semiotics, Literature, Deconstruction*. Ithaca: Cornell University Press, 1981.

de Man, Paul. "A Modern Master." *The New York Review of Books*, November 19, 1964, 8–9.

Díaz Rodríquez, Jesús. *Los años duros*. Havana: Casa de las Américas, 1966.

Donoso, José. *Historia personal del "boom."* Barcelona: Seix Barral, 1983. Translated as *The Boom in Spanish American Literature: A Personal History*. Trans. Gregory Kolovakos. New York: Columbia University Press, 1977.

Dumont, René. *Is Cuba Socialist?* Trans. Stanley Hochman. London: Viking Press, 1973.

Earle, Peter. *Gabriel García Márquez*. Madrid: Taurus, 1981.

Erisman, H. Michael. *Cuba's International Relations*. Boulder, Colorado: West-view Press, 1985.

Ester Gilio, María. *La guerrilla tupamara*. Havana: Casa de las Américas, 1970.

Faustino Sarmiento, Domingo. *Facundo*. Buenos Aires: Espasa-Calpe, 1951.

Fernández Retamar, Roberto. "Apuntes sobre revolución y literatura en Cuba." *Unión*, no. 4 (1972): 34–45.

Foley, Barbara. *Telling the Truth: The Theory and Practice of Documentary Fiction*. Ithaca: Cornell University Press, 1986.

Foster, David William. "Latin American Documentary Narrative." *PMLA* 99, no. 1 (January 1984): 41–55.

García Alvarez, Alejandro. "El testimonio: su divulgación en Cuba revoluciona-ria." *Revista de la Biblioteca Nacional José Martí* 27, no. 1 (1985): 107–18.

García Lorca, Federico. *Libro de poemas*. Madrid: Alianza, 1984.

García Márquez, Gabriel. *Cien años de soledad*. Buenos Aires: Sudamericana, 1967. Translated as *One Hundred Years of Solitude*. Trans. Gregory Rabassa. New York: Avon Books, 1970.

Genette, Gérard. *Narrative Discourse: An Essay in Method*. Trans. Jane E. Lewin. Ithaca: Cornell University Press, 1980.

————. *Narrative Discourse Revisited*. Trans. Jane E. Lewin. Ithaca: Cornell University Press, 1988.

González de Cascorro, Raúl. *Aquí se habla de combatientes y de bandidos*. Havana: Casa de las Américas, 1975.

————. *El hijo de Arturo Estévez*. Havana: Unión de Escritores y Artistas de Cuba, 1975.

————. "El género testimonial en Cuba." *Unión*, no. 4 (1978): 78–89.

González Echevarría, Roberto. "*Biografía de un cimarrón* and the Novel of the Cuban Revolution." In *The Voice of the Masters*, 110–24. Austin: University of Texas Press, 1985.

Goytisolo, Juan. "Twenty-Six Rue de Bièvre." *Partisan Review* 51 (1984): 680–91.

Guerra, Angel Luis Fernández. "Edipo y Cayo Graco (Para leer a Miguel Barnet)." *Casa de las Américas* 30, no. 180 (May–June 1990): 45–53.

Guevara, Ernesto. *El socialismo y el hombre en Cuba*. Havana: Ediciones Revolu-ción, 1965. Translated as "Man and Socialism in Cuba." In *Man and Socialism in Cuba*, edited by Bertram Silverman, 337–54. New York: Atheneum, 1973.

————. *Paisajes de la guerra revolucionaria*. Translated as *Reminiscences of the Cuban Revolutionary War*. Trans. Victoria Ortiz. New York: Monthly Review, 1968.

Guibert, Rita. "The Tongue-Twisted Tiger." *Review 72* (Winter-Spring 1972): 11–16.

Hoffman, Banesh. *Albert Einstein: Creator and Rebel*. New York: Viking Press, 1972.

Hollowell, John. *Fact and Fiction: The New Journalism and the Nonfiction Novel.* Chapel Hill: University of North Carolina Press, 1977.

Hutcheon, Linda. *Narcissistic Narrative: The Metafictional Paradox.* Waterloo, Ont.: Wilfrid Laurier University Press, 1980.

Huxley, Aldous. *Brave New World.* New York: Harper & Row, 1969.

Iser, Wolfgang. *The Act of Reading: A Theory of Aesthetic Response.* Baltimore: Johns Hopkins University Press, 1978.

Karol, K. S. *Guerrillas in Power: The Course of the Cuban Revolution.* Trans. Arnold Pomerans. New York: Hill and Wang, 1970.

Kristeva, Julia. *The Kristeva Reader.* Edited by Tori Moi. New York: Columbia University Press, 1986.

Levine, Barry B. "Miguel Barnet on the Testimonial." *Caribbean Review* 9, no. 4 (1980): 32–36.

Lewis, Oscar. *The Children of Sánchez.* New York: Random House, 1961.

———. *La Vida: A Puerto Rican Family in the Culture of Poverty.* San Juan and New York: Random House, 1965–66.

———. *Anthropological Essays.* New York: Random House, 1970.

Lewis, Oscar, Ruth M. Lewis, and Susan M. Rigdan. *Living the Revolution: An Oral History of Contemporary Cuba, Four Men Four Women.* Champaign: University of Illinois Press, 1977.

Lezama Lima, José. *Paradiso.* Edited by Eloísa Lezama Lima. Madrid: Ediciones Cátedras, 1980. Translated as *Paradiso* by Gregory Rabassa. Austin: University of Texas Press, 1974.

López, Ramón. "El danzón de Rachel." *Casa de las Américas* 57 (1969): 122–23.

Luis, William. "The Politics of Memory and Miguel Barnet's *The Autobiography of a Runaway Slave.*" *MLN* 104, no. 2 (March 1989): 475–94.

Mañach, Jorge. *Indagación del choteo.* Miami: Mnemosyne, 1969.

Marshall, Peter. *Cuba Libre, Breaking the Chains?* London: Victor Gollancz, 1987.

McMurray, George R. *Spanish American Writing since 1941.* New York: The Ungar Publishing Company, 1987.

Medin, Tzvi. *Cuba: The Shaping of Revolutionary Consciousness.* Boulder: Lynne Rienner Publishers, 1990.

Méndez, Adriana. "Conversación con Miguel Barnet." *Areíto* 5, no. 18 (1979): 37–43.

Méndez y Soto, Ernesto. *Panorama de la novela cubana de la Revolución (1959–1970).* Miami: Ediciones Universal, 1977.

Menton, Seymour. "La novela de la revolución cubana." *Casa de las Américas* 4, nos. 22–23 (1964): 150–56.

———. *Prose Fiction of the Cuban Revolution.* Austin: University of Texas Press, 1975.

———. *La narrativa de la Revolución cubana.* Trans. Marisela Fernández. Madrid: Playor, 1978.

————. *La narrativa de la Revolución cubana.* Mexico City: Plaza y Janés, S. A., 1982.

Molloy, Silvia. *Las letras de Borges.* Buenos Aires: Editorial Sudamericana, 1979.

Nietzsche, Friedrich. *The Will to Power.* Trans. Walter Kaufmann and R. J. Hollingdale. New York: Random House, 1967.

Olema García, Daura. *Maestra voluntaria.* Havana: Casa de las Américas, 1962.

Onetti, Jorge. *Cualquiercosario.* Montevideo: Arca, 1967.

Orwell, George. *1984.* New York: Harcourt Brace Jovanovich, 1949.

Padilla, Heberto. *Fuera del juego.* Buenos Aires: Auditor, 1969. Translated as *Sent Off the Field.* Trans. J. M. Cohen. London: Deutsch, 1972.

————. "Heberto Padilla: intervención en la Unión de Escritores y Artistas de Cuba." *Casa de las Américas,* nos. 65–66 (March–June 1971): 191–203.

————. *La mala memoria.* Barcelona: Plaza y Janés, 1989. Translated as *Self-Portrait of the Other.* Trans. Alexander Coleman. New York: Farrar, Straus and Giroux, 1990.

Paz, Octavio. *La estación violenta.* Mexico City: Fondo de Cultura Económico, 1958.

Perera Soto, Hilda. *Mañana es 26.* Havana: Lázaro Hermanos, 1960.

Poe, Edgar Allan. *Selected Writings.* New York: Penguin Books, 1979.

Quevedo Pérez, José. *La Batalla de Jigüe.* Havana: Instituto Cubano del Libro, 1971.

Rodríguez Monegal, Emir. *El Boom de la novela latinoamericana.* Caracas: Editorial Tiempo Nuevo, 1972.

————. "Tradición y renovación." In *América Latina en su literatura,* edited by César Fernández Moreno. Paris: Siglo XXI, 1972.

————. "La nueva novela vista desde Cuba." *Revista Iberoamericana* 41, nos. 92–93 (1975): 647–62.

————. *Jorge Luis Borges: A Literary Biography.* New York: E.P. Dutton, 1978.

Schwartz, Kessel. *A New History of Spanish American Fiction,* vol. 2. Coral Gables, Fla.: University of Miami Press, 1971.

Shils, Edward. *Tradition.* Chicago: University of Chicago Press, 1981.

Sklodowska, Elzbieta. "La visión de la gente sin historia en las novelas testimoniales de Miguel Barnet." Ph.D. diss., Washington University, 1983.

————. "Aproximaciones a la forma testimonial: la novelística de Miguel Barnet." *Hispamérica* 40 (1985): 23–33.

Smorkaloff, Pamela María. *Literatura y edición de libros.* Havana: Editorial Letras Cubanas, 1987.

Soler Puig, José. *Bertillón 166.* Havana: Ministerio de Educación, 1960.

Todorov, Tzvetan. "The Typology of Detective Fiction." In *The Poetics of Prose,* 42–52. Trans. Richard Howard. Ithaca: Cornell University Press, 1977.

Unamuno, Miguel. *Niebla.* Madrid: Cátedra, 1982. Translated as *Mist.* Trans. Warner Fite. New York: H. Fertig, 1973.

Vargas Llosa, Mario. *La casa verde*. Barcelona: Seix Barral, 1966. Translated as *The Green House*. Trans. Gregory Rabassa. New York: Harper & Row, 1968.

Viñas, David. *Los hombres de a caballo*. Mexico City: Siglo XXI, 1981.

White, Hayden. *Metahistory: The Historical Imagination in Nineteenth Century Europe*. Baltimore: Johns Hopkins University Press, 1973.

Wilde, Oscar. *Oscar Wilde, Lord Arthur Savile's Crime and Other Stories*. New York: Viking Penguin, 1985.

Woolf, Virginia. *Orlando*. New York: Harcourt Brace Jovanovich, 1956.

Young, Allen. *Gays under the Cuban Revolution*. San Francisco: Grey Fox Press, 1981.

Zavarzadeh, Mas'ud. *The Mythopoeic Reality: The Postwar American Nonfiction Novel*. Urbana: University of Illinois Press, 1976.

INDEX

Mella, Julio Antonio, 48
Méndez y Soto, Ernesto, 169n.9
Menippean satire, 53–54, 168n.7, 170n.7
Menton, Seymour, 14–23 passim, 25, 157n.2, 158n.4
Metafictional literature, 127, 176n.6
Mimesis: of process, 51–52, 66, 94, 167n.1; of product, 51–52, 54, 66, 86, 94, 167n.1
Molloy, Sylvia, 113
Morir en junio y con la lengua afuera, 154, 155n.1
Mother (theme), 73–74, 99, 101, 102, 143–44, 170n.19
Mundo alucinante, El, 1, 4, 18, 56, 92, 131–33, 140, 145, 148, 159n.7, 169n.14, 172n.4
Mundo Nuevo, 17, 158n.5

Necesidad de libertad, 137, 152
Nietzsche, Friedrich, 167n.3
Novela-testimonio. See Documentary novel
Nowell-Smith, P. H., 133

OLAS (Organization for Latin American Solidarity), 17
Olema García, Daura, 25, 37
Olivares, Jorge, 65
Onetti, Jorge, 37
Onetti, Juan Carlos, 37
Orwell, George, 88
Otero, Lisandro, 151
Otra vez el mar, 4, 7, 13, 35, 39, 40, 42, 48, 52, 62, 156n.6, 157n.12, 166n.8, 170n.19, 172n.4; chronology in, 94–98; contradictory passage in, 114–15; documentation in, 108–9; doubling pairs in, 67, 148; English translation of, 150–51, 169n.15; *entremeses* in, 97–98; first-person narrative voice in, 65–68; "Monstruo," 124–28; parody in, 97; possible readings of, 94, 148–49; sequence of time in, 144; story of, 66, 174n.3; struggle for expression in, 120–28; Tedevoro

story, 67–68, 145–46; vicissitudes in writing, 157n.8; witnesses in, 85–86

Padilla, Heberto, 20, 21, 22, 160nn.11, 14, 161n.17
Palace of the White Skunks, The. See Palacio de las blanquísimas mofetas, El.
Palacio de las blanquísimas mofetas, El, 4, 7, 13, 35, 39, 40, 42, 48, 52, 123, 141, 142, 145, 156–57n.6, 169n.10; chronology in, 92–94; death in, 94; documentation in, 105–108; doubling pair in, 61–65; first-person narrative voice in, 56–65; multiple narrative "I's" in, 57–58; newspaper articles and advertisements in, 174n.2; third-person narrative voice in, 70–71; witnesses in, 84–85; writing as a refuge in, 117–19
Palais des très blanches moufettes, Le. See Palacio de las blanquísimas mofetas, El.
Paradiso, 4, 143, 158–59n.6
Paz, Octavio, 97
Pedro Páramo, 146
Pentagonía, 1, 15, 35, 39, 42, 44, 45, 47, 48, 52, 81, 91, 103, 111, 142–43, 146, 154, 156n.6, 157n.12; Arenas's determination to complete, 5–6; contradictory statements and passages in, 112–15; neologism of, 4; questioning historiography, 130, 133–36; typography of, 90
Perera Soto, Hilda, 15
Piñera, Virgilio, 8, 17, 174–75n.5
Pinochet, Augusto, 154
Poe, Edgar Allan, 3, 155n.3
Portero, El, 147, 149, 157n.12
Post-revolutionary Cuban literature, 13–25
Princeton University library, 106, 149, 156n.4, 176n.2
Prose Fiction of the Cuban Revolution, 14; editions of, 157–58n.2. *See also* Menton, Seymour
Proust, Marcel, 153